THE ULTIMATE COACH

THE ULTIMATE COACH

foreword by Iyanla Vanzant

AMY HARDISON
& ALAN D. THOMPSON

The Ultimate Coach

Copyright © 2021 by Amy Hardison

Zeebroff Books
Mesa, Arizona

Website: theultimatecoach.com

Editing and interior layout: Chris Nelson
Cover design: Angela Hardison

ISBN: 979-8-9851461-0-3

Library of Congress Control Number: 2021921850

First Edition

Dedication

Amy Hardison:

To Steffany, Lil, Clint, and Blake

———⌒✇⌒———

Alan D. Thompson:

This book is for you.

Table of Contents

Part One: The Life

Part Two: The Ultimate Coach

Part Three: Steve Hardison—the Man

Before You Begin

Steve Hardison

Note: Thank you for reading the back cover and the first two pages each time before you read this book.

I never wanted to write a book. And I haven't. I never wanted to have a book written about me. But here it is.

This book is a gift from my wife, Amy, who wrote it, and my friend Alan D. Thompson, who conducted the research and interviews on which it is based.

And it's not just a gift to me, but to you too.

And now you're reading it. So with your permission I'll give you some suggestions on *how* to read it.

You see, this isn't an ordinary book. It's not simply a biography. It's not a self-help book. It's not a literary classic. It's definitely not a book about how to coach. In fact, it's not a book about *doing* anything.

It's a book about being.

And it's a book about *you.*

To access *this* book, ask yourself these questions as you read:

Who am I being as a partner, parent, or friend?
Who am I being as a leader?

Who am I being as a member of my community?

Who would I need to be to have miracles show up in my daily life?

Who would I need to be to create value in the work I do?

Who would I need to be to generate a life of abundance?

Who would I need to be to alter my relationship with fear?

Who would I need to be to be at peace with my past?

Who would I need to be to step powerfully into my future?

Who would I need to be to be present as a way of being?

Who would I need to be to live the most extraordinary life I can live?

Who would I need to be to know that my life makes a difference?

Who would I need to be to be fully in love with myself and my life?

Who would I need to be to improve my relationships with the most important people in my life?

Who would I need to be to read *The Ultimate Coach* and have a personal breakthrough in being wonderful me?

The best part about *this* book—this book about *you*—is that it is endless. The story goes on. And it's written by your being.

Loving you. Be Blessed. Be you.
Steve Hardison

P.S. Remember, every time you reread this book, please read the back cover and the first two pages before you begin! If you do this, your experience of this book will be totally different.

SFH/kab

Foreword

Iyanla Vanzant

The Reverend Dr. Iyanla Vanzant is an American life coach, celebrated spiritual teacher, six-time New York Times *bestselling author, inspirational speaker, Emmy Award-winning television personality, and host of* Iyanla: Fix My Life *on the Oprah Winfrey Network. She is one of the most recognizable life coaches in the world.*

Have you ever had a serving of macaroni and cheese that was so amazing that it made you want to pee?

Maybe mama or grandma made it. Maybe it's the right combination of cheeses, the creaminess, the balance, the beautiful warmth, the taste. In the future, you will compare every other dish of macaroni and cheese to that amazing dish. And nothing you compare it to will ever measure up.

I haven't found anyone that measures up to Steve yet, not even me. And I'm good. I don't hold a candle to Steve Hardison, because he's otherworldly. I don't know what planet he came from. Even though he might be able to walk on water, I think that he usually takes a boat. Plus, then he doesn't mess up his shoes—because he and I are shoe whores!

He re-structured my DNA. Steve Hardison told me that I was powerful and brilliant. He told me: "You are by far the best public speaker that I've ever heard in my life."

How you telling a black girl out of Brooklyn that I'm a better speaker than Werner Erhard? You gotta be kidding.

"You are powerful."

Every time this man would say to me something like, "You're powerful," it would take me about three weeks to process that in my system.

This is what I know to be true:

Some things speak to your mind.

Some things speak to your heart.

Some things speak to your soul.

And some things speak *into your spirit.*

And when something is speaking into your spirit, your mind can't comprehend what it is. Your heart can only feel it, and your soul allows it, but it is your spirit that responds.

Nothing that anyone has said, can say, or would say can describe the experience of coaching with Steve Hardison. Every experience is unique and authentic to who you are and what your spirit needs. Not your mind, your heart, not even your soul, but your spirit. That part of you that's connected to the angelic realm.

Trying to articulate what happens in the experience of Steve Hardison goes beyond a place that your intellect can hold in the moment. When you go back and think about it, you can get the words that can describe it intellectually or mentally. Except that it's really at the molecular level of your spirit.

I won't do anything big unless I call Steve first and tell him what I'm considering. And he'll have the same response every time.

"How can I help? Is there anything you need me to do?"

I just want him to hold that space, because he is a mystic and he is otherworldly.

For me, it's enough just to know he's holding my project or concept in his space. I don't even have to think about it. I don't think I've ever asked him to pray either. He *is* the prayer.

Anybody reading this book has a blessing that many of us didn't have. Authors don't usually write about most mystics until they're dead. Steve is here, now. This book is preparation. It readies your mind. It moves the ego out of the way. Because if you read these words and are open to the experience, you're ready.

Remember that you are stepping into the presence of an angel. It's not going to be anything like your imagination.

What do you wear when you go meet an angel?

My invitation to you would be to show up naked.

Rev Dr Iyanla Vanzant
Maryland, USA
November 2021

Chapter 1

Enigma

The employee sitting at the conference table was despondent. He had, in his own words, "a long history of failure, addiction, bankruptcy, and real chaos." But those were the old issues, the resolved ones that only rumbled occasionally. Currently, his tectonic plates were in motion. His wife had just been institutionalized. He was raising four kids by himself. He was in debt to TimeMax, the company he worked for.

It would be so easy to be swallowed up.

"If you could do anything," asked Steve Hardison, the coach who had recently been engaged to work with the executives at TimeMax, "what would you do?"

"I would write books and I would speak."

"Have you done either of those things?"

The man shook his head.

"You do realize that you work for a company that sells speaking and training?" said Hardison.

"I asked the company president if I could be a speaker, and he said no."

Hardison was quick to respond. "One guy tells you that you can't speak, and you quit? You have to do better than that. Look, I'll arrange for the room and you can speak next Thursday night."

On Thursday night, Steve Chandler showed up to speak. Steve Hardison showed up to listen. He was the entire audience. The next Thursday night, ten people came to listen to Chandler. One of the ten was Patrick Provost, a friend of Hardison's. Patrick recalls, "It was grim and dull." By his own admission, Steve Chandler was a terrible speaker with crippling stage fright. He had a lot to overcome.

One day, Chandler came to TimeMax after attending one of Landmark's personal development seminars. It was about creating your future. He had bounce in his step. When he saw Hardison, he announced, "I now have a five-year plan for becoming a public speaker."

"If that's what you want, that's fine," said Hardison. His words poked holes in Chandler's exuberance.

"Is there something wrong?" asked Chandler.

"You could take five years to become a public speaker if you want. Or you could do it in five months."

"I'm not you, you know," Chandler said. "I have to take a public speaking course. I have to get over my stage fright. That takes time."

"That's all in your head."

It all seemed so logical, so real to Chandler. Did Hardison always bend reality? Would it be as pliable for Chandler? Chandler was willing to find out.

Chandler passed out flyers to the businesses near TimeMax, inviting people to attend a free talk on achieving goals. He made up a booklet with some of his favorite quotes from Stephen Covey,

Napoleon Hill, and Tony Robbins. Chandler would build a discussion on the quotes, which was much less terrifying than standing on his own expertise.

As a single father with full custody and no money for babysitting, his kids would attend. They would be their dad's official pencil runners and his unofficial cheerleaders.

To counter his stage fright, Chandler practiced his presentations whenever he could, at home, in the car, during dinner. Before his kids went to bed, he would gather them and say, "I want to give you one of my talks."

They groaned.

"Only for ten minutes. That's all," insisted Chandler.

Just as Chandler was hitting his stride, he was interrupted with "Dad, this is so boring."

"Count your blessings," he replied. "You only get ten minutes. Grownups get an hour."

One day, Hardison read a booklet on fundraising that Chandler had cowritten before he worked at TimeMax. "This is amazing," he said to Chandler. "Why don't you present these ideas to the whole TimeMax team?"

Chandler blanched. "I could never stand in front of the whole company and speak."

"Of course you can," insisted Hardison.

Chandler did it, but his nerves were espresso jittery. He was relieved when it was over. Chandler thought he did all right. Hardison thought he was wonderful. He asked Chandler to autograph his booklet.

"I thought he was mocking me," says Chandler. "I felt like the kid with ALS who plays on the school football team because of the coach's compassion. The other team lets him score a touchdown out of pity and because they are way ahead. The crowd is cheering, not because the kid is wonderful, but because he showed great heart."

"Why do you want my autograph?" asked Chandler. "After all, I'm in the company—and this isn't a real book."

"I want you to remember this moment," replied Hardison. "Something miraculous is going to occur out of what you did today. You will be a world-famous speaker one day."

Chandler didn't believe him.

Today, Chandler is a highly sought-after speaker. He is the author of over forty books, which have been translated into twenty-five languages. He has created in-person and online coaching schools that are in high demand. He is known throughout the world as the "Godfather of Coaching." When he speaks and writes, he consistently acknowledges the coach who was integral in helping him become who he is today. He says things like: "Hardison is known in coaching circles, and business circles, and personal growth circles and any circle you can think of as 'The Ultimate Coach.' He coaches way beyond the normal concept of coaching. To call him a mere life coach is like calling The Beatles a garage band."

Trent La Marsh kept encountering Steve Hardison in Steve Chandler's books. La Marsh writes: "I was intrigued by this fellow Steve Chandler kept mentioning, this 'Ultimate Coach,' who coached Chandler for nearly thirty years. I was in awe of the fees he commanded and the people he coached. My main question was 'What on earth does he do to warrant such respect and admiration?'"

That question may well be in the minds of those who pick up

this book. La Marsh found his answer "slowly, as bits and pieces and stories about this man surfaced."

Within these pages are bits and pieces and stories that reveal Steve Hardison. There are stories about Hardison's childhood and family of origin, the people and disciplines that shaped his thinking, and the path that led to his coaching. There are principles that are fundamental to his coaching. There are stories from people Steve has coached. These stories are the warp and woof of this book. They approximate, as much as possible, stepping into Hardison's office and experiencing his coaching.

Beyond that, there are stories of Steve Hardison the man, stories that delight, stories that evoke a giggle or even a belly laugh, stories that baffle, and stories that astound. There are stories that leave readers inspired to live big and bold, alight with the fire of their own possibility.

Perhaps we, like La Marsh, can start to understand Hardison through these stories. Or perhaps we will understand him when we read about the things that nearly crushed him. Or perhaps we will never totally understand this enigmatic force, this Tasmanian devil of passion and power. Perhaps we don't need to. Perhaps all we need is to inhale some of his energy.

Part One

The Life

Chapter 2

Roots

Two handsome airmen stood on the side of the road with their thumbs in the air. It was 1944. The war still raged. Maurine and her girlfriend were driving by Hill Air Force Base when they spotted the airmen. Should they stop? Why not? It was a split-second decision that lasted a lifetime.

Maurine Forbes was a Mormon girl from the small town of Clearfield, twenty-five miles north of Salt Lake City. She had green eyes and auburn hair. She was vivacious and intelligent, the valedictorian of the class of 1944 at Davis High. She played the organ, the violin, and the piano. She adored jewelry and had a flair for fashion. She also had a little bit of attitude and just the right amount of kick-ass.

Roy Hardison was a paratrooper in the air force. He was handsome, slender, and tall—just over 6'4". He was raised in Kentucky by God-fearing parents who walked several miles each Sunday to the local Baptist church. As sharecroppers, they lived a hardscrabble life, made harder by not knowing how to read or write. On payday, others helped them cash their paychecks, skimming the top off a check that barely covered necessities.

Roy did everything possible to erase all traces of his humble origins from his life. His shoes were polished and his fingernails manicured. He was impeccably dressed. He was rough around the edges, but that was hardly noticeable when he cut such a striking figure. And it wasn't just his appearance. He had charm. Later, Maurine would frequently say, "He could talk the birds out of the trees." Maurine was smitten.

At eighteen, Maurine still had to be home at 10:00 every night. Roy was adventurous and exciting— the opposite of Maurine's tamped-down life. They eloped on June 9, 1945. Not ready to tell her parents, Maurine returned home as if nothing had changed. When her parents found out that Miss Maurine was Mrs. Hardison, they sent her to her husband. She had made her bed; she would lie in it.

Roy Hardison

Children

It wasn't long before Maurine was expecting, a two-for-one pregnancy. Unfortunately, her twins came too early. She delivered them in her bathroom, attended by her mother and a local doctor.

Sammy and Danny didn't live long. The doctor dropped them in a bucket. Maurine's soul shuddered. By the next year, a healthy and robust baby boy, Rob, joined the family. He was followed by sisters Jayme and Teresa.

In 1953, Roy was deployed to Bitburg, a small town in Germany. Phil was born in June, 1954. Thirteen months later, Steve was born at the military hospital in Bitburg. He weighed 11.5 pounds (5.2kg) and was the biggest baby born in that hospital as of 1955. A year later, the family was in Mountain Home, Idaho, and the year after that, Roy was deployed to Spain.

Maurine and Roy's marriage was difficult. They both had strong personalities. Roy was fond of playing poker and played often with the officers from the air force base. His losses strained the family finances. And he was a bit of a libertine.

In the 1950s, it was routine and reasonable for Americans living abroad to employ household help. One morning when living in Germany, Maurine walked into the kitchen and said good morning to the maid. The maid spat in her face. Why this sudden contempt? It seems Roy had forced himself on the maid.

In Spain, Roy and Maurine went out to eat with another couple, whom we will call John and Mary. During dinner, Roy announced that he and Mary were in love. They were leaving their marriages and going off together. While Maurine grappled with this betrayal, Mary said, "I've changed my mind. I'm staying with John."

Roy turned to Maurine and said, "Well, I guess I'll stay with you."

Maurine longed to divorce Roy, but with five young children and no college education, her options were limited. She stayed in the marriage.

Maurine and Roy (center), and friends

Throughout his adult life, Roy was good at making money, but he was better at spending it. He frequently picked up the tab for steak dinners and rounds of drinks, propping up his image as a high roller with deep pockets. At home, Maurine barely had enough money to put food on the table.

Roy's excessive spending and gambling debts caught up with him when they were living in Seville, Spain. He resorted to writing bad checks, sixteen of them for a total of $810.00 (worth about $8,000 today). He faced a military investigation. To avoid the possibility of a dishonorable discharge, Roy resigned from the air force.

The family returned to the States and moved to Indiana, where they lived in East Gary, Hammond, and Griffith. One of Steve's earliest memories occurred at this time. He was young, still waddling in diapers. He was outside on the front porch. It was snowing. He couldn't get into the house. His diaper was soiled. No one was there to help him. They *should* be there to help him. He felt abandoned. This was not the most traumatic abandonment Steve would experience, but it was the first. It etched into his soul.

Civilian life wasn't going well. Homelife became violent, loud, explosive, uncertain, and stressful, especially when Roy had been drinking. And he drank a lot. Steve remembers a family dinner abruptly ending when his dad launched a bowl of mashed potatoes across the room, potatoes flying everywhere.

If Roy wasn't drinking, he could be fun. Jayme remembers him playing kick the can with them. He liked practical jokes. However, his play edged to cruel. He short-sheeted his kids' beds, crumbled up cornflakes and put them in their sheets, and put tabasco sauce inside of Oreos. Rob, Steve's older brother, learned never to take anything his father offered him. Roy taught Rob to play baseball by throwing baseballs as hard as he could at Rob. He taught Rob to swim by throwing him into a river in Germany and walking away. Nothing Rob did was ever good enough for Roy. If Roy raised his hand quickly, Rob ducked. By the time Rob was fourteen, he had peptic ulcers. Roy was gentler with his girls. He doted on Teresa. Phil and Steve were too young to pay attention to.

The most traumatic event of Steve's young life occurred late one night when Roy, under the influence, was beating Maurine. All five kids were in the house, lying petrified in their beds. When Maurine screamed for Rob to help her, Roy threatened, "If you get out of bed, I'll kill you." They all took him at his word. No one moved.

Clearfield

Several states away, Ellen Forbes fretted. Her daughter was in trouble. She was sure of it. Ellen and John (J. P.), Maurine's parents, asked their son, Myron, to go to Indiana and assess Maurine's situation. Despite a debilitating fear of flying, Myron braved the three-hour flight. When he got to Maurine's house, the kids were home alone. Maurine was working at a bar and Roy had been missing for several days, presumably on one of his benders. Myron reported back to Ellen. Ellen and J.P. scraped together the money for six train tickets to Ogden. Maurine and the kids fled before Roy returned.

Ellen and J. P. were almost finished building a house next to their current one. When Maurine and the kids arrived, Ellen and J.P. moved into the new house and gave Maurine their old one instead of selling or renting it. Maurine had come full circle. She was back home, under the watchful eyes of her parents, in the small town where she had grown up. It was a relief. However, she didn't return to the religion of her youth, keeping her slightly out of step with her Mormon community.

Ellen and J. P. were sixty-eight and seventy-three, respectively, when Maurine moved in next door. At an age when others might be retiring, Ellen and J.P. were still running their small farm, eleven acres just west of the railroad tracks. They had chickens, cows, and a small orchard with apple, apricot, and cherry trees. They grew beets, green beans, tomatoes, wheat, and hay. Their primary income source was from the milk their cows produced, but they also sold some of their produce. They didn't have the time or energy to raise a second family. But they were there for emergencies.

Maurine started waitressing full time and going to school. She was proud and independent. She did everything she could to make it on her own without church or government assistance. She didn't quite pull it off. They had industrial-sized peanut butter from the church's welfare center in their pantry and milk from J.P.'s cows.

Steve hated that the milk often had cow hair floating in it, but the milk and the peanut butter were enough to keep hunger at bay. Still, Steve hoped his friends would invite him home after school so he could get a snack and, on a really good day, an invitation to dinner.

Work and school pulled Maurine out of the home for most of her children's waking hours. Jayme says there were long periods of time when they never saw their mom, except when she came home to sleep. Rob and Jayme were in charge of the younger siblings, but they were going to school and working at local restaurants. Rob worked as a busboy at the Officer's Club at Hill Air Force Base from 6:00 p.m. to midnight and then tried to stay awake at high school the next day, often unsuccessfully.

Minimal supervision had its perks. Steve explored the farms, the culverts, and the town. No one was restraining his curiosity or his propensity for mischief. No adult was hovering. No parent was pushing compliance. He had ample space to be himself. But there were definite downsides. There were few family dinners and no family vacations. As far as Steve was concerned, they were a group of lone wolves living in the same house.

Steve's dominant memory of his childhood is being alone. He came home from school to an empty house. When he played sports, no one was there to cheer him on. If he was sick, he was home alone. Once he had an adverse reaction to a medication and suffered hallucinations. He had to sort out reality from terror by himself. Often, Steve had to figure out his homework by himself. He had questions about life, his body, and his future. Usually, there was no one around to ask.

The worst time to be alone was night. Sometimes he called Grandma Ellen and asked if he could come over. She normally said

Family picture: Steve (left), Jayme, Rob,
Teresa, Phil, about 1962

yes, but Steve was terrified of the dark, a fear that lasted until he was fifteen. To get to Grandma Ellen's, Steve had to cross the sector of terror between his back porch and his grandma's back door. It wasn't far, but it felt like three miles.

Steve's fears weren't groundless. Sketchy-looking men frequently walked by Steve's house after working at the nearby Job Corp, a job-training program for at-risk young adults. One night, an intruder entered their home through Steve's window. Steve feigned sleep while the man hovered over him. The intruder's intentions, whatever they were, were derailed when Maurine shrieked, "Rob, get your gun. Someone's in the house." Her bluff worked. The prowler bolted out the window.

Steve was not the only one afraid in the Hardison household. From time to time, Roy called Maurine and threatened to come to Utah and take the kids. Because of this, Maurine never insisted on child support. She never received one dollar from Roy to provide for his children. It was worth it to keep him away.

Once, Roy did show up. Steve was young, about five. He remembers his dad putting him up on the back porch. Steve pointed to the mountains and said he would like to go there. Roy said he would take him. Steve never saw his father again.

These experiences left their mark on Steve. When Maurine left Roy, Steve lost the father figure in his life, but he also lost his mother. Her heart was with her family, but her time and energy were committed to temporal survival. Deep down, Steve knew that when you are five years old, adults should be there to help you. He also knew that when a dad says he will take you to the mountains, he should do it. How disappointing. How infuriating.

Chapter 3

Growing Up

S teve was taking in his environment: desks, chalkboard, potential friends, and a teacher with an uncanny resemblance to Granny on the Beverly Hillbillies. First grade was going to be okay. Then he saw his mother walk by the open door of his classroom.

She was leaving?

Steve darted out the door and wrapped his arms around her legs. It took a bevy of adults to pry him loose. His teacher, Mrs. Smith, scolded him. His mother walked away. Steve steeled his soul. He was going to have to do this thing on his own.

Steve wasn't totally alone. Because of their frequent moves and the emotional turmoil in the family, Steve's brother Phil struggled in school. Maurine thought it best for Phil to repeat first grade. Since Steve and Phil were only thirteen months apart, they both started first grade at Pioneer Elementary in 1961. They would attend all twelve grades together, often in the same classes.

In many ways, school was a trying time for Steve. He couldn't

Steve (left), Phil (right), Rob (center), about 1963

tell the difference between a lower case "L" (l) and the number one (1). He struggled with long division. In junior high, he missed the day when his algebra teacher explained variables. When he returned to school and saw x's and y's on the chalkboard, he was baffled.

More challenging was Steve's frustration. When Steve's mom was home in the evenings and available to help him with his homework, too often the experience was a corkscrew to hell. When Steve didn't understand something, he got frustrated. When he got frustrated, he would scream and throw things. When he screamed and threw things, his mom refused to help him and walked away. When she walked away, Steve felt like his words and frustration were shoved down his throat. Unresolved, they became combustible. Sometimes he punched holes in the walls.

Steve remembers hearing his mom say that he was "hyperactive." He didn't know what "hyperactive" meant, but he was pretty sure it wasn't a compliment. He also knew that sitting at a desk for seven hours a day and only talking when his teachers called on him was a formidable task. Some teachers were understanding. Mrs. Gailey extended extra love and kindness to him. Other teachers said things like, "Put a rag in that kid's mouth." That was humiliating, but Steve concealed it with bravado.

There were parts of school that Steve loved: math, physical education, recess, story time, and all the social aspects of school. He also enjoyed the expanded opportunities for mischief. Steve and his friends often put a rock on the threshold of the cafeteria door so the door wouldn't completely shut. Later that night when all the teachers, janitors, and administrators had gone home, Steve and his friends crept back into the cafeteria and helped themselves to all the cookie dough, chocolate milk, and orange juice they wanted.

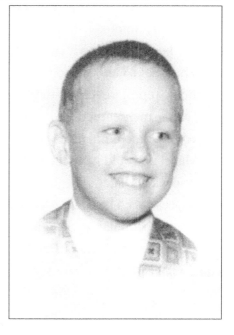

Before Pioneer Elementary School had centralized heating, they used fireplaces to heat the classrooms. Many of these fireplaces had been bricked in by 1960. In Steve's sixth grade classroom, the fireplace was

Steve, 1962.

extant, but was used to store the soccer balls and sports equipment used during recess. One time when Steve's teacher left the room, Steve and a friend climbed into the fireplace and up the chimney, using the casing for the electrical wiring as a handhold. The ascent was going well until Steve accidentally pulled the casing from the wall. The school was immediately shrouded in darkness. Steve and his friend dashed to their desks and assumed innocence. No one ratted them out, showing the influence Steve had with his peers. It took the school maintenance man a long time to pinpoint the source of the outage.

Maurine

Maurine completed a bachelor's degree in Business Administration and secured a job as an executive housekeeper for the Rodeway Inn. Presumably, a day-time job in management would significantly improve the family finances and give Maurine more time at home. It helped. But Maurine was now commuting to and from Salt Lake City each day, and she worked long hours. The 1963 Kennedy report revealed that women earned 59 cents for every dollar that men earned and that the more lucrative positions were closed to women. Finances were still strained.

Maurine would have thrived had she come of age professionally a few decades later. She had an intuitive sense for business. Her employees loved her and worked hard for her. If they fell short, she held them accountable. She had an uncanny ability to size people up after speaking with them for a few minutes. She had a work ethic equal to her pioneer ancestors and her indefatigable parent farmers. She boosted her natural abilities by reading business and motivational books and participating in business associations. She was capable, decisive, and astute—a natural leader.

Maurine dated and had offers to marry, but she was hesitant to complicate the family dynamics. She would eventually remarry, but not until all her children had married. In the meantime, she enjoyed the honks she got from passing cars as she mowed her lawn in her short shorts and low-cut T-shirts. Steve was mortified, especially when his friends drove by.

Working hard was the norm for everyone in the Hardison household. Each Saturday, Maurine left the kids a long list of tasks to complete. Sometimes Steve would ask for extra jobs to earn money to buy something he longed for. On one occasion, he wanted cowboy boots. Steve did all the contracted tasks, but when it came time to pay him, Maurine didn't have the money. It was a bitter pill. Steve also worked for his mom's approval and to appease his tendency to OCD. He brushed the carpet in his room with a hand brush to get the nap to lie just right.

Before cell phones and their predecessor, cordless phones, phones were either mounted on walls or attached to walls via cords. If you wanted to talk, you were tethered to the wall. If Maurine got a phone call, Steve would take advantage of her temporary stillness. He would lean across her lap and lift up the back of his T-shirt so she could rub his back. These were solid-gold moments—attention from his mother and being touched. They were rare. Also rare, but definitely a part of Steve's childhood, were those times when the stress was too much. Maurine could snap. "I'm losing it. . . " she warned. Once unhinged, she could be fierce.

Maurine thought it was important that her children get religion. She just didn't want to be the one to do it. She would send the kids to church with Ellen and J.P. or she would drop them off. Steve lingered at the door of the church until Maurine was out of sight, then he made a beeline to the nearby Chevron station, shinnied up the tree, and perched. For the next hour, Steve watched cars go by and daydreamed. That was the way he liked his religion. On one occasion, Steve intentionally left his dress shoes at school, in spite of his mother's reminders to bring them home so he could wear them to church. Not to be outmaneuvered, Maurine insisted Steve wear his sister's shoes. Steve kept those pointy canvas shoes tucked deep beneath the pew. He couldn't get out of church fast enough.

For years, Maurine's life had been physically hard and emotionally stressful. She wore out too soon. At least once a quarter, she would come home from work too weak to get out of the car and walk into the house. She would honk and Steve would come out and help her in. When Steve was twelve, he was playing baseball at Pioneer Elementary School. He was up to bat. Waiting for the pitch, he heard someone say, "We need Steve Hardison. His mom is sick." He dropped the bat and sprinted through the alfalfa field, the shortest way home. When he got home, his mom was in bed. Steve does not remember what laid her low, but he was terrified.

When Steve was seventeen, Maurine had a stroke. She was only forty-six. She lost her eyesight and was paralyzed on one side. Steve bathed her and helped her to the bathroom. Eventually, her sight and mobility returned. In between these health crises, Maurine frequently lamented that she was sure she was dying. Each time she foretold her demise, Steve blanched. What would happen if Maurine died? There was no father to turn to. Steve was terrified.

The Farm

Steve and Phil spent a lot of time on the farm. J.P. recruited them to pick beans, pull weeds, and be his gofers. Sometimes Steve had to help J.P. castrate bulls and cut the horns off cows. Steve watched as grandpa picked up chickens and wrung their necks and as Uncle Myron put a bullet in a cow's head so it could be butchered. Such things are part and parcel of farm life, but they disturbed Steve's sensitive soul.

Steve managed to have fun, even while working. One day when J.P., Phil, and Steve were picking string beans, Steve pelted his grandpa with beans and then quickly returned to picking, feigning innocence and industry. J.P. stood up and looked around, but couldn't identify the culprit. After the third assault, J.P. walked to the nearest grandchild and kicked Phil in the butt. He fell into the green beans, puzzled by his grandpa's random smack. Sometimes, Steve was at the receiving end of the jokes. Rob recalls, "Our grandfather's farm had milking cows. Cows leave fresh cow pies. Once, I held Steve up by his ankles, and dipped his head into the cow poop. Steve didn't think it was funny."

Ellen and J.P.'s house, as well as Maurine's, sat on the western edge of the farm. Behind the houses were all the structures of a small farm: a barn, a milk house, a chicken coop, tool sheds, storage for their wheat, and a garage-like structure for their farm equipment. Behind the tool shed was an 8 x 10-foot lean-to that grandpa used for extra storage. It didn't have a door, just an opening to walk through. The floor consisted of slats of rough-hewn wood. Sunlight filtered through the spaces between the one-by-fours of the walls. Inside were horse bridles, harnesses, and odds and ends.

This lean-to, or "the shed" as Steve called it, was a refuge for Steve. He would sit there for hours. He would meditate. He would watch the dust particles float in the sunlight and think the image looked like the universe. Sometimes he would cry, but mostly he thought. And he thought about his thoughts. Steve says, "I would sit there and ask, 'What's life all about? Why is it like this?' I've always been thoughtful about thinking. I remember wondering, 'There's thoughts in here. Who's doing that?'"

Sports

Steve's favorite way to channel his energy was through sports. Steve's father had been a Golden Glove boxer and an outstanding baseball player. Steve and Phil inherited that natural talent. By the time Phil was in the ninth grade, he could throw a runner out at home plate from center field. Steve, who played catcher, could zing the ball to second base when a player on first base attempted to steal. The opposing teams weren't expecting arms like that on fourteen-year-olds. Steve and Phil spent hours playing baseball, but also watching pro baseball on TV. Afterwards, they went out and practiced the strategy they observed. One coach told Rob that he worked hard to get his players to understand the strategy that Phil and Steve instinctively grasped. The coach also left a word of warning with Rob about Steve. "That brother of yours, he better watch his mouth. He's a smart ass."

Steve's favorite baseball memory was hitting three home runs in an all-star game. Steve also loved football and basketball. He was a gifted athlete, but what gave him his edge was his desire and intensity. Steve remembers, "I would take out all my frustration and all of my disappointment on the football field. I remember tackling one guy and accidentally breaking his leg."

Music

Steve channeled his energy through sports, but he soothed his soul through music. He was constantly listening to music through all the mediums then available: the radio, record players, and eight-track tapes while in the car. He would listen to music to fall asleep.

He would listen to music as soon as he woke up. He could identify a song after hearing two chords.

The first concert Steve attended was an Atomic Rooster Concert, a hard rock band from London. This was a big deal for Steve, and he wanted to look his best. He wore his white bell-bottom pants with creases down the front. When he walked in and looked around, Steve saw everyone was in standard hippy attire—ripped jeans, beads, and leather vests. It looked like Donnie Osmond had just walked into a Metallica concert.

Girls

Steve was a charmer and a bit of a heartbreaker. Jayme recalls, "Every day, as soon as he got home from school, the phone at our house would start ringing. The girls were calling." At that time, the place to be in Clearfield on Friday nights was the Admiral Theater, where the preteens would hang out and catch the current movie. Right next to the Admiral Theater was Chandler Rexall Drug, where kids would stock up on candy for the movie. They also sold friendship rings for $1. Steve bought one each Friday night and gave it to a new girl each Saturday. Occasionally, he bought two and had two "girlfriends" at the same time. These were not deep relationships. They couldn't even qualify as puppy love. Still, it is telling that Steve can count sixty-six girlfriends of this variety.

Carol McGrath remembers Steve inviting her into the tree house in his back yard. Eleven-year-old Steve leaned in to give her a romantic kiss. Just before their lips touched, he whipped out a Kleenex from his pocket and put it between their lips. You can never be too careful about germs.

When Steve was fourteen or fifteen, he went to Cedar City, Utah, to play in a state championship tournament in the Babe Ruth

Baseball League. After practice, Steve and his teammates hit on the local girls. The girls flirted back and soon the Clearfield boys and the Cedar City girls were walking together down Main Street. Things were going well until the hometown boys saw them and their alpha anger surged. The Cedar City boys jumped in a car, drove towards the outsiders, and gunned it. Steve and his friends fled into a park and shook off their pursuers.

Steve was cute and his baby blues were framed by eyelashes that looked like he had crimped them with an eyelash curler. He was athletic, magnetic, and already had a vibe that said he was going places. Just underneath that vibe, there was one that said, "Don't mess with me." With all that, it was easy for Steve to pull off cool. He naturally had it. However, in sixth grade his cool was threatened. "I thought anybody wearing glasses looked dorky," Steve recalls. Yet, he knew his vision was subpar. On the day of the school eye test, he memorized the eye chart. "It seemed smart at the time. I started wearing glasses in eighth grade and I needed them in sixth."

Talking

Steve inherited traits from both his parents that have served him well his whole life. From his mother he got a keen intuition and a sense for business, leadership, and managing people. She instilled in him a prodigious work ethic. Most propitiously, he inherited her ability to read people. Steve got his father's athleticism, a persuasive charm, an outgoing nature, and a penchant for talking. By the time he was twelve, he could wax lyrical about *anything*. On his second-grade report card, his teacher Mrs. Guiver comments, "Steven is a good student. The only thing that is any problem is his talking." A mother of one of Steve's friends banned him from sleepovers because he talked too much.

North Davis Junior High

Two photographs of Steve from junior high are telling. The first is a picture of the eighth-grade class officers. Steve is the class president. He is positioned between his vice president and secretary, two girls who look more like juniors in high school than eighth graders. Since the girls tower over him by at least six inches, it looks like Steve is sitting down. Steve is standing. The second picture is Steve's eighth-grade photo. Steve is wearing a suit. He was the only boy in junior high wearing a suit for the sheer pleasure of it. Maybe ever. It's hallmark Steve Hardison.

Eighth grade was a banner year. Steve started on the football, basketball, and baseball teams. He was a class officer. He was confident, even cocky, adored by girls, gregarious, and popular. But in ninth grade, things started to unravel. By tenth grade at Clearfield High, his inner world was shattered. All his male friends' voices were cavern deep. They were adding muscles and inches to their frames. Steve looked like a little boy. It's a hard thing to hide, especially in the locker room.

One game day after a tough loss against a rival junior high basketball team, Steve's angst came out in tears. His coach, Carl Clayton, approached him. "Hardison, are you upset about the loss?"

"No. It's not that . . . Coach, what if I never grow?"

"You don't need to worry about that," responded Clayton. "You are going to be at least 6'4". I played baseball with your dad at Hill Field. Your body is just like his. You are going to grow."

Steve was shocked on two accounts. First, he had never met anyone, outside of family members, who knew his father. Second, he was astonished at the prediction. Steve graduated high school at 5'8". Three years later, he was 6'4".

Steve's crisis of confidence must be put in context. His innate confidence may have taken a hit, but no one other than Steve noticed it. He still had his swagger, certainty, and arrogance. That is as fixed in Steve as his blood type. Consider an incident that occurred when Steve was in eighth grade. He was walking down the hall at North Davis Junior High when he spied a boy flirting with his girlfriend. Infuriated, Steve walked up to this boy, who was much bigger than Steve, with his dukes in fighting position. Steve demanded to know what he was doing. Next, Steve barked, "Do you wanna fight?" thinking his rival would back down.

The boy landed an uppercut right in Steve's jaw. Steve's bottom teeth went through his tongue. There was blood everywhere. One punch had taken Steve out. Indomitable as ever, Steve spat out, "Have you had enough?"

Chapter 4

At Risk

Steve was strutting his stuff. After all, a cute girl was watching. He went for "wow" and threw his bicycle into a skid. He miscalculated. He crashed into the glass door of the donut shop. Lying in razor-sharp rubble, bleeding and stunned, Steve felt compelled to move. Seconds later, the glass that was still in the upper frame of the door came crashing down like a guillotine.

Steve escaped serious injuries, but he needed a trip to the hospital to stitch up the gashes. Maurine ran in. She saw Steve sitting on the counter, his hand wrapped in a towel that was oozing red. He was alive. Whew. Her next thought: "How are we going to pay for this?"

Another day in the life of Steve Hardison.

Maurine held her breath when the phone rang, especially if Steve was out and about. Too often, the caller said, "Steve has been hurt."

It's not that Steve was clumsy or unlucky. Steve's intensity created a higher probability for injuries. Add an adventurous spirit, a penchant to impress, and a laser focus that ignores caution, rules, and sometimes just plain common sense and the plethora of injuries starts to make sense. Steve suffered two concussions while on the junior high football team and another when he fell while hiking in a canyon. When he was in eleventh grade, he knocked out his front teeth in a basketball game. A year later, he was water-skiing and took a spill. The ski hit his bottom teeth, laying them back, nearly horizontal. The dentist had to wire his bottom teeth back into their sockets and Steve subsisted on baby food for several months. He has also broken his wrist and his collarbone, and torn a ligament in his ankle, all for the love of sports.

Steve did not invite all his injuries. His favorite store in Clearfield was Melvin's Shoes on Main Street. He often lingered at the front window. He would have loved to do more than window shop, but the shoes all cost more money than he had. One day, Steve broke away from his shoe gazing to go home. As he stepped into the street, his brother Phil yelled something about watching out. Steve stopped and turned to Phil. The car did not stop. The impact sent him flying through the air. He landed hard. Steve jumped up and started walking around. When the policeman asked Steve how he was doing, Steve said, "I'm okay. Really. It's no big deal." What he was thinking was, "We don't have money to go to the doctor." The policeman let Steve walk home. When he arrived, he crawled into bed. It wasn't until his mom got home from work that evening that he dissolved into tears.

When Steve was seven, Maurine's boyfriend made little wooden boats for Steve and Phil. These weren't just basic boats. They had a cabin, a mast, and a crafted hull. They were painted candy-apple red.

Steve had never had anything so exquisite. After bundling up in his heavy, dark blue parka, Steve ran to the culvert at the end of the street to launch his boat on its maiden voyage. It had been raining. The water was flowing with unusual volume and force. The current tumbled and tossed the little boat and shot it downstream. Steve ran along the culvert until he found a spot where he could retrieve his boat. He reached out as far as he could. Too far. The water was deeper than Steve was tall. The insulation inside the parka sopped up the frigid water and the jacket got anchor heavy. Steve thrashed. He reached out to grab something, anything, but got only a handful of water. And terror. There was plenty of terror to grab. Suddenly, Steve was out of the culvert, sitting on the path. No one was around. Steve had not climbed out. Steve *could not* have climbed out. Maybe it was an angel. If so, the angel's saving power was reserved for Steve. Steve never saw his red boat again.

Twice, Steve was in serious car accidents and walked away unscathed. When Rob was newly married, he bought a new Volkswagen Beetle. Steve longed to drive it. When he asked, Rob handed him the keys and said, "Just don't get in a wreck."

An hour later, Steve called. "Rob, I've been in a wreck." It hadn't been snowing when he left, but it was winter in Utah. A storm rolled in. The roads got slick. Steve lost control. Steve was fine. The car did not fare as well. Steve had just totaled Rob's new car.

In addition to the accidents and the sports injuries, Steve did plenty of rowdy and reckless things, the kinds of things that have parents scratching their heads and citing the studies about teenagers' brains not being fully developed until they are twenty-five years old. For instance, when Steve and his friend Larry Belnap were seniors

Steve's senior picture, 1973

in high school, they went to Salt Lake City for a rock concert. Steve asked his mom if she could get them a room at the Rodeway Inn so they wouldn't have to drive home late at night.

At the hotel, they met a group of girls who were there as a part of a church event. The girls invited Steve and Larry up to their room. They would have to be discreet to avoid detection by the girls' chaperones. They weren't discreet enough. Larry relates:

> All of a sudden, an adult was pounding on the door and saying, "Girls, what's going on in there?" One of the girls said, "You guys have to go out on the balcony." It was the middle of winter. It was late at night. It was freezing cold. But we climbed out on the balcony. It was no more than two feet wide. We were freezing, but we couldn't go back in until she left.

The chaperone started looking around. She was obviously suspicious. She said something about checking the balcony. So, Steve and I had to climb over the railing of the balcony and hang on to the outside of the balcony. We were on the twelfth story! We were shaking so badly, trying to hold on to this railing. The woman slid the curtain open and stepped out on the balcony. She couldn't see us because we were hanging off the side. I guess she figured that she was hearing things and finally left the room.

Not all of Steve's teenage adventures were this perilous, but many included a sense of daring, adventure, and mischief. During church services, Steve and his friends would skip out and go into the parking lot where they would hunt for unlocked cars. Once found, they put the car in neutral (something that could be done in the 1970s) and pushed it into the junior high parking lot, which was adjacent to the church parking lot. Then they would hide and watch the churchgoers exit the church and start looking for their car. Sounds a little like tabasco sauce in Oreos.

Steve and his friends also enjoyed launching apples from the local apple orchards at passing cars on Friday nights. Sometimes the drivers slammed on the brakes and chased the offenders. Sometimes they called the police. The boys learned to scatter. The police learned where Steve lived. Steve quips, "When there was trouble in Clearfield, the policed showed up at our door."

Some of Steve's devilry was more serious. He became adept at shoplifting. Steve never tried drugs, but he drank plenty of alcohol, a dangerous practice for the son of an alcoholic. Drinking was typical weekend entertainment for Steve and his friends, not unusual for high school boys, but sometimes they drank *before* school. While working at the Rodeway Inn as a linen boy, Steve would pour the leftover alcohol from the mini bottles people left in their rooms into a gallon bottle. When the bottle was full, they had enough for their weekend party.

In reality, many of Steve's antics were not atypical for a teenage boy, especially one who had an abundance of energy, little supervision, a love for adventure, and wasn't afraid to bend—or break—the rules. But for Steve, there was more going on. Underneath the bravado, the cool, and the charisma, Steve was lost. He was uncertain about his future. He was afraid he would never grow. He felt alone. He had several unresolved issues from his childhood that he had stuffed down inside, down to his toes, so far down he didn't know they were there, so far down they wouldn't see light for another thirteen years. But they were still there, messing with Steve, like radiation.

Chapter 5

Finding God

It was an unlikely place to find Steve Hardison. Seminary was a class for religious instruction for members of The Church of Jesus Christ of Latter-day Saints. It was a non-credit, release-time class, held during the school day because of the high concentration of church members in Utah. It wasn't Steve's thing, but it was an easy class and all his friends were taking it. He sat towards the back with his feet kicked up on the chair in front of him. Lorrie Weeks, one of the cutest blondes in the senior class, sat behind him. Sometimes she pulled out her comb and combed his hair. It was like having his back rubbed. Steve was in total bliss. Somewhere at the front of the room a religious guy was droning on, sounding like the adults in the Charlie Brown cartoons.

One day, his teacher yanked Steve out his reverie and out of the classroom. In the hall, Brother Fraser probed, "Steve, why are you here?"

Steve pointed over at Lorrie. "Right there . . . And no homework . . .

And I want one of those fancy graduation certificates."

"That's not why you come to seminary. You come to seminary to learn about God and Jesus Christ." Looking hard in Steve's eyes, Brother Fraser asked, "Steve, do you believe in God?"

Tipping his chin up, Steve said, "Well, if there's a God, He hasn't been around my house much."

After a minute, Brother Fraser said, "Steve, instead of coming into our class, why don't you go in my office and read the Book of Mormon. Find out for yourself if it's true. Find out if God is real."

Steve's relationship with The Church of Jesus Christ of Latter-day Saints was complicated. His grandparents were devout members. Steve had gone to church on and off throughout the years. It was the culture of his community. But Steve still smarted from being kicked out of his congregation's Boy Scout troop for punching a fellow scout. Steve made sure he attended enough church to qualify for playing on the church basketball team, but attendance wasn't the same as worship. During the most sacred moments of the Sunday service, Steve was crawling around in the rafters, having accessed the attic through a crawlspace he discovered. When he fulfilled the duties given to fourteen- and fifteen-year-old boys to help prepare the Sacrament, he used rusty water that had a bad taste and pushed the Sacrament cups down extra hard so people had a hard time getting them out of the tray without spilling them. Every month representatives of the church (called home teachers) came to check on the Hardison family. When they rang the doorbell, the family hit the floor so they couldn't be seen. It was easier to find alcohol in the fridge than scriptures in the house. In spite of all this, something in what Brother Fraser said, or in his way of saying it, or something Steve couldn't explain, cut through Steve's insolence. He accepted the invitation.

Within weeks of immersing himself in scripture, Steve began to have profound insights and personal revelations. He felt the Spirit. His mind was opened. His heart was softened. He cut his hair. He quit drinking. He started cleaning up his life. He began studying, directing his hallmark intensity and focus to the pursuit of religious knowledge.

Steve's ecclesiastical leader, Bishop Doug Barrus noticed. He called Steve in for a visit. He started with some general chit chat, then asked, "What are your goals for the future, Steve?"

Steve had no vision for his future. The thought of college had not entered his mind. Not once. He was floating. He was buying time. He was trying to not think about the future. When Steve didn't answer, Bishop Barrus moved on. "What are your thoughts about a mission?"

A mission? Serving a two-year mission is expected of most Latter-day Saint boys when they turn nineteen (currently eighteen). It is a mark of devotion and a spiritual rite of passage. Boys who grow up in families active in the Mormon faith start thinking about missions early, even before they start grade school. They sing in Sunday School, "I hope they call me on a mission, when I have grown a foot or two." They put their quarters and nickels in piggy banks dedicated for mission funds. The topic had never been broached in Steve's family. Steve was gobsmacked.

Bishop Barrus again changed tack. He asked Steve to spend the next week thinking, praying, and making a list of all the things he needed to repent of. This was something Steve got. He was eager to take this on. When they met the next week, Steve's list was several legal pages long. Bishop Barrus explained that Steve would need to ask God for forgiveness, and he would need to make restitution. For instance, Steve had once pulled up to the stands where golfers leave their clubs at golf courses and loaded a set into his trunk and drove off. He still had the owner's name tag. He called the owner, explained what he did, apologized, and offered to pay for the clubs.

Stolen golf clubs, pilfered eight-track tapes, and purloined belts—those were the easy things to make right. Some things were more abstract. Some things were mortifying.

Steve called or visited every single person on his list. He repented for every single transgression he could recall. The response was consistent. People were not angry; they were moved. It took Steve six months. The process was life-altering.

Steve was now ready and had a burning desire to serve a mission. He wanted to share the transformation he experienced with others. Phil thought his brother was crazy and needled him regularly. When Steve walked by, Phil fell on his knees, made the sign of the cross and said, "Forgive me, Padre, for I have sinned," appropriating Catholic piety, not Mormon. The other members of his family didn't get it, but they didn't hassle him. It wouldn't have mattered if they had. Steve was on fire.

Chapter 6

Gainfully Employed

Steve had his first job when he was nine years old. There was a convenience store near Steve's house called the Milk-O-Rama. They sold milk, gasoline, sundries, milkshakes, and donuts. One day when he was in the Milk-O-Rama, ogling the donuts, the woman working at the counter asked Steve if he would like to make some money. He belted out an enthusiastic "Yes!" Soon, Steve had a wire basket with a strap that went around his neck. Each day, his boss would fill his basket with boxes of donuts and Steve would go door-to-door selling donuts. If he sold them all, he would come back and get more. He got a percentage of the donut sales. He sold a lot of donuts.

When Steve was ten years old, he asked his mom for twenty dollars to get a football uniform so he could play Pop Warner football. She didn't have the money. Building on his donut success, Steve found a job selling magazine subscriptions. The company that hired him drove him and several other young salespeople to Logan, about forty-five minutes away, and dropped them off. They descended on Logan like ants. Steve relates:

> I loved this job and the opportunity it gave me to talk to so many people. Yes, I sold magazine subscriptions, but I also started polishing my ability to connect with people. This wasn't just a technique. I genuinely cared about the people I met. One day I was talking to a woman at her doorstep when I saw she had a clock just like one we had. When I mentioned it, she said her clock didn't have a key. Well, we had a key, but our clock didn't work. The solution was obvious. I promised her I would bring her our key. Logan is a long way from Clearfield if you don't have a driver's license or a car, but I got back there and took her the key. We forged a friendship. Years later, she came to my mission farewell.

When Steve was seventeen, he worked at Murdock Manufacturing in the Freeport Center. They manufactured bombs for the defense department. He stood at a machine and drilled holes into cast iron. He did this over and over and over. It was monotonous and mind-numbing. He lasted three days.

Steve soon found another job. This one entailed a long commute, an hour's drive each way. Steve went to his friend Larry Belnap and told him about the job. Steve enjoyed working with Larry. Plus, Steve didn't have a car. Larry did. Steve handed Larry a pair of white patent leather shoes and a white leather belt and told him to wear them to the interview, which Steve had set up for the next day. White shoes for a factory job? That seemed strange, but Larry trusted Steve. When he showed up to the interview, Larry "noticed that all the men were from Indianapolis, Indiana, and they all had white belts and white patent leather shoes." He fit right in and he got the job. They would both be working at Balkamp, Incorporated, an automotive parts distributor.

Balkamp was a step up from Murdock Manufacturing, but it was not in any way Steve's dream job. After working at Balkamp for about six months, Steve opened up the newspaper one day and saw a big, two-page ad: "Max Factor Coming to Clearfield, Freeport Center. Jobs available." That looked promising. On the appointed day, he went to the location listed in the newspaper. He saw dozens of long tables with hundreds of people filling out applications. Once they finished, they put their applications in a box.

Steve walked over to the man who looked like he was directing things and asked, "Who is in charge here?"

He responded, "I am."

Steve said, "I am not very old. I don't have anything to put on that piece of paper that will give you an idea of who I am and what I can do. If I put my application in there, you are going to miss the talents I have."

This got the man's attention. He interviewed Steve and offered him a job as the inventory control manager. Steve loved this job and he did it well. Although he was just eighteen, he set up the entire inventory control system at this location.

Steve had worked hard for several years. He had no other choice. If he wanted to buy something, he had to make it happen. He and his siblings needed to contribute to the household expenses. Since his religious conversion, he had been saving money to pay for his mission. He was on target to have the money he needed—until Maurine had her stroke. She fought back from death's edge, but it took time. She was out of work for months. She had no disability insurance. She received no paychecks when she wasn't working. Steve drained his savings account to help keep his family afloat. Steve was sure that God would provide.

Chapter 7

A Man on a Mission

Missions are an integral part of The Church of Jesus Christ of Latter-day Saints. They have their own language and culture. Without a brief explanation, Steve's mission experience would be enigmatic to all but members of his church.

Young men of good standing in The Church of Jesus Christ of Latter-day Saints are expected to serve a mission when they are eighteen. Girls can serve a mission, but it is optional. Missionaries do not choose where they go. They receive a letter (now an email) that tells them where they have been called to serve. Often, they need to learn a new language. They serve for two years. They are not paid for their work. They pay their own living expenses.

A missionary leaves his young adult life behind. At the time Steve served his mission, a missionary communicated with his family only by letter; he could call home only on Christmas and Mother's Day. A missionary does not date. He doesn't watch television. He doesn't return home for weddings or funerals. He is *always* with his companion, another missionary who is assigned to be his coworker. These two missionaries form what is called a "companionship." They work together, study together, eat together, and live in the same apartment.

Missions are divided into geographic areas. The smallest is called an "area." It is the place where a missionary is assigned to live and work. Several of these areas make a district; several districts constitute a zone. Several zones create a mission.

In a companionship, one missionary is the senior missionary. Missionary companionships that are particularly effective, obedient, and hard-working will serve in leadership capacities, as district leaders and zone leaders. The top missionaries of the mission serve as assistants to the presidents. Mission presidents are men who are called to serve for three years, without pay, to oversee the mission. A mission president is accompanied by his wife and children, if they happen to have children under the age of eighteen. They are the only adults providing supervision for the approximately two hundred missionaries in their mission. The mission president assigns the missionary companionships. Typically, he will change the companionships every six or twelve weeks, though there are exceptions.

A missionary's objective is to teach the principles and precepts of The Church of Jesus Christ of Latter-day Saints. Those who accept these teachings join the faith through baptism. Baptism is performed for those who are eight years old or older. Missionaries may provide support in helping a family transition into involvement in the church, but with baptism, their primary responsibility is complete. Within the church's belief system, there is still one more step. They believe families will continue to exist in heaven. For this to happen, they must receive sacred ordinances in their temples. This is the pinnacle of their faith.

Steve had been checking the mailbox daily. Finally, the oversized white envelope with the words "The Church of Jesus Christ of Latter-day Saints" in the upper left corner arrived. He didn't wait to gather family or friends. He went straight to Grandma Ellen and together they opened the letter that would chart the next two years of Steve's life. He read the words: "You are hereby called to be a missionary . . . to labour in the England London South Mission. You are scheduled to enter the Mission Home in Salt Lake City on Saturday, 12 October, 1974 . . . We ask that you please send your written acceptance promptly."

Steve's first thought was, "I'm teaching The Beatles. I'm teaching the Queen."

Steve's first visit was to Brother Fraser, whose wake-up call had set Steve on a path that few would have predicted. Steve's pace on that path was about to hit Mach speed.

Three months later, Steve landed at Heathrow airport. He was eager to plunge into one of the greatest experiences of his life. He was committed to not waste a minute. It was a commitment he made the minute he determined to serve a mission. His commitment ratcheted up when his congregation stepped up to help finance his mission expenses.

Reality hit quickly, and it hit hard. Steve recalls:

I remember my first week in my first area. I was in Leighton Buzzard, a little village about fifty miles north of London. It looked like somebody rolled the clock back two hundred years. I was thousands of miles away from my home, my family, and anything that was familiar. I was tired. I was overwhelmed. I was scared. I was homesick. I was lonely. I was experiencing major culture shock. I remember kneeling down to pray and crying, but trying to hide it from my missionary companion. I didn't cover it up very well, because about ten minutes later he said, "Pray your heart out, elder. Pray your heart out."

Serving as a missionary for The Church of Jesus Christ of Latter-day Saints is not easy, but it is simple. There is only one thing to do: share the gospel of Jesus Christ for ten to twelve hours a day. Before the ten-hour shift of knocking on doors and talking to people begins, the missionary and his/her companion spend a couple of hours studying the scriptures and the lessons they will teach. They have an allotted time for the routine parts of life, like showering and meal prep. Most of Steve's meals consisted of Weetabix cold cereal. Why waste time on meal prep when there are people to teach and lives to change? This led some of his companions to call and beg the mission president to be transferred. "This guy doesn't even stop to eat!"

Missionaries spend their days talking to people on the streets. Walking up to complete strangers and starting a conversation out of the blue was daunting for many missionaries, especially when they were new. Steve was in seventh heaven. He loved meeting people. He was never at a loss for something clever or fun to say. He was talking the birds out of the trees.

Missionaries also knocked on a lot of doors. This is called "tracting." It can be hard. Missionaries get a lot of doors slammed in their face. This can be demoralizing. Steve had become inured to knocking on doors and rejection years before when he sold doughnuts and magazine subscriptions. This was no different, except now he had something much more valuable to offer.

One day, Steve looked around at the town where he was tracting and realized that missionaries had been tracting there since 1842. If he wanted someone to listen to him, he had better get creative.

Steve and his companion, Paul Waite, knocked on a door. The woman who answered didn't even open the door. She flicked open the mail slot and said, "We know who you are. We aren't interested."

Steve said, "My name is Elder Hardison. What is your name?"

"Doreen Crook," she responded.

"Is your husband home? Could we talk to him?" asked Steve.

"I'm ironing his trousers. He's not available. He's in the back room with his trousers down."

"You're telling me that you have a crook in your house with his trousers down and you haven't called the police yet?"

Steve could hear a man laughing. "Let them in," Mr. Crook said as he slipped on his pants.

Steve baptized Mr. and Mrs. Crook and five of their seven children.

Steve loved missionary work and he made it fun. Missionaries in Steve's mission, which included London and its southern suburbs, tracted in a lot of apartment buildings. Sometimes, Steve would have his companion walk up one flight of stairs above Steve. Steve would knock on the door and when someone answered, he would say, "We are here to tell you about a book from heaven." On that cue, his companion would drop a Book of Mormon and it would land in Steve's hands. Every now and again, the book would hit Steve's glasses and knock them off-kilter.

Steve had fun, but never at the expense of working hard and working effectively. Scott Parker, who served with Steve in the England London South Mission, says, "Steve was the same height he is now, but take off about forty pounds, maybe fifty pounds. He was very skinny, not just lanky, but skinny on skinny. But he was fearless. He was fun. He was funny. He was incredibly articulate. He was dynamic. He was hardworking. He was very diligent. There was no screwing around. There was no playtime." What happens when fearless, funny, and indefatigable unite? "Steve was far and away the most effective missionary I ever experienced," says Scott. "He out-found, out-taught, and out-baptized everyone in the mission!"

One day, Steve and his companion met a woman named Julia Burgess. She was receptive and was later baptized. Years later when Steve and Amy returned to England and visited Julia, their conversation turned to their first meeting. Julia asked, "Did I ever tell you the rest of the story?" She hadn't.

The night before Steve met Julia, she was sitting on her front porch smoking a cigarette. She was divorced and was raising two young boys. There wasn't enough money for their basic needs. Julia was exhausted and discouraged. It all seemed like too much. She groaned a prayer. "God, if you are there, you are going to have to tell me. You are going to have to help me. Otherwise, I'm going to end it all." Steve and his companion knocked on her door the next morning. When she answered, they told her they had a message from God.

Steve's two years were filled with experiences like these. These years were a period of intense growth. Steve drew close to God. He used and developed every talent he had. He found that the difficult events of his life had deepened his soul and enabled him to understand and empathize with people whose lives were difficult.

Steve's talents were evident. It wasn't long before Steve was given leadership positions. Steve served with two different mission presidents, Donald Livingstone and Richard Eyre. Typically, mission presidents are mature men in their fifties or sixties. Sometimes they are in their forties. Richard Eyre was thirty-one. Eyre was a Harvard-trained management consultant and a truly extraordinary man. After his three-year service as a mission president, Richard and his wife Linda wrote *Teaching Your Children Values*, which was the first family and parenting book in fifty years—since Dr. Spock—to reach number one on *The New York Times* bestseller list. They were named by President Reagan in the 1980s to direct the White House Conference on Children and Parents. They have appeared on Oprah's television show. Richard Eyre exerted a powerful influence on Steve's life.

Here are Richard and Linda's accounts of meeting Steve, in their own words.

Linda Eyre

Steve Hardison was the first smile I saw as we disembarked from our very long flight to London with our four little children, age five and under. We had flown through the night from Salt Lake City and I was bleary-eyed and exhausted! I had never dealt with jet lag, as this was my first overseas flight and, sparing the details, I will say that it had not been a pleasant experience! With four needy preschoolers in tow, and a husband excited for the task ahead (even though he was only about ten years older than many of the missionaries), I must admit to being a bit daunted! I was about to be a "mission mom" to two hundred young missionaries, which for starters meant learning their names, a little about their families, their hometowns and a bit about their lives, as well as learning to run a new home, which involved feeding multitudes of missionaries and dignitaries. That beaming smile of Steve's saved me that day! He was so kind and encouraging to me while engaging so enthusiastically with our kids.

Richard Eyre

We were young ourselves at the time. I was thirty-one and Linda was twenty-eight.

Our flight was met by the two "Assistants to the Mission President" (the two top leaders of the two hundred missionaries serving in the South of England). Their names were Glen Foreman and Steve Hardison. While they had been chosen by my predecessor, it quickly became apparent to me that they would have been my selections as well. Steve was the younger of the two, just twenty-one years old, and was in the final few months of his missionary service. He had the respect and allegiance of the missionaries he led, particularly the "middle management" of the mission's district leaders and zone leaders. He also knew all of the missionaries and had perceptive and accurate opinions and assessments of their abilities, and of their strengths and weaknesses.

I leaned a lot on Steve and on his knowledge and insights. I felt like he had particular gifts in listening and evaluating. This not only helped him lead the mission, it made him a good teacher, assistant, and counselor—far beyond his years in his maturity, responsibilities and abilities. It was clear even then that he was more interested in people and in helping others succeed than in compiling personal accomplishments and accolades.

Steve brought all his focus, intensity, and passion to his missionary work. He never squandered a minute. His dedication was total and complete. Every day of his mission he prayed, "God, I'm giving everything I've got. Every day I am teaching people about eternal families. Please, when I get home, help me find someone I can create a loving and eternal family with."

Chapter 8

Meeting Amy

Steve knew nothing about Arizona except that it had cacti and Native Americans and it was where his mom now lived. She had moved there while Steve was in England. She had found a higher-paying job in Phoenix. Plus, Steve's mission had spurred Maurine to return to her faith. It would be easier to live a new life in a new place. Spiritually and financially, Arizona was a good move for her. It also left Steve homeless since he had no intention of living anywhere but Utah, where he had friends, contacts and opportunities. Still, Steve wanted to see his mom, and so he made the thirteen-hour drive to the valley of perpetual sunshine. He never intended to stay long.

In The Church of Jesus Christ of Latter-day Saints, the myriad responsibilities (called "callings"), from major leadership roles to teaching three-year-olds in Sunday School, are filled by members of the congregation. All serve without pay. No one requests a calling. All callings are rotated every few years. At the time Steve returned from his mission, Maurine served in a calling that enabled her to work closely with the stake president, a local leader who presides over approximately eight local congregations. Steve's mother was an impressive woman and a capable leader. When she hinted to the stake president that Steve would be a valuable asset in a class that prepared and trained future missionaries, the stake president jumped at the opportunity. Shortly after he met Steve, he asked him to help with the class. Steve agreed and extended his visit.

The class was led by Gordon Jennings. Steve and another young man named David Bedford were called to help and support Gordon. As Gordon got to know Steve, he saw a man with fierce spiritual conviction, just like Gordon's sister-in-law, Amy Blake. The longer Gordon knew Steve, the more convinced he was that Steve and Amy should meet. Amy relates:

> Gordon had told me a couple of times that he had met someone he really wanted to introduce me to. It wasn't happening, so Gordon got creative. He asked the two guys who were helping him with the stake missionary prep class if they were okay if they stopped by his in-laws so he could drop off the cookie sheets they had used that night.
>
> I didn't know about the cookie sheet ruse. I just knew that when I got home from a meeting there was a note sitting on the counter from my sister. It said, "Gordon is bringing someone for you to meet about 8:00. Be there. Look cute."
>
> Shortly thereafter, Gordon walked in with two gentlemen. One was the most handsome man I had ever seen. He was movie-star good looking.
>
> The other was Steve Hardison.
>
> But Steve was dazzling. He had charm, charisma, and confidence. He definitely had confidence. It wasn't love at first sight for either of us. But it was "interest at first sight,"

at least for me. Gordon said Steve would call me.

He didn't call—not the next day and not the next week. About the time I wrote him off, the phone rang. We had a fun conversation, and we set up a date. On my mom's birthday, February 10, 1977, Steve came over and we made doughnuts. Four days later, I got a Valentine from him. On it, he wrote:

February 14, 1977

Amy,

I hope you have a lovely Valentine's Day.

Thank you so much for the most enjoyable evening. Needless to say, your fantastic doughnuts didn't last long.

Perhaps Gordon, Melinda, you, and I could get together for an after-Valentine's Day tennis match?

By the way, I'm impressed with your many talents. I'm looking forward to hearing you play the piano.

RSVP

Steven F. Hardison.

Twenty years later, Steve told me he had passed out a dozen Valentine's Day cards that day. He ended up with one extra and decided to drop it by my house. It's a good thing I didn't know at the time that I was an afterthought.

I brainstormed for a fun way to respond to this tennis invitation and decided to write my RSVP on a tennis ball and send it to Steve in the mail. Steve liked the creativity.

By date two, magic was starting to happen. It didn't take long until we both determined we had found the person we wanted to spend the rest of our lives with. There was only one complication. I was seventeen and still in high school. Meeting the man of my dreams at seventeen had definitely NOT been in my life plan. But what do you do when you meet someone so amazing, loving, talented, fun, creative, charming, powerful, full of dreams and potential, and simply too good to let go?

Couples have their stories, the ones they laugh about over the years, the ones their kids ask them to tell over and over, the ones that brand their life with their unique imprint. The cookie sheet encounter and the Valentine's card are two of Amy and Steve's. Another is the peanut butter-honey-and-banana sandwich date. Amy writes:

Helen Keller said it. Steve lives it. I am swept away in its current. "Life is either a daring adventure or nothing." I should have known. There were signs from the very first.

We hadn't been dating long. We were nearly engaged. It was a beautiful spring day and Steve had planned our date. He said he would handle lunch, but when he showed up, he was traveling light. Oh well. I can always eat later. We jumped on our bikes and pedaled away.

We ended up at the playground of a grade school. The merry-go-rounds I had loved as a kid were not to be found, but there were swings and monkey bars. I had to wad my legs up grasshopper-like to sit in the swing. We were substantially out of scale, but we still got lift. Our setting prompted stories of our childhood.

"Have you ever had a peanut butter-honey-and-banana sandwich?" Steve asked.

"No. Do they put all those on one sandwich?"

"They're delicious," Steve assured me.

"Hmmmm." No comment.

After swinging and talking, Steve said he was hungry. I raised an eyebrow.

"I have an idea," Steve said. "I'll go ask someone if they will make us lunch, maybe even peanut butter-honey-and-banana sandwiches."

"Would he really do that?" I wondered. "I hope he wouldn't really do that. . . . Oh no."

Steve was knocking on the door of a house across the street from the park. A middle-aged woman opened the door. Steve made his request and she stared at him and then said, "Are you serious?" Steve assured her he was. She started to shut the door and then in mid-motion changed her mind. "Are you really serious?" she asked once more.

"Now's the time," I thought. "Here is where you say you were just kidding. . . . Here. . . .Right now. . . .Oh crap."

In about ten minutes, she reappeared with a paper sack. I peeked in. There were two sandwiches. It looked like some peanut butter and the edges of a banana were poking out from between the bread. And something else . . . Was it a salad? And drinks? This is weird.

"Now, all we need is a blanket," said Steve.

This was too much, too over-the-top. Steve dragged me to the next house. A gruff-looking man opened the door. "Sir, do you have a blanket we could use for a picnic."

He grunted, handed us a blanket that was sitting by the door, and turned away.

Steve had a nice lunch. I had too much to digest. Why would strangers do that? How do we sufficiently thank them? Does Steve always do stuff like this?

Low-grade bewilderment escalated to full-blown anxiety

when Steve packed up the blanket and our detritus and started riding in the opposite direction from the man's house.

"Where are you going? We have to take the blanket back." I said.

Steve kept pedaling.

"Steve, we need to take the blanket back."

He kept peddling.

"I'm not joking. We have to take the blanket back to its owner. Really."

Finally, Steve turned his bike around. "I am."

It all came together. He was taking the blanket back to its owner. *He* was the owner. This was no casual ride to the park. It was carefully planned and well-executed. It was Steve's riff on a basic date. I should have known Steve would never be conventional. I could count on fun. I could count on unique. I could count on Steve talking to strangers and dragging me out of my comfort zone. This will be an adventure.

Before meeting Amy, Steve had dated women who were in college, and college graduates who had already launched their careers. He saw in seventeen-year-old Amy a depth that was unique. He loved how her eyes sparkled, especially when she smiled. She filled a need he didn't know he had. When he was with her, he felt safe. The clincher for Steve occurred when they were deciding what to do one Sunday afternoon. Somewhat sheepishly, Steve said he would like to study the scriptures. He had just spent two of the most intense years of his life absorbed in spiritual things. He had been thrust back into a workaday world and he missed the light. When he saw the knowledge and love Amy had for the scriptures, he knew he had found his wife.

In the Mormon faith, teenagers don't start dating until they are sixteen. Amy had just turned seventeen when she met Steve. During her one year of eligibility, she hadn't dated a lot. She was an old soul and, in some ways, had matured out of high school before she ever got there. Add a move from Phoenix to Mesa during her junior high years that was socially traumatic and a profound spiritual awakening at fourteen, and it is clear why Amy always felt a little out of step with other teenagers. When she met Steve, she met someone who was four years older, who had experienced a soul-expanding mission, who loved the Gospel of Jesus Christ with passion and commitment, and who adored her in a way she had never experienced. Clearly, their primary connection was spiritual. But underneath that, some deep emotional needs were exerting a magnetic pull, strong enough for Steve and Amy to know they belonged together, strong enough to make them think they were alike.

Their first meeting was on January 23, 1977. Their first date was February 10, 1977. On April 20, 1977, Steve asked Amy to marry him, but by that point they had already known for a month that they had each met their one and only. The breakneck speed is astounding, scary even—downright terrifying if you were Amy's mom, especially since Amy was only seventeen, especially since Steve had just barely rolled into town. He was a sweet talker, but was he as good as he looked? Carol Blake was apprehensive. Amy's dad, Kent, recognized that Steve would be successful and would take care of his daughter. Amy had always been mature. He thought marrying young would work for her. The only comment Kent ever made that was slightly negative was that Steve had the most unusual hairstyle he had ever seen. But that is what everyone thought—everyone but Steve. Steve could only find one barber in Mesa who could cut his hair so it looked like a yarmulke perched on top of his head.

Once Steve asked Amy for her hand in marriage, the next step was for Steve to ask her father for his permission. Steve told Kent that he didn't know how to be a husband or a father. He had had no role model in his home. He had seen more divorces than

Engagement, 1977

successful marriages in his family. Kent, a successful attorney, was not ignorant of the risks. However, he saw Steve's heart and his potential. He gave his nod of approval.

The next day, Steve drove away. He felt the weight and responsibility of finding a place to live and a way to support his soon-to-be bride. Utah, where he had contacts and opportunities, was definitely the place to do it. He enrolled in Weber State University in Ogden, Utah, found work at Hill Air Force Base, and got licensed to sell real estate. In June, he met up with Amy and her family at Lake Powell, Arizona. As they sat under the evening stars, he slipped a ring on Amy's finger. They were officially engaged.

Throughout that summer, Steve and Amy dated long distance. Once or twice they saw each other. Sometimes they called each other—but long-distance phone calls were expensive. Mostly they wrote letters, real postal mail that took three or four days to travel between Arizona and Utah. They wrote nearly every day.

At the end of August, Amy moved to Provo, Utah, to attend Brigham Young University, something that had been arranged before she had met Steve. Now they were only seventy-two miles apart. Steve drove from Clearfield to Provo to see her every weekend until they got married. On one Saturday in December, Steve drove from Clearfield to Provo to pick up Amy and take her back to Clearfield, then returned her to Provo and drove back to Clearfield, all in a blizzard. It was important. It was her birthday. And for months he had been planning an astounding surprise.

In the summer, on one of the occasions when Amy had traveled to Utah to visit Steve, they sat in a park and Steve pulled out his handouts from a marriage preparation class he had taken. One paper had a list of a hundred different items. Each prospective marriage partner was to mark each item as a "want" or a "need." Given the vast differences in Amy and Steve's backgrounds, this exercise had the potential for acute divergence. Surprisingly, they mostly agreed, until they got to "piano." Immediately Amy said it was a "need." At the same time, Steve said it was a "want." Amy felt that it was essential for a family to be raised learning to play musical instruments. Steve thought that owning a piano was a luxury. No big deal. Next.

When Steve picked up Amy from Provo in December and took her to Clearfield, he opened the door to their little house. She walked into the living room. There was no furniture, but there was a piano. It had taken almost all the money Steve had set aside. He was not going to start out their marriage without something Amy considered a need.

The house with the piano became affectionately known as "the little pink house," due to the color of the siding. Steve's grandma had inherited a 700-square-foot house from her sister, Lavina. It was functionally obsolete for most families. It had only one bedroom, a kitchen, a living room, a bathroom (with a tub, but no shower), and a small laundry room. It was located in what Amy and Steve called the "devil's triangle." It was surrounded by railroad tracks. If you timed it right, you could be stuck inside the triangle for thirty minutes. Grandma Ellen had been renting out the house for $80 a month. It was tattered and frayed.

In the summer of '77, Steve was visiting Grandma Ellen when she complained that her renter had missed several months' payments. He was a snarly, unpleasant sort of fellow. She might just sell the house. When Steve asked her how much she was thinking of selling it for, she said $8,000. Steve's mind was clicking.

"Grandma, I would love to buy your house and I will pay you $10,000—$2,000 more than you are asking. I will pay you $100 a month, $20 more than you are getting for it now, if I can buy it without interest." Grandma was happy to be out from under the house, free from the snarky renter, and to have a little more money in her pocket. Steve was happy to have a home for his bride. He carpeted it, painted the interior walls, poured a rather thick patio (his first and only foray into cement work), and generally spiffed it up. Seventeen months after he and Amy moved into it, they sold the little pink house for $32,777. Their profit margin was over two hundred percent.

Steve and Amy had chosen December 20 for their wedding date. Amy and Steve would leave immediately after Amy's last final on

December 18 and drive to Arizona. They would arrive the night before the wedding. But there was a snag. At that time, in Arizona you had to have a wedding license at least forty-eight hours before a wedding. The solution was to get their wedding license when they went to Arizona for Thanksgiving. When Steve and Amy went to the county Superior Court's office the day after Thanksgiving, the employee took one look at Amy's birth certificate and said, "I can't give you a marriage license unless a parent signs for her. She is only seventeen."

Chagrinned, they returned to Amy's house and asked Carol to come with them and sign for Amy to get married. It's a good thing Carol had warmed up to Steve and the idea of her daughter getting married so young. Two weeks later, Amy turned eighteen. Two weeks after that, Steve and Amy got married.

Steve and Amy

1977

Chapter 9

Newlyweds

They were young. They were poor. They were freshmen in college. But they were in love. Just like the movies, right? Happy ever after, right?

Maybe. Eventually.

Amy grew up in a loving, functional family. She relates, "My mom and dad were head over heels in love throughout their marriage. I come from a family of six kids and none of us ever saw mom and dad fight. It wasn't because they fought behind closed doors. They simply didn't fight. My siblings and I all say the only disservice mom and dad ever did was to make it look so easy."

Steve, as he told Kent, grew up without a role model for marriage. By the time Steve was twenty-one, he had five divorces in his immediate family. As far as Steve was concerned, his father was a cipher—not that this was a bad thing. Steve's oldest sibling, Rob, has plenty of memories with Roy and considers the day his mom left Roy the happiest day of his life. Steve's mom was rarely at home. When she was, there were times of rage, dysfunction, and drama, but mostly Steve remembers being alone. From this void, Steve created his own ideas of what marriage and family would be like. They were radically idealistic.

Not only are Steve and Amy's backgrounds diametrically opposed, their personalities are polar opposites. Amy is a rule-keeper. Steve challenges authority. Amy is peaceful. Steve is high energy. Amy needs her own time. Steve would tuck Amy into his pocket and have her with him every minute. Amy hates conflict. Steve tackles conflict head on, with a lot of passion and volume. Amy is conventional. Steve is not just outside the box. He has no box.

Things were about to get bumpy.

Amy and Steve attended Weber State University together. The little pink house wasn't exactly energy efficient. Ice formed on the inside of the windows. When they studied at night, Amy the desert dweller was swaddled in her coat and a scarf. They drove a 1971 Duster that sported a huge dent in the front and squawked with right turns. They carried power steering fluid in the trunk for when the screech got too loud. When the heater went out in the car, they didn't have money to fix it. The morning drives to Weber State University in the winter were bone-chilling. On occasion, they splurged and went out to eat at Tony's Pizza in Ogden or bought a Cosmos burger at the hamburger joint down the street. Mostly, they spent their nickels and dimes sparingly. But they were in love and happy, most of the time.

Their first house improvement project was painting their kitchen cabinets. Steve didn't like the way Amy painted. He snapped at her. She was shell-shocked.

One day, Steve was talking to his close friend, Paul Waite, on the phone and venting his frustrations with married life. He said, "These women, they're extra baggage." Steve didn't realize Amy could hear him—until he heard the front door open and close.

Steve hung up quickly and went to find Amy. She hadn't gone far. She was sitting on the front step crying. When Steve came out and sat beside her, she said, "I'd run away, but I don't have anywhere to go."

Like all newlyweds, they had to figure out how to be with each other and how they were going to deal with their problems. Some of the patterns they established weren't optimal. Steve snapped. Amy withdrew. Steve got angry. Amy, who looked like a deer caught in the headlights, shut down.

Suffice it to say, they made it through the adjustment period where they ironed out the differences common to newlyweds. But some of their challenges were fundamental and substantial. They tried to deal with them, but the solutions were elusive. At eighteen and twenty-two years old, neither Steve nor Amy really understood how to fix what was wrong. Nor did they recognize that Steve had a wounded soul.

It took decades for Amy and Steve to work out their challenges. At times, the challenges almost won. In an interview with matchmaker Roseann Higgins, Steve spoke candidly about their lowest moments:

On more than one occasion, we almost called it quits. Amy's dad is an attorney, and I remember looking at her and saying, "Hey, this can be easy. Just have your dad write up the papers and we can just split this thing up and go." I was upset because of my own inadequacies and immaturity.

Another time, we'd been married fifteen years. We had four kids. We were building a new home. I was traveling all over for business—Japan, Delaware, Silicon Valley. It all overwhelmed me. I remember driving down the street, stomping on the brakes, throwing the car into park, getting out, slamming the door, screaming, and walking away, leaving my wife and four kids in the car.

Amy had her own moments of despair. On one occasion she laid down an ultimatum: "Handle your anger or we're finished." She is quick to point out that their children "have not grown up with the idea that marriage is easy and that parents don't fight. However, they have also seen that marriages have ups and downs, you can work through tough problems, and you can have a sweet, loving relationship—even when you are very, very different."

What is remarkable about this candid glimpse into Steve and Amy's marriage is that those who have seen them together or have heard Steve speak for more than a few minutes are likely surprised, probably in shock. Most people who experience "Steve and Amy, the couple" say things like, "I don't think I have ever met a more beautiful, loving, and joyful couple who have so much love and devotion to one another. They are magical, to say the least" (Darlene Loves); "The reason I wanted to meet you is because of how you speak about your wife"; "What I want out of our coaching is to have the kind of relationship you have with Amy"; and, "I bet you guys never fight." Steve and Amy spoke frankly because they are madly in love with each other. They cherish and enjoy each other. They are unflinchingly committed to each other. And they have worked damn hard to get there.

But *how* did they get there? There are a few answers. One is they simply didn't give up, even when it would have been easier to do so. Another is the recognition that relationships are hard. You have to bring your A-game and you have to do so over and over and over. Having a successful relationship is one of the toughest things most people will ever do. Finally, it is essential to acknowledge that relationships are a daily creation—but that is for another chapter.

Chapter 10

Weber State

Steve stepped into a furniture store in a little strip mall on Main Street in Clearfield. The owner, Jim Barlow, greeted him, hoping he was a customer. Hovering at the end of the aisle were Jim's mother and two other salespeople. The salespeople outnumbered customers four to one. Four to one is not a good ratio. Five to one is worse. But Steve needed a job, something he could do after his morning classes at Weber State. Steve shared ideas with Jim on how to increase foot traffic and offered to work for thirty days on straight commission. At the end of thirty days, Jim could decide if he wanted to keep Steve. What was there to lose? Within days, Jim knew that he definitely wanted to keep Steve. He paid him $4.37 per hour, plus commission. In an exceptional month, Steve brought home $800. In his downtime, Steve could do his homework.

Jim notes that Steve had the perfect personality for sales. He was "always upbeat, smiling, and happy. He wasn't the least bit inhibited and he got along well with customers. He was fun to be around."

Steve served his customers well—and no one figured out that he was actually colorblind, even after he helped them with their fabric choices.

Not everyone who walked into the store walked out with a purchase. Sometimes, they didn't find what they wanted. Sometimes the price was out of their budget. Steve saw an opportunity. Jim let Steve buy furniture at cost plus ten percent. After Steve and Amy had been married about a year, Steve started buying things for their house at the employee rate, a little here and a little there. Sometimes, Steve had a piece of furniture at his house that fit the needs of a customer, one who couldn't pay full price at Barlow's. Steve could sell it at a price that was affordable for the customer and profitable for him. Jim agreed. Later, when Amy was eight-and-a-half months pregnant and couldn't sleep, she got out of bed. Steve asked where she was going.

"I'm going to rock in the rocking chair. Maybe that will help me fall back asleep."

"You can't," Steve responded. "Remember, I sold it today."

When it came time to pay their obstetrician for delivering their firstborn, Steve worked out a trade in furniture.

Weber State University

Steve and Amy went to school together year-round. Steve majored in business and communications and Amy majored in English. Amy was always excited about what she was learning in her classes. She would talk most of the way home about this short story or that fascinating theme. When she would ask Steve about his classes, he would say, "They were good." This became a pattern that would play out over and over throughout the years. Amy was excited about what she learned. Steve was excited about the people he met.

Steve loved attending Weber State's football and basketball

games, and the cost fit right into their budget—free. They rarely missed a game. One crisp, autumn night, Steve and Amy attended a Weber State football game with Amy's sister and brother-in-law, Melinda and Gordon, who had come from Arizona to visit them. During the game, the announcer informed the fans that if they had a star on page twenty-three of their program, they could enter the half-time field goal contest. The prize was $250, a third of Steve's monthly income. Steve's program had a star. "This will be a piece of cake," Steve said to Gordon. "I kicked extra points in junior high." Steve beelined it to the meeting point. As the first one there, he would get to kick first.

The contest was structured so that the contestants started on the thirty-five-yard line. If no one hit the field goal, they would move up five yards and kick again. This process would be repeated until someone kicked the football through the goal posts. However, the person directing the contestants got confused and started them off at the ten-yard line. Steve was sure this would be the easiest $250 he ever earned. Steve lined up, approached the ball, connected—off it flew towards the bleachers. He shanked it.

After one year at Weber State, Amy was taking Saltines with her to every class, hoping she wouldn't throw up before class was over. Steve and Amy were going to become parents.

The little pink house was cute, but very little. In a few months, it would be too small. Steve and Amy started looking for a new home. With their daytime hours packed with work and school, they did a fair share of tromping through the snow and peering into new-builds with a flashlight at 10:00 p.m. Eventually, they found the perfect house about five miles west of Clearfield, in Syracuse.

A few months later, on a Sunday morning, Amy kept looking out the front window. Steve had gone to a church meeting. He should have been home by now. All the other neighbors were home. Finally, Amy called their friend who lived across the street. "Rick, do you know where Steve is?"

"Is it time?" shouted Rick.

"It's time."

Minutes later, Rick was speeding to the church building to retrieve Steve. Ten minutes later, Steve was home. An hour later, they were a family of three.

Steve and Amy were besotted with Steffany. When she was about three weeks old, Scott Parker, Steve's close friend and former mission companion, visited the Hardisons for the weekend. When Steffany woke up at 2:00 a.m. to nurse, Steve took her into Scott's bedroom to show him how adorable she was. Scott was not all that impressed, not at 2:00 a.m.

Steffany conveniently arrived between the summer and fall quarters. Amy had twenty-seven more credit hours until she got her bachelor's degree. This was decades before online classes existed, so Amy arranged with her professors to take some of her classes as home study. Others she took at night. Occasionally, she had to go to the campus to take a test. At that time, Steve took Steffany with him to his class. He became known as "the business guy with the baby."

A Diagnosis

When Steffany was born, Amy's mom, Carol, flew to Utah to help her for a week. Before she returned to Arizona, she joked, "Well, I think Steffany will make it through the night, but I don't know if Steve will." Steve was consuming an inordinate amount of food—day and night. He was drinking gallons of liquid. His preferred beverage was milk, but that much milk stressed their budget, so he switched to Kool-Aid. And he was losing weight. Having dropped over forty pounds, he was skeletal. He finally agreed to visit the student health center. They sent him straight to the hospital. A glucose tolerance test revealed a blood sugar level of 832, eight times that of a non-diabetic. Steve was diagnosed with juvenile-onset (type 1) diabetes.

This was a life-changing diagnosis. Steve, who hates having anything slow him down, was now tethered to insulin and constant blood testing. Steve, who found eating a frustrating interruption and had often wished he could take a pill instead of having to stop and eat, now had to be mindful of meals and make sure he always had sugar with him. Steve, who had swings in mood, now had to manage swings in blood sugar. His life just got more complicated.

Once Steve adjusted to life with diabetes, things returned to normal, aka busy. He had a new daughter, a new house, and a full schedule at Weber State. He was working nearly full time and had a time-consuming church calling.

National Extemporaneous Speaking Competition

One day when Steve was sitting in a business class, his professor announced a speaking competition sponsored by the business fraternity. Steve didn't think much about it until his professor pulled him aside and pressed him to sign up. Steve did, and he won first place in the extemporaneous speaking category and advanced to the state level.

As the representative from Weber State, Steve would be going up against the winners from Brigham Young University, Utah State, University of Utah, and Southern Utah State. Steve didn't prep for the match up and he definitely didn't worry about it. Talking the birds out of the trees—what could be more fun?

When Steve took second place for the state of Utah, he learned that the state winner went on to compete at the national level in Washington, DC, in July. At that point, Steve started to realize that maybe this was a big deal. He also thought that he could have won the state competition if he had taken it more seriously. In hindsight, he knew exactly what he could have said that would have made the difference. Too little, too late—except that the first-place winner for Utah got sick right before the national competition. They called Steve. Off he flew to DC.

The event started out with a Friday evening meet-and-greet. The room oozed with pomposity. It was cloying. Steve recalls, "Everyone was flinging around who their mom or dad was. One guy made sure everyone knew his father was a U.S. senator." Steve's first thought was, "This is a big deal." His second thought was, "I am winning this thing."

The next day, Steve advanced through the four rounds of competition. He and four others moved on to the finals. The finalists were isolated in different rooms. Fifteen minutes before they were to speak, they were given the question: "If there was one thing you could do to change the world, what would you do?"

Steve laughed. "This is so over." Steve had been thinking about this question his whole life. He thought about it in the shed. He grappled with it on his mission. He knew exactly what he was going to say. This is the essence of the concluding words of his speech:

I would change all the sacred texts that teach the world must end with an Armageddon or some cataclysmic battle. I would change all the holy scriptures that say one group of people has the truth and another doesn't. I would change what parents teach their children so that any teachings that divide and alienate people of different races, religions, and countries vanished overnight. In their place I would insert the teaching that all people are equal. All people are valuable. When we come together to work for the common good of all people, we have community instead of separation. We have unity instead of divisiveness. We have love instead of hate.

Steve won first place. It was a big deal.

The phone rang. Amy picked up. It was Steve. "Guess who is the National Extemporaneous Speaking Champion of 1980?"

"Are you serious? You're not joking?" squealed Amy. "Tell me all about it."

Steve gave Amy the blow by blow. He recreated his winning speech.

"I am so proud of you," Amy said. "This is amazing. You are amazing. Congratulations!" They reveled in his accomplishment, but not too long. Long-distance phone calls were expensive. Amy hung up. She stared at the phone. "That isn't what we believe. Is this going to be a big deal?"

Chapter 11

From Proctor & Gamble to Xerox

In the fall of his junior year, Steve saw a posting in the business department at Weber State that Proctor and Gamble was coming to interview. Steve was interested. Proctor and Gamble (P&G) was a solid company, selling leading brands that were embedded in American life. It was a great organization with room for advancement. Steve thought this just might be the career path he was looking for.

Steve showed up for his interview, looking sharp in his suit.

"So, Mr. Hardison. You are all set to graduate in May?" asked the interviewer (whom we will call "Mr. Smith").

"No. I don't graduate for one more year," responded Steve.

"Mr. Hardison, we aren't interviewing juniors."

"Mr. Smith, are you familiar with Weber State's basketball team?"

"I am not. But what does that have to do with anything?"

"Mr. Smith, they start three juniors and two sophomores. Can you imagine if the administrators told the coach he had to start a senior, just because he was a senior, even though it would weaken the team? There is someone in your organization that would want to hire me, even as a junior."

There was one person who could do that. They flew him in. He hired Steve on the spot. They offered Steve his choice of three territories. One happened to be Mesa, Tempe, and Scottsdale, Arizona. Steve's mom still lived in Arizona and all of Amy's family lived there. It was an easy decision. Steve reminded Amy that they were headed to P&G's ivory tower. Arizona was a temporary stop.

Steve and Amy and fifteen-month-old Steffany relocated to Arizona. They bought a new-built house and lived with Amy's parents for a month while it was being finished. Steve would finish up his degree at Arizona State University. They were elated.

Amy recalls:

I was excited all day to see how Steve's first day with P&G went. [This was before cell phones.] Steve walked in at 5:00 and I took one look at his face and my stomach dropped.

Steve said, "I made a big mistake."

I'm sure that P&G was a good job for the right person, but Steve loved sales. Nothing Steve did impacted how much the grocery stores ordered. That was determined by management. Steve felt like all he was doing was stocking the shelves with diapers.

Steve stuck with it for six months while he looked for another job. The best part of the job was that he could keep any of the boxes of diapers that were damaged. This was helpful, because Amy and Steve had another one on the way.

Steve's next job was at Safe and Sound, a mom-and-pop business that sold and installed alarm systems. It wasn't ideal. It was a stop-gap job to get him out of P&G before it drove him crazy.

Safe and Sound shared office space with another business. One day, a Xerox rep came in and pitched a copier to someone in the other business. Sitting at his desk, Steve saw and heard the whole thing.

Steve thought, "That's the worst sales presentation I've ever seen." He picked up the telephone and made a call.

A perky voice greeted him. "This is Jody. Welcome to Xerox."

"Jody, can you tell me who's responsible for sales in your company?"

Steve was transferred to Helen Hermann. Steve told Helen what he had just observed. She invited him to come down to the Xerox offices. After they spoke, Helen offered Steve a job.

The environment at Xerox was fun and competitive. Most importantly, Steve was really selling. Compared to having doors slammed in his face in England, cold-calling local businesses seemed like a walk in the park. Plus, Steve was working with some superb salespeople. The sales manager, Bill Brebaugh, was extraordinary.

It wasn't long before Steve was selling twenty, thirty, and sometimes even forty copiers every month. The average was five to ten. Often, Steve led the sales team for sales that month. He was always looking for ways to improve the current system. Steve said, "Nearly all of the salesmen would present to the office managers, who were pressed against the wall to make a $3,000 decision. I found that it was much easier to talk to someone who had the power to make a $100,000 decision. By jumping up the ladder, I could sell ten copiers at a time."

Xerox was a great experience. Steve was good for Xerox and he was compensated for his ability. However, about two years later, Steve was ready to move on.

It was at this time that he read a book that had an enormous impact on his thinking. It wasn't the first. That honor goes to Napoleon Hill's *The Laws of Success*. Steve found *The Laws of Success* on his mom's bookshelf shortly after coming home from his mission. He devoured it. It aligned with the fundamental principles that Steve had lived for years, especially on his mission. Seeing these principles written down by someone else and designated as "laws of success" was eminently satisfying. This book was so significant that Steve insisted that he and Amy read it together, out loud, which they did between Weber State's summer and fall quarters in 1980.

In 1982, Steve's friend, Rick Glauser, sent him the book *How to Solve All Your Money Problems Forever: Creating a Positive Flow of Money Into your Life* by Victor Boc. Amy read it first. When Steve came home from work that day, she was lit up. Steve immediately began the book. He read it multiple times. It moved Steve to the next level in understanding the power of the mind.

In 1982, Steve took out an ad in the local paper. Like Steve, it was unconventional. It read simply: "Do you need some help solving a problem? Do you need someone to talk to? If so, call me. Steve." Steve delighted in talking to a variety of people with diverse concerns and helping them. It was pure, unadulterated fun.

An entry in Steve's journal dated November 18, 1981, reads: "I am looking forward to developing a company by the name of Thought Process Inc., a concept in mind teaching. I think this will be big one day. I plan on setting up an office in my home for one-on-one instruction."

Coaching was starting to emerge.

Chapter 12

Family

Fatherhood was not easy for Steve. He listed towards meticulousness and found noises and commotion unsettling. His acute senses were assaulted by the chaos that comes with four young children. Sitting around the table and talking after dinner was a foreign concept to Steve. Eating dinner as a family was a foreign concept for Steve.

Sometimes parenting brought up pain. The kids knew that no family member had ever watched their dad play in any sporting event. (There was one exception. Rob attended one junior high football game, the one when Steve was knocked out and got a concussion.) They knew their dad had never gone on a vacation. They knew no one bought him the hottest basketball shoes or gave him money for a movie. They knew he walked to school in the snow and that it was uphill, both ways. They laughed when he made light of his childhood and rolled their eyes when Steve launched into "just like Roy did for me" when he bought them something or gave them money. They didn't know that at night, in bed with Amy, sometimes

Steve cried. When he provided his children with the things he never had, he relived his pain.

Without a role model, and with some extra baggage, Steve had some missteps as a dad (as do parents who have stellar role models and travel light). Still, Steve was an extraordinary father. He particularly excelled at preparing his children to make it in the world. He passed on business and people skills both genetically and through teaching. He taught his children to work. He educated them on how to harness the power of their minds and how to create their world. He taught them to be their word. He loved them fiercely.

The following are some of the Hardison children's memories of their father, in their own words.

Steffany

By the time I was ten years old, Dad and I launched my first business, "Steffany & Stinklwinkle's Special Stuff." Stinklwinkle was the quirky nickname I called my dad. Far be it from me to remember where it actually came from. What I do remember is choosing and designing my little business cards, which were fluorescent pink.

The business model was simple. We bought items in bulk from Price Club (like popcorn & water thermoses) which I sold door-to-door. I worked the neighborhoods in walking distance, using a little red wagon to pull my product. I was fearless and well-received by my customers.

I quickly graduated from selling popcorn and thermoses to $30 bottles of perfume. I remember one time especially well. My Dad and I were at the car wash and he encouraged me to use it as an opportunity to do business.

I didn't actually have my product, but he insisted I didn't need it. He taught me to overcome each and every objection. So, with some on-site coaching, we prevailed, and I sold a perfume bottle to a man at the car wash. Later, my mom and I delivered it to his home.

As a ten-year-old kid, I learned from my Dad how to work hard, close deals and run a business. Thirty years later, I am doing just that. In looking back, it's clear to see how much my dad, Steve Hardison, has influenced and shaped every aspect of my life. Who I am today, my talents, my capabilities and my professional accomplishments are because of him.

Lil (Lindsey)

My dad was always fun. We would build tents out of blankets and have tickle fights. Sometimes we would sleep outside in sleeping bags. Often, my dad would pop in at my elementary school during lunch. That always made me feel special. One day when he came, there were ropes hanging down from the ceiling. They had used them during P.E. My dad said that he had never been able to climb the rope as a kid. Before I knew it, he was halfway up the rope. He made it to the top and touched the ceiling. Then he loosened his grip and slid down. He had rope burns on his hands, but it was worth it.

When my dad worked at Rodel, he often missed my birthday because they always had "Rodel Days" in Delaware that week. So, when I was eight, he took me to Delaware with him. It was exciting to fly across the country. At the airport, he taught me the power of asking. He told me the worst that can happen is someone will say no. He walked up to the agent and asked if we could be bumped to first class. She agreed! The flight attendants went out of their way to make me feel special. When we went to Rodel Days, the employees made a big deal over me. My dad had told them that it was my birthday. They had a big birthday cake and they sang to me. They even gave me a beautiful porcelain doll.

When I was a teenager, we had a few rough patches, but we laugh about them now. We had a strict midnight curfew. We had landscape lights in our front yard that were on an automatic timer. They were set to go off at midnight. If we got home and the lights were off, we were late.

One Friday, I had gone out with my friends for the evening. We wanted to stay out later, so we came up with a plan. I would go home and check in and then ask if I could spend the night at Courtney's house. Then we would go and hang out with these boys. So, I went into my parents' room, and said, "Hey, I'm going to spend the night at Courtney's house. Is that okay?"

My mom said it was alright. I later learned that as soon as I left, my dad turned to her and said, "She's lying to you."

"She wouldn't do that. She wouldn't lie."

My dad said, "You want to bet?"

We got to Courtney's house and called the boys. In a few minutes, they picked us up. We were maybe a mile away from Courtney's house and we saw this white minivan coming up quickly.

I said, "Oh, no, it's my dad. Whatever you do, don't stop!"

They couldn't outrun my dad. He was never going to give up. He was in a minivan, dressed in a robe, and he was chasing us down the street.

It turned out that after he left our house, he didn't go towards Courtney's house. He felt compelled to drive in another direction. He didn't know the friend's car; he didn't even know the boys! Yet he somehow found the car I was riding in. He just *knew* it was us.

He pulled us over. He began lecturing the three of us girls. Then he started with the boys. He scared them so badly. He took each of the girls to their homes and had them tell their parents. My friends' parents thought, "What's the big deal?"

When we got home, my dad woke up my brothers and my sister. Everybody was a part of the discussions in our home. It was not a one-person thing. It felt so extreme, and so embarrassing.

Afterwards, my friends teased me a lot. They said, "Is your dad a cop? Because he literally pulled us over, and we listened to him!"

I didn't always appreciate his commitment to me when I was a teenager, but now as an adult, I am moved by it. My dad has always been there for me, including when I became an adult. I went through a divorce when I was thirty-four. I had four-year-old twins. It was devastating and the transition was rough, but eventually I told my dad, "I am really pleased with where I am. You have been so supportive. You are here for me. I'm happy. I have everything I need. I don't need a relationship."

I thought he would say, "That's great. I'm so happy for you." Instead, he said, "That's great to hear, but you are playing it safe. Relationships are where the growth is." It was at about this time that my dad introduced me to a guy he knew from his gym. We got married five months later.

Clint

I remember nights lying in the backyard with dad, looking up into the night sky. I'm sure he couldn't name a single constellation. But it wasn't about looking at the stars. It was really about contemplating eternity and your place in it. He would ask questions like: "What's beyond space?" and "Do you think Adam had a belly button?" followed by the more traditional, "Which came first: the chicken or the egg?" He would also say, "Take as long as anything has ever been and then multiply that by infinity." He wanted to cultivate a curiosity in me and my siblings. But also, he is just really fascinated by these questions.

My dad played basketball with me and my brother from the time we were really little. We love basketball and still play. I remember him teaching me stuff when I was five years old that I'm pretty sure no other dads are teaching their five-year-olds, things like, "It's not a foul unless the ref calls it." That is such a funny thing to teach a five-year-old, but he really instilled it in us. He spent a lot of time working with us on our mindset about basketball. He taught us to play aggressively. When we were playing basketball in kindergarten and first grade, both my brother and I would steal the ball from other kids. At that age, nobody else did that. The kids just waited for the kid with the ball to shoot or pass. Years later I realized that my dad was teaching us to bring intensity to whatever we are doing, to be focused and committed, because that produces amazing results.

My dad taught my brother and me things that allowed us to be really good missionaries. My dad was in the ninety-ninth percentile as a missionary in terms of his ability to get stuff done. It's a very hard thing to do, to go out and proselytize to people, to be a young, pretty ignorant kid and go tell people they should make these sweeping life changes. Unless somebody has done it, it would be hard to understand how difficult that is. And it would be hard to get anybody other than a nineteen-year-old with no life experience to sign up for that, because it's a heavy lift. It's really tough. And my dad was super excellent at it, at the far, far end of the bell curve, and he taught us a lot of ways to think and things to do to help us be effective.

One of the things about my dad that is really impressive to me is all that he was able to accomplish with very little guidance and with very few resources. I remember when I was four years old and he came home with a brand-new BMW. I remember how much it meant to him. It wasn't until years later when I got my first, kind-of-nice car and I knew how much it meant to me that I started to understand. And he had so much farther to travel to get to that point than I did. He really had to pull himself up by his bootstraps.

My dad is one of the world's foremost practical exemplars of the idea that life is what we make of it. Much of what we think of as fixed and concrete is actually arbitrary and malleable. Life and our experience of it is created by us, so why not be intentional in that process to make life what we want it to be? Every day, for as long as I've known him, he's posed that question with almost every act.

Here are some of the things my dad has taught me over our thirty-seven years together:

- If you do what you say you will do, you can become what you say you will be.
- Measure twice, cut once.
- Do more than you're paid for.
- Rely on agreements, not expectations.
- It's not as much what you're doing as who you're being.
- Hire a handyman.
- Live beneath your means.
- Don't take no for an answer.
- Dumb rules bind only those who aren't willing to question them.
- Get outside your own paradigm.
- A well-timed curse word can be rather cathartic.
- Be the same "you" wherever you go.

Blake

As a kid I played competitive baseball. Practically every day I was on the baseball diamond. My dream was to become a professional catcher, so I would spend hours in the Arizona summers catching and throwing, sacrificing my body to stop wild pitches, and improving my swing. It was at this time that my father taught me how to create a future that I could live into. With a giant sharpie, we wrote on the back of my catcher's mitt "THE VACUUM." It was a declaration that there wasn't a wild pitch that I couldn't scoop up or suck out of the dirt. I don't believe that I was the most naturally talented catcher on the first day of tryouts, but I became the best catcher on our team because my dad helped me develop a tenacious work ethic and a mindset that gave me confidence.

I also loved basketball. I played in my first basketball league when I was six years old. At that age, they didn't let you guard the kids until they passed half court. So, I stood at the half-court line, and as soon as I could, I tried to steal the ball. In one game, the player crossed the half-court line and I stole the ball, ran down to the hoop, and laid it in. The very next play, the same kid was bringing the ball down. He took a step over the half-court line and I stole the ball from him and scored. The third time the same kid was coming down the court, I went to steal the ball and he punched me in the face. He clocked me. The kid got kicked out of the game and the whole thing stopped. I remember going to the sideline and saying, "Dad, why did he hit me? I wasn't trash-talking him or anything." I was just being a kid who loved the game of basketball.

My dad said simply, "He didn't like you stealing the ball." He didn't sugarcoat it. He didn't pity me so that I felt like a victim. He just said, "You did this. He did that. Now, it's your turn to choose. Do you want to keep stealing the ball?" So very early, I learned that you can play it safe and never get punched in the face, or you can play all out. I chose to play all out. Yes, there are risks, but the payoff is an extraordinary life.

Another thing that made a big impact on me also occurred at this time. I was about five or six years old when my dad came home with a 9 x 6-inch notebook called *The Cash Keeper* for each of the kids. Inside were plastic dividers, pouches labelled "spending," "saving," and "giving," and a general ledger on the side. Even as a young kid I thought, "This is the coolest thing ever!"

Dad sat all of the kids down and explained a principle he called 10/10/80. The idea is that whenever you earn money, you give 10 percent of your money to someone else (tithing), you save 10 percent of your money, and you use 80 percent to cover your bills. And if you can put more in savings, you do it. I was young—I was still watching cartoons—but I caught the vision of it. I was excited. I was doing a general ledger as a six-year-old.

I earned a dollar a week. I remember taking that dollar, looking at the pouches, and thinking, "Okay, ten percent goes to tithing. Ten percent goes to savings. . . Now I don't have my dollar anymore!" I realized I was going to have to be paid in dimes to make this work. Then I got a better idea. I went back to my mom and negotiated getting paid $1.25 each week so I could give ten percent away, save ten percent and still have my $1 bill!

Not only did my dad teach me what to do with the money I earned, he taught me to be creative about earning it. One day he was golfing, and he noticed that golfers often hit balls into the back yards of the houses that backed up to the golf course. That triggered an idea. I could make money by reselling these golf balls at a discount price. First, I had to get the golf balls.

The obvious approach was to ask the homeowners for a few of the golf balls. But my dad said, "Blake, go and knock on their doors and tell them you are offering them a service by taking the golf balls away." I ended up with bags and bags of golf balls. I had my inventory and it didn't cost me a cent. I washed and cleaned the balls and then I researched them, figuring out which ones were the most valuable. My dad guided me on all of this.

Next, I needed a marketplace. My dad asked the owner of the gym where he worked out if his son could ask him a question. Of course, he said yes. I asked him if I could set up a table by the front door and sell my golf balls. He said, "Sure, why not?" So, I did. I sold a good amount of golf balls. I don't remember how much I made, but it seemed like a lot at the time.

In my teenage years, I became fascinated with skateboarding. My father didn't see my skateboarding as a waste of time or a sign of rebellion, but rather as an opportunity to grow closer to me. He bought a matching skateboard and went to the skate parks with me. Later, he broke his collarbone trying to go off a ramp.

In my early twenties my passion for business exploded. I wanted to get my dad's coaching. I was surprised when he told me that he would be glad to coach me—if I paid the same fee as his other clients. It was a huge sacrifice and I had to really humble myself, but I decided to hire my father to coach me. The hours of coaching I spent with him transformed my life. Thanks to my father, I developed the skills that have not only helped me close millions of dollars' worth of business, but also build a loving relationship with my wife and be at peace in a very fast-paced world.

Really, my dad has been coaching me my whole life. He has never tried to shape me to be someone other than who I wanted to be, but he has always helped me to be the best version of myself. And if, for whatever reason, I decided to leave business behind altogether and become a hippie, I'm sure he would be right there supporting me in our matching tie-dye T-shirts.

Chapter 13

Rodel

"Amy, can you help me with my computer?"

Amy hears this a lot. Steve is not a technical whiz. Nor is he an engineer. Or a handyman. When Blake was about twelve, the light bulb in his bedroom was flickering. The light bulb was new, so Steve figured it was probably the connection. He had a brilliant idea, something his grandpa had done. He covered the metal base of the light bulb with foil and screwed in the light bulb. He turned on the light switch. The light bulb exploded and the electricity in the house went out. Steve hadn't noticed that his grandfather made a hole in the foil for the base of the light bulb to go through. So how did Steve, a low-tech guy without a PhD in chemistry or engineering end up being the president of Rodel Products, a high-tech company that supplied chemicals and pads for polishing silicon wafers?

In 1983, Steve was ready to leave Xerox. Mike Koether, the branch manager of Xerox, asked Steve about his plans. When Steve said he had not yet decided on his next step, Mike called his friend and former fraternity brother, Don Budinger. He told him he had a young, sharp employee who was leaving Xerox. Don needed to see him.

Steve recalls his first meeting with Don. "The minute I saw Don, I was impressed. He was impeccably dressed. As we visited, it was clear he was polished, articulate, and brilliant. Everything about him was impressive. I knew I would learn a lot from him. Not long into our conversation, he stopped and said, 'What would it take for you to come to work for me?'"

Steve was hired to work in sales, but Don never intended for him to stay there. At their very first meeting, Don drew on a piece of paper the pathway for Steve to become the general manager of the company.

Steve had a lot to learn. "When I looked at the Rodel products brochure, I thought, 'I need a dictionary to understand this!'" On one occasion, Steve was in a manufacturing facility and started to put his finger into some liquid. A stunned engineer pulled Steve's hand away just before he submersed it in a vat of hydrochloric acid. Indeed, Steve had a lot to learn. He also intuitively knew how and where to go to learn the most essential things. He went into the plant in Delaware and talked to the people who worked on the assembly lines. He asked questions about how the products were made and how they worked. He asked the line workers what they needed to make their job easier. He went into the Research and Development lab, gowned up, and learned how to use the polishing machine. Steve spent more time at the plant than any salesperson ever had.

Steve mastered the nuts and bolts. Then he brought in his expertise: how to bring warring parties to consensus, how to solve problems, how to listen for answers, and how to enroll people in a vision.

Don Budinger recalls:

We got to the point where we had thirty percent of the worldwide market for what we did. We were the number-one market shareholder. So, I decided that we would take a risk. We had a company meeting in Delaware every month. I said, "Congratulations. But we don't want to be the business where seventy percent of the people buy from somebody else. If you want a prosperous, secure, challenging, rewarding future, we need to have over half of the people in our technology space buy from us and not somebody else."

I made this great speech and their response was, "You don't appreciate what we're doing." So, Steve would come behind me and explain that they were appreciated, that what they had done was great, but we needed to do better to have a future we want. And frankly, he could make that case better than I could.

Terry Hays-Sapp recalls that Steve was "one of the strongest-communicating Rodelians." Along with his listening and speaking skills, Steve brought creativity and a pit bull tenacity to solving problems. If salespeople complained that they couldn't get a certain foreign customer because they only bought from local venders, Steve's response was that it didn't matter. They had to be better than whatever was in the way.

In 1986, Steve was promoted to national sales manager. One day, Mike, one of Rodel's salespeople, came into his office. The world's largest manufacturer of silicon wafers at that time had just fired Rodel. They were incensed because Rodel's products were scratching their wafers and ruining their yields. They were going to find a new supplier.

Steve told Mike to get two plane tickets for that afternoon or as soon as possible and they would go and talk to them. "I don't think you understand," Mike responded. "They aren't happy. They don't want to see us. Ever."

"Just get the tickets," Steve said. They flew out the next morning.

When they got to the corporate headquarters, they were given a scant fifteen minutes to plead their case. Steve looked at the executives. It felt like a summer day in Arizona—111°F in the shade.

Steve took a deep breath and began, "We came to apologize. You have every right to be angry. You have every right to fire us. However, as I see it, you have two options. You can keep us, and we can work together as partners or you can fire us and get another vender—but you will have the same problem with the new vender. This is an industry-wide problem. You're so zealous in guarding your intellectual property, we don't know how you use our product. If you let us put an engineer in-house, right in your manufacturing facility, we can work together to get you what you need."

They liked the idea. They put a Rodel engineer in their plant. They improved the flatness of their wafers. They created a long-term working relationship marked by trust and respect.

In 1989, Steve was promoted to President of Rodel Products Corporation, the sales arm of Rodel Products.

Rodel was an incredible experience and Don Budinger was an unparalleled mentor. When he met Don, Steve was twenty-nine years old. He had pulled himself up by his bootstraps, but his boots were lacking some polish. Don supplied that. He boosted Steve from a life below the tracks into a more refined world. He shaped Steve's thinking, notably helping him shift to abundance mentality. Don's example and influence buffed up Steve without changing his essence. Steve was still Steve. He worked hard and laced his work with fun. He pressed the edges. He was creative. Don remembers:

We are back East in our main factory complex in Wilmington, Delaware. It's a Friday afternoon and we're tired. We have tickets for a return flight from Philadelphia to Phoenix. We arrive at the airport and go to check in. Steve takes his ticket and he tears it up. He throws it in the trash. I said, "What are you doing?"

He says, "I'll see if I can get on the plane without a ticket." Obviously, today you couldn't do this. But things were different back then. Still, I have had a long week. I just want to get back. I'm sitting in the first row in coach. The plane is filling up. They are getting ready to close the door. I'm thinking, "Steve's not here. He's not going to get on." I look in first class. There's one row with one empty seat. I'm not paying much attention. I'm just worried about Steve getting on the plane.

Before they close the door, in walks Steve. Guess what seat he has? Yes, he has the first row in first class. He comes back to me and asks if I want the first-class seat. I'm his boss. I say, "No, absolutely not. You earned it. You figured out how to do it. You got it."

That's who he was. He pushed the envelope like I've never seen anybody. He's uniquely skilled and I admire him tremendously. I had the privilege of being his boss, perhaps helping in his development in some way, but he's a unique critter. There's just no question. That whole concept of listening powerfully and listening out of commitment and love, nobody's done that like he's done it. I've worked with two presidents of the United States and Werner Erhard. I've worked with a lot of gurus back in the '80s and '90s. Steve is at the top of that whole list of personal development experts.

Chapter 14

Werner

Steve and Amy were staying at a local resort, celebrating their tenth wedding anniversary. At 2:00 in the morning, Steve woke up in incredible pain. He picked up the hotel phone and dialed his friend and dentist, Dr. Andy Shumway. Andy picked up on the first ring.

"Are you awake?" asked Steve.

Andy, coincidentally, was awake, and offered to meet Steve at his dental office.

While Andy performed an emergency root canal, he told Steve about a remarkable patient. Every time she came in, she talked about something called "The Forum," the brainchild of a man named Werner Erhard. Andy was animated. He was going to attend the next Forum. Would Steve like to go with him?

The Forum? Steve had never heard of it. Would he like to go? Absolutely.

The day after his root canal, Steve registered for the next Forum in Phoenix. It would be in four weeks. The Forum staff—all volunteers—phoned Steve on multiple occasions to confirm the location, the directions, and to ask Steve what he wanted to get out of his Forum. "This is overkill," thought Steve. "Just give me the address. I'll show up." The third time they called, Steve told them to leave him alone. "I know how to get there. You've got my money. I'm coming." He thinks he hung up on them.

When Steve arrived, he walked up to the registration area where several tables held three hundred name tags. Steve looked for his name tag, twice. He turned to one of the volunteers and said, "I can't find my name tag."

"I can help you. What is your name?"

"Steve Hardison."

Heads popped up. The volunteer found his name tag. It was set off, all by itself on a separate table.

A different volunteer, Nancy Groben, approached. "Hi Steve. We're going to give you a refund for The Forum. We don't think you would get much out of it."

"What are you talking about?" demanded Steve.

"You haven't taken it seriously."

Was Steve being kicked out of the course? Before it even started?

"What would I need to do to stay in it?" Steve asked. As if on cue, a small, dark-haired woman wearing a name tag that said "Linda" stepped in. Linda was crisp and clear about what he needed to do and who he needed to be. Steve liked her precision. He agreed and found a seat in the front row. In moments, The Forum leader made her way to the front of the room. It was Linda.

After a short introduction, Linda stepped down from the stage, and walked through the audience. She called on a woman sitting next to Steve and began having a conversation with her. The woman described her brutal home environment, the tense atmosphere, and her difficult partner. She began crying.

The participants squirmed. Some looked like they wanted to jump up and hug the woman.

"Is this the bullshit you pull on your husband?" Linda said without emotion.

The woman stopped crying immediately. "Yes," she said coolly. Steve was enthralled. Here was candor that cut to the core. By the first break, Steve was certain of one thing: this was the best thing he had ever sat through in his life. This was transformation with teeth. This was commitment to possibility so big that it was borderline ruthless. It was in-your-face, wake-you-up transformation. This was holding people accountable with grit. This was being your word. This was like coming home.

Within a few months, Steve had shared The Forum with hundreds of people. Steve and Amy went on to participate in multiple seminars and events, from The Six Day to The Mastery of Empowerment to Openings. Steve continued to study Werner's material for ten years. He continued to share The Forum and its next iteration, Landmark, introducing more than a thousand people to the work. Stepping into The Forum was a pivotal moment in Steve's life. And he had come so close to getting chucked out.

The technology of The Forum helped Steve distinguish between events and his thoughts about the events. It helped him recognize his winning formulas. It helped him comprehend choice in its purest form. It gave him the tools to help him forgive and to complete his past. But before Steve could be totally at peace with his past and at peace in his soul, he would have to go to nothing.

Chapter 15

The Build-Up

His voice had an edge. He snarled at Amy. Maurine's head snapped up. Steve stormed out of the room. "You know, Amy," said Maurine, "that's not acceptable. You need to let him know that." It was out of character for Maurine to say anything that edged into how Steve and Amy lived their life.

"He doesn't do it often. He must have something going on."

Indeed, he did have something going on. But it was not a passing frustration. Steve was starting to come unwound.

When Steve and Amy dated, Steve had disclosed that as a kid, he had a bad temper. He threw bats when umpires called a third strike. He punched holes in walls. His mom frequently told him that he was in the right but how he handled the situation caused him to lose his point. He loathed it when she said that. But these were things of the past. He had mastered his anger on his mission. Now, twelve years post-mission, Amy was starting to sense that perhaps "master"

wasn't the right word. He had shrunk it, like radiation shrivels a tumor. It had gone into remission. But evidence of a relapse was surfacing.

It wasn't just anger. Steve had a lot gurgling inside of him. He was traveling a week or two each month, flying to Delaware, Silicon Valley, Cincinnati, and Japan for business. Travel messed with Steve's blood sugar and it required Steve to handle details. So many details. And paperwork. And life's minutiae. They buried Steve. He could do things no one else could do. And the things most people could do crushed him. Plus, Steve burned bright. To rekindle, he needed down time and space. Lots of it. His walls were closing in.

When he was at Rodel in Scottsdale, Steve started going to the park and taking naps during his lunch hour. He always loved naps, but these weren't power naps to recharge; these were escapes into oblivion for survival. On Sunday nights he started going to bed at 7:00 p.m. The house needed to be pin-drop quiet. Amy lay by him and rubbed his arm. He was on edge about the workweek starting. His nerves were amped on anxiety.

Four kids. A wife. A job. An avalanche of details. Soul-sucking travel. Questions about faith. Building a custom home. Feeling unappreciated. Monotony. Ruts. Steve was a pressure cooker. He was going to blow. The question was when.

Chapter 16

Demolition

"He's good. Amazing, actually. He could help us," Steve thought.

Steve was sitting in a Landmark Forum seminar. At the front of the room, leading the seminar, stood Lloyd Fickett. Lloyd was impressive. He was distinguished in appearance, articulate, and masterful in leading the seminar participants from breakdowns to breakthroughs. He had a keen understanding of Werner Erhard's work, something no doubt honed when he had worked for Werner in San Francisco. Lloyd's job had been to make sure all the telephone cords were consistently straight and untangled on every phone in the seven-story building. In a world of cell phones, sans cords, the difficulty of this task might be undervalued. Before 1990, the possibility for a tangled cord existed every time the phone was hung up. Lloyd could not run around the building straightening every cord after every call. He had to enroll every person into the commitment to untangled cords. He had to get people to see that impeccability existed in the smallest of actions. This was rigorous training in getting everyone in a company in alignment. It was perfect training for what Rodel needed.

At first, Don Budinger was hesitant to hire Lloyd as an executive coach. He wasn't sure they needed an outsider to come in and help them. Plus, Lloyd was expensive. Steve was insistent that hiring Lloyd, who could see with clarity *because* he was from the outside, was exactly what Rodel needed. Eventually, Don hired Lloyd to work with the executive team. Together, Lloyd and the team created the Rodel principles (which Lloyd later developed into his Collaborative Way). They were:

1. Listen generously to each other.
2. Speak straight to each other.
3. Be *for* each other.
4. Honor our commitments.
5. Be a source of acknowledgement and appreciation.

Rodel was already doing these things to some degree, "but the organization wasn't quite 'we,'" explains Lloyd. These Rodel principles, or commitments, established a context for how they would work together and support each other. Lloyd's work with Rodel was exceptional.

After the company's culture was in place, Lloyd took groups of key employees into the wilderness where they jumped off cliffs, ran through a ropes course, and participated in activities that pushed them physically and emotionally. But that came later. First, Lloyd was about to rock Steve's world.

Early in July 1991, Lloyd entered Steve's office at Rodel and closed the door. He held his tightly clenched fists in front of his chest and said, "Steve, what's this about?"

"What are you talking about?" asked Steve.

Lloyd raised his eyebrows. It was so obvious. Lloyd came at it from another direction. "You're constantly on edge and stressed. What's behind that?" Steve had no answer. Lloyd continued, "Almost all of us are born belonging. At some point, an event occurs and we—all of us—find we are alone. We're not prepared for that moment. It's disconcerting. We respond based on patterns that are already in place. Over time, these patterns solidify and form our fundamental approach to life. They usually have a very strong emotional anchor."

Lloyd had a process to heal this break in belonging. It consisted of two sessions. In the first, Lloyd helped his clients remember the early events in their lives, the decisions they made about those events, and the patterns that emerged. Lloyd usually held the second session a week later. This session included breathing exercises, exploring what the client had learned during the week, and further processing of the early experiences. Everyone Lloyd had taken through this process found it to be a fundamental turning point in their lives, including Lloyd himself. He asked Steve if he was interested in doing it. Steve was all-in.

Steve arrived for his first session the next Friday evening. Lloyd and a gentleman named Ron sat in Lloyd's home office. They both had yellow legal pads. Steve took a seat in the middle of the room.

"When were you born?" "How many siblings do you have?" "What do you remember about. . . ?" Lloyd's voice was calm. His questions were constant, like an escalator. For three hours, Lloyd queried, Steve responded, and Ron and Lloyd captured Steve's answers on legal pads.

Lloyd flipped to the first page of the legal pad and began to read Steve's answers back to him. Any of the following could have been written down: "Your uncle constantly berated you and told that you would never amount to anything." "You were jumped by a group of teenagers and beaten up, egged on by a family member." "There was the young-adult man who preyed on younger boys." And so on. There were some darker things.

Steve felt dazed. He knew about those things. He had lived those things. But when they were all laid out with their jagged edges exposed, with his soul naked, there was no pretending it didn't matter. There was no imagining it was a one-off. So many people had injured him. No one had protected him. No wonder he was angry.

The first part of their process was complete. Steve drove a few streets away and parked under a tree. Tears welled up, then surged over their margins. Steve felt like he did when the water-ski bashed into his bottom teeth, laying them flat and leaving the nerves exposed to the cold air. His whole body was his teeth.

July 17, 1991. Round two. Steve knocked on the office door. A very pregnant woman greeted him warmly. Lloyd introduced her as Carrie and explained she was there to hold the space of love and to guide Steve in some breathing exercises.

The office now had a large mattress on the floor. It was for Steve. Lloyd settled into his office chair. Steve relaxed into the mattress. Lloyd picked up the list of last week's questions and responses. He read the list slowly, pausing to ask how Steve felt and if there was anything he wanted to say. There was so much to say. Steve's emotions began to seethe, like magma.

Lloyd read Steve's description of his experience of having his ear bitten, gnawed, and twisted by a family member. It had happened over and over until Steve's ear became grotesquely misshaped, like a pixie ear. He had to have surgery to fix it. The pregnant woman gently touched Steve's ear.

Steve hurled a defiant scream. The rage spewed. Steve bolted to his feet. "Stay on the mattress!" Lloyd called. Steve obeyed, but his energy defied containment. He thrashed. He kicked. His foot connected with Lloyd's file cabinets. The wood splintered. Lloyd relates:

> The anger that came up was overwhelming. I had never met that much anger. I was looking at how to dispel it. I handed him a couple of legal pads. He ripped them up, but that did nothing to curb his anger. So, I handed him a phone book. It was too big to rip up, so he just tossed it. It was pretty clear to me that this wasn't going to stop. The only way to stop it was to enter his energy field and risk what might happen. And so that's what I did. I got down on the floor with him and, fortunately, we were able to connect. He calmed down.

Steve remembers curling into the fetal position and Lloyd wrapping his arms around him. Lloyd whispered, "Steve, there's nothing left for you to prove. You're okay. Everything's all right. There's nothing left to prove."

Eventually Steve's breathing slowed. His energy ebbed. He felt purged. Lloyd felt it was safe for the expectant Carrie to be close to Steve. Together, Lloyd and Carrie nurtured Steve. When Steve was grounded, he and Lloyd went to lunch and they continued processing. Food tasted different. They went for a walk in the desert. Everything looked different. Steve felt like he had just experienced a rebirth.

Before driving home, Steve reclined his seat all the way back and took some deep breaths. He reflected on his experience. Instead of basking in the afterglow, his peace started to disintegrate. He picked up his car phone and dialed Amy. He tried to describe what he had gone through. His words crumbled. He began to sob. When he arrived home, Steve again folded into the fetal position. He stared at the wall for the rest of the day, and the night, and the weekend.

On Monday morning, Steve had to go to work. His body went. His heart and his soul were splattered. Steve limped along for six months. Each day, the thought of getting out of bed and going to work became more and more oppressive. Finally, Steve went to Don and told him he had to quit. Don offered him thirty days off. Steve took them. For thirty days, he sat and stared and cried. It bought him ninety more days at Rodel, but by then his golden boy image was tarnished. For Steve, that hardly mattered. He had nothing more to give Rodel. He barely had enough to live.

Lloyd helped negotiate the departure. He says:

Steve was a powerful part of Rodel. He played a big role in the Rodel merger. He was a tremendous source of inspiration and leadership. He loved so many of the people there, and they loved him. Separating wasn't going to be an easy thing. And there were also economics involved. It was a very challenging process, one of the hardest I've been through personally in terms of trying to make it work for him and work for the company.

The details were handled. The dissolution was achieved. The relationship between Steve and Don was smudged, but it would heal with time. What were Steve and Amy going to do with the house they had just moved into, the one they had been building for two years? What were they going to do with their lives?

The future looked bleak.

Chapter 17

The Birth of Coaching

As of 2020, there are an estimated 71,000 life coaches worldwide. There are coaching schools, coaching certifications, and credentialing organizations. One website lists twenty-one types of life coaches. There are business coaches, career coaches, and relationship coaches. And if the relationship coaching doesn't work, there is divorce coaching. But none of this was happening in 1991 when Steve was deciding what to do with his life.

Steve was sitting on the deck, staring out at the mountains. He had been doing this a lot over the past few months. If only he could unplug forever. In the house were his four children and his wife. He had a modest severance package from Rodel, but he could not afford the luxury of an endless breakdown. He had to do something. They could sell the house, but that would be a temporary solution. At some point, Steve would have to do something to provide.

When Steve was at Weber State, he was constantly being recruited for multi-level marketing. He knew he would have done well at it. He loved sales. He was good with people. But Amy was strongly opposed. He still resented that she had clipped his wings. Maybe now was the time. Amy was worried enough about him to offer no resistance.

Steve stepped into multi-level marketing. Soon he stepped out. Steve learned that he was not constituted to nudge, encourage, and prod people who weren't serious or who needed support every step of the way. He was great if people caught the vision and could fly. He could provide lift and momentum. He could keep eagles focused on the sun. People who weren't sure if they could get off the ground drove him crazy. The foray into multi-level marketing had consumed some of their precious savings, but Steve now knew without a doubt that it was not for him.

Steve was at the car wash. As usual, he was talking with people. He met Keith, who was struggling with his business. By the end of the conversation, Keith was Steve's first client. He came to Steve's house and they sat at the dining table. Steve helped him solve his problems. Steve saw a glimmer of possibility. It was enough to break the white-knuckled grip of despair. It was enough to resurrect his energy. Steve was back in the saddle.

Steve's phone rang. It was Bill Brebaugh, Steve's former boss at Xerox. Like Steve, Bill had moved on from Xerox. He was currently the sales manager at the University of Phoenix.

"Hi, Steve. Have you heard of a company named TimeMax?"

"No."

"Well, they're only about ten minutes away from you," said Bill. "They've done some work with us and I really, really like them. I think they could use you."

A few days later, Bill brought Dennis Deaton, the co-owner and CEO of TimeMax (a corporate training company that specialized in time management) to Steve's house. Bill made the introductions and took his leave. Steve asked Dennis questions about his company and learned that Dennis had a partner. Steve asked if his partner knew about this meeting. Within minutes of Dennis saying no, Steve and Dennis were driving to TimeMax.

In ten minutes, they picked up Reece Bawden. In ten more minutes, Steve said, "If you want a partnership, you are going to have to trust each other and talk to each other." Steve then gave them an irresistible offer. Steve would work with them for six weeks without being paid. At the end of six weeks, they could decide whether or not to hire him.

Steve did for TimeMax what he has never done since. He worked in-house, three days a week.

Steve also did for TimeMax what he *has* done before and after. He worked miracles.

For instance, one day Steve asked Reece how much business they did with Motorola.

Reece replied, "They're our biggest customer."

"How do they come to us?" asked Steve.

"Actually," said Reece, "I don't know."

"I think we should find out," said Steve.

Reece explained that as the president of TimeMax, he was a little uncomfortable going into Motorola's human resources department and asking those kinds of questions. Steve assured Reece that all he had to do was watch.

At Motorola, Steve introduced himself. "Hi. I'm Steve Hardison and this is Reece Bawden from TimeMax. I'm his coach. Could you help us understand something? We have one-hundred and twenty seats available in the courses we put on for Motorola, but only thirty people come. When we talk to your employees after a course, they say they loved the course and they had to wait for two months to get in because it was sold out. But we are definitely not at capacity. Could you walk us through how someone from Motorola gets into our courses?"

The HR employee explained, "The Motorola employee comes to us and tells us what training they want. We look up the company in the computer and see how many seats are available." She clicked a few keys on her keyboard. "We have thirty seats available for TimeMax. When those are filled, we don't put anyone else in."

Steve asks, "Who puts the 'thirty' in the computer?"

"I do."

"Can we change that to 125?" asks Steve.

Click.

Done.

Motorola enrolled employees in fifty courses each year. Each seat cost $225. Selling one hundred more seats for each of the fifty courses created a potential increase of $1,125,000 to TimeMax's annual revenue from Motorola alone, from one conversation. Not a bad miracle for starters.

Steve worked with TimeMax for five years. He coached several of the executives and key employees. He trained the executives and the sales team on the practical side of business and on their thinking. Reece Bawden said, "Steve could listen to me for five minutes as I described a problem, and then spend the next hour helping me to see the thinking that caused the problem in the first place. More importantly, he helped me see the thinking and the actions that would solve it."

Steve ruffled feathers when he first arrived at TimeMax. He was direct. He called people on their stuff. He cut out the deadwood. He changed the way things were done. He also solved huge problems.

One day Dennis and Reece came to Steve and said they wanted to handle their debt. Steve asked whom they owed money to. Reece mentioned a binder manufacturer. Such venders usually demanded payment in thirty days, but Reece had negotiated one hundred and eighty days. Steve said, "You're taking advantage of him. Put him at the top of the list. Who else?"

They listed every outstanding account. Before they finished, Steve again asked if there was anyone else that needed to be on their list.

"Well," said Reece, "there is one more debt. We owe $80,000 to an elderly woman."

"When is the money due?" asked Steve.

"There is no date."

"Get her on the phone." As Steve chatted with this sweet grandma, he asked her when she planned on being paid."

"Oh, whenever they can," she said. "I just love those boys."

"How about July 1?" responded Steve.

"Oh, that's fine. But there's no hurry. It doesn't matter."

"It matters to us," said Steve. "We are trying to clean up our ship." They gave their word for July 1.

When Reece asked how they were going to pay all these vendors, Steve said, "We're going to sell our way out of debt."

To do so, they needed a sales force. Steve helped them build one. It wasn't long before TimeMax was operating in the black. Reece relates, "My personal income doubled in 1994, the first year we hired Steve as a coach. It doubled again each year for the next two years. Our business profits soared. But his impact wasn't just financial. Being coached by Steve fundamentally changed who I was and how I thought and acted."

So how did Steve, who was sitting on his deck staring off at the mountains, leapfrog into being a successful business coach? The mountain-staring Steve was floundering in depression. He had reached the end of his winning formula. The Break in Belonging exercise had jarred his soul. Issues from his childhood were clamoring for resolution. All of these collided at one time. It was almost too much.

Almost, but not quite.

His work with Lloyd brought Steve to his nadir—and to his rebirth. Steve shook off his depression. He started resolving his past. He created a new way to win. He dropped off his baggage. He embraced without apology the man he was at his core: outrageous, bold, committed, loving, unleashed, unorthodox and brashly confident. He brushed off the gifts and experiences that had given him power throughout his life. He still had them. They had been in the attic of his soul, waiting. With newfound clarity, Steve 2.0 was ready to roll.

Leadership Principles I Learned from Steve

Reece Bawden

Here are just some of the leadership principles I learned from Steve.

Life is a creation. We create it with our speaking.

Leaders use their speaking as a way to create hope and possibility.

Every conversation is an opportunity to create a better outcome than would have occurred had you not been involved. Effective leaders bump up the conversation to a higher level.

Leaders bring positive things into existence through their speaking.

There are seldom quick, easy answers. Most solutions come through managing conversations.

Leaders complete one conversation before moving to another one. They don't pile conversations on top of each other.

Acknowledgments are a powerful form of creation. People will become what you acknowledge them to be.

When you transfer responsibilities, train the employee with the new responsibility to a new, higher level.

No assignment is complete until it is reported as complete. Returning and reporting is a powerful leadership principle. It gives a leader an opportunity to acknowledge the completion.

When delegating, establish an agreed-upon time for the assignment to be completed. Tuesday at 5:00 p.m. means the same thing to everybody. That discipline produces results that would not likely have occurred without a specific deadline.

No organization will rise above the level of its leader. My company is a reflection of me.

Making commitments creates opportunities to practice being your word. When you tell someone you will meet them at a certain time, it is an opportunity to practice keeping a commitment and being your word. Practicing this principle makes you a more effective, disciplined individual and leader.

We think we see life as it is. This is not true. We see life as we are. When we open our mouths to speak, we think we are describing the world as it is. This is not true. What we are really doing is describing ourselves. We are describing how the world looks to us.

Chapter 18

Steve Chandler

Dennis Deaton's speaking schedule was full, yet requests were coming in. Dennis was the CEO and co-founder of TimeMax (now Quma). He was also their primary presenter. Hardison recommended that Steve Chandler, the director of marketing, take the overflow. Chandler's deep desire was to be a public speaker, but he had a long way to go.

Whenever Chandler spoke, Hardison attended. Afterwards, he would give Chandler feedback. The most valuable was, "Don't try to be Dennis. Your resume and your experience don't support it. Be you. Let them hear about your failures. They will connect with them." Chandler brought authenticity, humor, and scrappy wisdom to his presentations. People related. Within a year, his courses at TimeMax were selling out.

Soon, Chandler was flying around the country to give his presentations. Chandler represented TimeMax, but the content of his courses was his own. When Chandler went into corporations, he set his own prices and paid his own expenses.

One day, Hardison and Chandler were sitting in the TimeMax conference room, looking at a map and discussing Chandler's out-of-state speaking schedule. Hardison asked Chandler how much he was charging. Chandler's price was $1,250 for the whole day.

"Steve, you have to raise your prices," said Hardison.

Chandler started shifting in his seat. "I don't want to raise my prices," Chandler said, barely loud enough for Hardison to hear.

"But you can't even cover your travel expenses at $1,250. You're going in the hole," insisted Hardison. "You'll $1,250 yourself to death."

Chandler took a deep breath. "Well, what's my value?"

"I can't tell you your value. You have to determine that yourself. Then you deliver on the value you set. If I were you, I would charge $40,000."

Chandler choked. "But what if they won't pay $40,000? I would rather get $1,250 than nothing."

"Steve," said Hardison. "They will pay you $40,000. You're worth it."

Chandler wasn't so sure.

Shortly after this, Motorola approached Reece and Dennis and said they had a problem with morale on their line. Did TimeMax have some programs that addressed morale and culture? Dennis said no. Reece said no. Chandler said, "Yes, we do." Dennis and Reece stared at him. Chandler had been working on developing a course to help people take ownership of their own morale and not make others, including their company, responsible for their attitude.

"When can we see it?"

They set up a time. Going for broke, they also invited several decision makers from Texas Instruments to come and observe. No one had any idea what Chandler was going to say. Motorola and

Texas Instruments were big companies. They were important clients. It was risky to use them as guinea pigs, and Reece and Dennis were nervous.

Chandler hit it out of the park. The Texas Instrument execs wanted Chandler, and they wanted him in Texas. They adjourned to the conference room to work out the details. Chandler stood at the white board. He wrote $1,250 on the board and started to explain his typical fees.

Hardison interrupted. "Do you mind if I make it a little easier for you to see what Steve Chandler is saying? Steve charges $1,250 per person for his course. But if you put one hundred people in the room, we can get the price down so it's closer to $400 per person." They didn't bat an eye. They booked ten dates for $400,000. Chandler had a new fee for speaking: $40,000 a day.

When Hardison first started coaching at TimeMax, Chandler was working as the marketing director. He wrote ads. He came up with creative ways to get the company's name and services in front of people. He helped with branding. And he hoped people would call. They had one salesperson. When Hardison came on board, he said, "You don't need marketing. You need actual sales." Hardison created a sales team, which Chandler joined. He wanted to be where he could really help.

It wasn't a natural fit. A salesperson that quaked at the thought of asking for money was going to have some hard days. This was one of them. Reece Bawden called Chandler into his office. Hardison was there. They let Chandler know that they were sending him out to collect money that was overdue on one of his accounts.

"Can't someone else do it? This is hard for me. Really hard."

"This is your account," said Hardison. "If you can't collect the money that is due us, you are a liability to the company."

"I'm not sure I can do it, but I'll try," said Chandler.

"I don't want you to try," said Hardison. "I want you to do it. Trying is an excuse."

"You know," said Chandler, "This client is tough. He runs a gym. He holds world records. I'm not good at asking for money."

"Then don't be you. Be someone who could do it. Be Brando, be Bruce Lee, be anybody who could get it done. I don't care who, as long as you do it. And don't come back to the company until you have the money."

"I do have a job here, you know," said Chandler.

"And you still will when you return with the money."

Chandler went to the gym and asked the owner for the money that was overdue. He tells the story:

The owner said, "I can't pay you right now. I might be able to pay in a couple of weeks." I knew I couldn't take that answer back to Steve. I told him I knew he might have a hard time paying, but I wasn't leaving until I got what he owed the company. We stared at each other for a few minutes. Finally, he said, "Are you threatening me?"

I said, "No, no threat. I'm just not leaving. We have to have the money today, not tomorrow. And you've already broken promises to pay. I understand that. But today, that promise can't be broken. I'm returning with the money or I'm not leaving the building."

The owner got up and left the room. I'm sure he was wondering if I was going to leave, but I didn't move. After a while, he came back in, shook his head, reached into his drawer, pulled out his checkbook and wrote a check for the full amount. He handed it to me. I said thanks. I went back to the company and handed the check to Reece. Hardison gave me a high five and said, "You're not the same person you were when you went over there. Do you get that?"

I said, "I kind of do get that. I kind of feel that." It ended up being a huge breakthrough for me in life because it showed me two things. First, the things I believed I couldn't do were only beliefs. They weren't really the truth. And second, I learned that it is always about who you need to be, not what you need to do. What you need to do will flow from who you are being.

On another occasion, Chandler walked into the conference room, sank into a chair, and lamented to Hardison, "I hate selling."

"Well, you'd better get used to it, because that's all there is."

Chandler winced, like he had just taken a bullet. "I could get a different job."

"Look," said Hardison, "If you think of selling as something a guy in a plaid jacket does when he's trying to convince you to buy something you don't need or want, you will always hate selling. You have to shift how you see it. Selling is enrolling people in your ideas. It's what goes on when someone asks their boss for extra time off. It's what goes on when someone makes a case for a larger office. It's what goes on when your teenager negotiates an extra hour on his curfew. Selling is not just about getting what you want. Selling is about serving someone."

This was a game changer for Chandler.

While selling didn't come naturally to Chandler, writing did. As a young boy, his play included writing make-believe newspapers. His first real job was as a sportswriter. In college, he majored in creative writing. He went into journalism, became a professional songwriter, and was a published poet. It was only natural for him to organize his course material into book form. He started with a booklet of ten ways to motivate yourself. When it grew to twenty-five ways, Chandler took it to Dennis Deaton, who had authored a couple of books. Chandler asked him to read it and tell him if he thought it had potential. Deaton came back and said, "I really don't think you have anything here. It's so disconnected. There's no unifying theme. I just don't see it. I don't think a publisher would be interested."

Chandler was disheartened.

He showed the manuscript to a friend who was a songwriter, who said, "I guess there's a market for this, but it's not me. I wouldn't read this book."

Chandler was crushed.

He showed the manuscript to Hardison. Hardison was over the moon. "Don't stop. This is great."

Chandler found hope.

That summer, Chandler's daughter, Stephanie, wanted to earn money for camp. Chandler wrote up a query letter, gave her the letter and a list of publishers, and had her send out his manuscript to see if anyone was interested. That's what he told Stephanie. In reality, it was just make-work. But Chandler started getting phone calls from publishers—in the plural. He called Stephanie at camp to let her know that seven publishers were interested in his book. After he spoke, there was a long silence. Finally, Stephanie said, "Only seven?"

Chandler had to come up with seventy-five more ways to motivate oneself to complete his book. When he did, *100 Ways to Motivate Yourself* was published and became a best-seller.

Hardison's support never flagged. If they went to lunch together, Hardison would call the manager of the restaurant over to their table and say, "Do you know who this is?" When the manager shook his head, Hardison would say, "This is a very well-known author. He has a best-selling book. I happen to have a copy of it in my car. If you promise to read it, I will give it to you. I promise you it will change how you run your business. It will make a difference in your life."

Hardison didn't just have one copy of Chandler's latest book in his car. He had a whole trunkful of them. When he went on vacation, he took an extra suitcase filled with Steve Chandler books. He gave them away to everyone he met, after committing them to read it. If the recipient hedged, he took the book back. He was planting seed books, getting Chandler's name out, and creating him. "Hardison was my greatest promoter," said Chandler. "He had me believe in myself all the way."

When Hardison received positive feedback from a client about one of Chandler's books, he would call Chandler on the spot and say, "Steve, so-and-so just told me what your book meant to her. I want her to say it directly to you. Here she is." Chandler says, "Calls like that kept me going."

Chandler's speaking and writing were going well. It was time for him to fly solo. He parted from TimeMax. He hired Hardison, who had also completed his work with TimeMax, as his personal coach. One of the first things Hardison tackled was Chandler's relationship with money. It had deep roots.

Chandler's grandfather abandoned his family, leaving his family penniless. Everyone in the family worked around the clock to make money. Chandler's dad learned early he could make money if he worked hard enough. It became his creed, and he eventually became a millionaire. Hard work was enshrined in the Chandler household. But young Steve Chandler needed room to dream and think. When his dad said "jump," he collapsed. He wasn't carved out of military marble. When his work lacked precision, which it always did, his dad chided, "You don't deserve your allowance. You don't deserve any money." That thought was superglued in Chandler's self-concept, right next to his resentment towards his father. Hardison helped Chandler identify the lies that kept his disempowering beliefs in place: he didn't deserve money, he didn't work hard, he couldn't do hard things. Chandler was finding freedom. Then Hardison said, "Stop making your father wrong."

"What?" asked Chandler.

"If he grew up poor, he feared you would too. He was afraid for you. Fear shows up as anger and sarcasm in men. He was afraid. He loved you. He wanted you to be strong and responsible when it came to money. He wanted you to be safe. He loved you."

Chandler began to cry. For the rest of their session, Chandler talked about his father. He resurrected good memories, memories without resentments. He told Hardison how his father "became a millionaire industrialist in Detroit, how he fought the unions, how he was approached by the Mafia and stood up to them and turned them down, how brave he was."

Before Chandler left that day, Hardison challenged him to write a song for his father. He spent a week writing the song. One verse reads:

> And I'd give everything I own right now
> Just to tell you how I feel
> Just for one more hour with my father
> Heart of gold, man of steel.

Chandler's praise for Hardison's coaching is copious. This is the abridged version: "I love his teaching and training. It is fierce. It is powerful. And it is effective." Chandler and Hardison currently have a lifetime agreement. They call it the "Can't-Fog-a-Mirror Agreement." Hardison will be coaching Chandler until one or the other of them is no longer breathing.

*Steve Hardison and
Steve Chandler,
outside Hardison's
office, 2019*

Chapter 19

University of Santa Monica

S teve has struggled with his anger his whole life. Lloyd's work helped. So did The Forum. But there was still a lot of work to do. Steve started searching. He found the University of Santa Monica. In 1999, Steve enrolled in USM's Master's of Spiritual Psychology program, where he met Drs. Ron and Mary Hulnick.

In traditional universities, students expand their horizons and gain valuable knowledge through lecture and study. They hone their intellect through papers and projects. USM does all this and has some dimensions that traditional education does not. At USM you learn *and* you heal. You are one of the textbooks. You are the case studies. Your life is the homework. Steve brought one behemoth of a case study to his very first weekend.

First Class

Five days before Steve's first class, the phone rang early in the morning. It was Phil, Steve's brother, calling about their oldest brother, Rob. He said, "I don't know any details, but Rob called and said Shara [Rob's nineteen-year-old daughter] has been killed. I'll call when I know more."

Killed? If she'd had a health crisis or been in a car accident, wouldn't they have said "died" or "been in an accident"? Steve and Amy paced and cried and wondered. An hour later, they got clarity, but no relief. Shara had been brutally murdered by her ex-husband.

Steve immediately flew to Utah. He held his brother and sister-in-law. He cried with them. He took over the funeral preparations that they weren't ready to deal with. He helped manage the people, flowers, and food that came streaming into their home. He did everything that could possibly be done to help Rob and his wife Debbie, and then he flew out on Friday, straight to USM.

To start Friday night's class, Ron asked the students why they were there and what they wanted to get out of their USM experience. There were the expected answers. People wanted to become better husbands, wives, fathers, and mothers. They wanted to be better listeners or kinder people. They wanted to kick-start their careers. They wanted to heal. They wanted to move forward. Then Steve shared about his week.

Steve's classmates responded with shock, sadness, and outrage. Then Ron spoke. He explained that we don't know what agreements we made before we came to this life. We don't know what people need to learn. Everyone—Shara, her ex-husband, Rob, Debbie, Steve, and even those in the room at USM—all had something to learn from Shara's death. On the first day, in the first hour, Steve's perspective took a massive shift. And he still had two more years to go.

The Amy Project

One of the first assignments Steve received at USM was the Manifesting Your Heart's Desire project. Fellow student, Dr. Carla Rotering recalls:

> His goal was to know his wife in the most intimate way available on the planet. Despite the fact that they had been married for a long time, despite the fact that they had four kids, he wanted to know her more. And he was willing to devote his entire year to that. He took notes on how she exercised. He witnessed the research that she did and the way that she wrote. He watched her teach. He followed her around at the grocery store. (He realized he had no idea how much milk cost—no idea!) I used to ask him, "Are you stalking her?" And I think he was, and I think he does. I think he stalks her for her wisdom, love, beauty, grace, and joy.

And what did Steve learn from his project? "I was stunned at all my wife did and all she managed and how well she did it. Not only is she beautiful, kind, and loving, she is eminently capable. I realized that I had won the wife lottery." But didn't he already know that? Absolutely. "But," Steve says, "it is so easy to lose sight of those things in the midst of everyday life. My Amy Project at USM didn't just remind me of what I knew. It created a shift in my being so that I will never take her for granted."

The Student

Steve is constituted to make a difference, to share, to inspire others, to be noticed, and to become personally connected with whoever is leading an event or course. He could walk up to the

President of the United States and feel he has every right to talk to him or her—and that the president is lucky to meet him. It is his signature confidence. It is part of his power.

It is why fellow USM student Lisa Haisha says, "Steve really intrigued me. Anytime he spoke, he had something intense to share that I think helped shift everyone. He had a beautiful way of tapping into whatever the conversation was in the room, and then taking it to the next level with his sharing." It is also why Steve was named USM's "Student of the Year" in 2001, along with Dana Dunbar and Iyanla Vanzant.

Steve loved his experience at the University of Santa Monica. He reflects:

> One of the greatest things I got from USM was a principle called "heart-centered listening," which means that when I'm listening to a person, I am listening not just with my ears, but also with my heart. I'm trying to get where they are coming from, instead of judging them or being right. It changed how I listen to everyone, from the people I love the most (my wife, my kids, my grandkids) to strangers (an employee at the car wash or someone in the grocery store).
>
> The most powerful tool I acquired from USM is compassionate self-forgiveness. It works like this. Perhaps I think, "Amy doesn't appreciate me." It's not a pleasant thought. I can take that thought through the compassionate self-forgiveness process. I breathe it in. I realize I'm the one judging her as unappreciative. She's over there, happy as a clam, and I'm upset because I think she isn't appreciating me. Then I forgive myself for judging my wife as not appreciating me. My frustration leaves. My world becomes peaceful.

I introduce compassionate self-forgiveness to all my clients. We work miracles once they see the judgments they place on themselves and the world. The result is personal peace.

Lifelong Learning

Steve completed his courses at the University of Santa Monica in 2001. In addition to USM and the decade immersed in the teachings of Werner Erhard, Steve spent two years studying the Enneagram with Dr. David Daniels. He and Amy participated in several Enneagram courses.

Steve's learning is not restricted to formal courses and programs. He reads and studies extensively about belief systems, personal development, and the creation of personality. Two of his favorite, self-directed courses are *A Course in Miracles* and *The Way of Mastery*. He also reads the holy writings from different religions. Steve's oldest son, Clint, provides an insight into this part of Steve:

He doesn't study academically; he studies for experience. He studies to expand himself. I've seen my dad constantly working on himself my whole life. Consistent growth and improvement seem totally normal.

I don't think he ever read books to be a better coach. I think his coaching is an outgrowth of who he is as a person. He has been driven to become a better person. His coaching is just the natural manifestation of that.

Chapter 20

Iyanla Vanzant

R honda Eva Harris was born in the back of a taxi in Brooklyn, New York. At the age of thirty, she was given the name "Iyanla," which means "great mother," after being initiated and ordained as a priestess in the Yoruba religion. She is an inspirational speaker, a lawyer, a life coach, a best-selling author, a television personality, and the CEO of Inner Visions Institute for Spiritual Development. "In 2000, she was named one of the '100 most influential Black Americans' by *Ebony* magazine . . . In 2012, Vanzant was listed at #7 on *Watkins Mind Body Spirit Magazine*'s list of the 100 most spiritually influential living people."

In 1999, Iyanla appeared over twenty times on *The Oprah Winfrey Show*. Audiences around the world watched as she served as a spiritual mentor and coach. Iyanla is warm, wise, incisive, and powerful. The audiences loved her, and so did Oprah. Oprah and Iyanla discussed the idea of Iyanla having her own show. The issue wasn't *if* she should have her own show, but *when*. Both decided there were things Iyanla still needed to learn about the television industry and the inner workings of a show. Iyanla was content to wait.

While waiting, Barbara Walters offered Iyanla the opportunity to have her own show on Buena Vista Television. Being wanted by the two most powerful women in television was a heady experience. Iyanla was torn. When Iyanla told Oprah about the offer and explained why it looked like a great opportunity, Oprah and her executive producer felt betrayed. They wished Iyanla good riddance, with little warmth or goodwill.

Iyanla went to New York City, but the dream opportunity turned out to be a nightmare. Her producers were not aligned with her vision for her show. She had no say in critical decisions. They tried to twist, bend, and shape her into someone she was not. She was too black, too in-your-face, too inner city. They wanted a vanilla talk show host to speak to the housewives of Middle America. They wanted a bland interviewer who read the teleprompter without inserting herself. Iyanla and the executive producer, Bill Geddie, were on a collision course. When the showdown came, Geddie won and Iyanla was demoralized and broken.

"The day after the Bill Geddie meltdown, I hired Steve to coach me—Steve Hardison, a brilliant man who is extraordinarily sensitive and downright psychic, although he would never represent himself as such. We had met during our master's program in spiritual studies at the University of Santa Monica. Steve could see directly into my heart. I flew him to New York to get the lay of the land."

For two days, Steve shadowed Iyanla, talking to everyone involved in the show. At the end of those two days, Steve said to Iyanla:

Iyanla, these people do not know who you are. They do not know, because you have not told them. Most of them respect you and they respect the work you did on *Oprah,* but they do not know your vision. If this show is going to work, you have to let them know who you are, get them enrolled in your vision, and make this process life-giving for you, or you might as well walk away. If this process does not give you life, it will steal your life, and nothing is worth that.

Iyanla wrote, "Over the course of three months, Steve coached me on how to stand up for myself within myself, and how to take a powerful stand on my vision for the *Iyanla* show. It was one of the most powerful experiences of my life."

More than a decade after the rift between Iyanla and Oprah occurred, they reconciled—and they did so in front of the world. Oprah dedicated the last two episodes of her show to broadcasting this rapprochement. It was real. It was raw. It was grace. Iyanla reflects:

Many of my conversations with Steve are etched into my soul. Many I don't remember. I just know the outcome. I can't tell you the words. But by the time I sat down with Oprah, I was her equal. I didn't need anything from her. I didn't want anything from her. I was: "I am Iyanla."

I had made a mistake, and I had to own it and acknowledge it. And that's what I did. The first thing I said to her was, "I have to ask you for your forgiveness." It was my stuff. She's got her own stuff. But it was my stuff. I had already healed up the unworthiness. All of that was a result of my work with Steve.

The Oprah Winfrey Network—OWN—was created soon after.

Oprah gave Iyanla her own show, *Iyanla: Fix My Life*. In an email to Steve, Iyanla wrote "[This time] I am doing what you and I did together, creating the vision." Iyanla's series ran for ten seasons, with one hundred and forty-two episodes. Oprah Winfrey calls Iyanla "the most powerful spiritual healer, fixer, teacher, on the planet," and has referred to her show as the heart of the Oprah network. In 2014, Oprah surprised Iyanla with a total home makeover that ran into the millions.

Ever since their meeting at USM, Iyanla and Steve's relationship has been exceptionally close. She calls him *brother*, sometimes "my FINE white brother." They share an obsessive love for shoes. They share a commitment to help people see clearly and access their power. They own a little piece of real estate in each other's hearts. "He's just a part of me," says Iyanla. "And I like to think I'm a part of him. I just love him deeply." Steve consistently sends Iyanla packages in the mail: articles, books, gifts—things that say, "You are on my mind."

Their coaching experiences have welded a permanent link of love and respect, tinged with wonder. Iyanla says, "I haven't found anyone that measures up to him yet, not even me. And I'm good. I'm really good at what I do. I don't hold a candle to Steve Hardison because he's other worldly. I don't know what planet he came from. I don't know."

Iyanla and Steve in Sedona, 2012
(Photo: Sean Lopez)

Chapter 21

Byron Katie

A my lives the adage "So many books, so little time." She always has a long list of books to read and a shelf or two of books she has already purchased and is hoping to get to. When her sister, Melinda, gave her *Loving What Is* by Byron Katie for her birthday in December of 2005 and told her it was the most powerful book she had ever read, Amy catapulted it to the top of her queue. As soon as she finished it, she handed it to Steve, saying, "This book bent my mind. You're going to love it." He devoured it.

After Steve read *Loving What Is* twice, he got on the internet to find out more about Katie. He learned she was coming to Phoenix in a couple of weeks. Steve and Amy rearranged their schedules to be there.

The stage was sparse, just two comfortable chairs and a small table with fresh flowers. The event began at 7:00 p.m., sans puffy introductions. Katie simply walked out and said, "Who's ready to do The Work?" A hundred hands went up.

For two hours, Steve and Amy observed people who grappled

with titanic troubles—a mother whose son was schizophrenic, a woman in a toxic marriage, another with multiple sclerosis, a man with cancer, a woman who as a child had been locked in an attic for days at a time by her parents. Katie invited each of them up to the stage and into the chair. She walked them through her signature four questions for defusing stressful thoughts. Katie's words were peppered with "Oh, sweetheart." Her eyes twinkled.

As Katie went through the inquiry process, she did not simply ask her four questions. She had a conversation in and around and between the questions. It was in these conversations that Katie's humor and immense love beamed. It was in the conversations that the principles of The Work were explicated. It was in the conversations that Katie said the following:

> We see thoughts as unwanted children. We medicate them down. We meditate them down. We chocolate them down. What if we met them and embraced them?

> Except for your thinking, you're just fine.

> If I take off all my clothes and my husband screams, *he* has a problem. I hope he works on that.

> That's reality. We don't have to like it. When I think, "This shouldn't be . . ." I'm at war with reality, and it feels terrible.

Steve was enthralled. Once again, he found himself in the presence of a master.

As the event finished, Steve knew he wanted more. In asking around, he learned about Katie's nine-day School of You. There, participants experienced The Work more intensely, from morning till night. The next school was in two weeks. For Amy, that was a deal-breaker. Steve was determined to be there and moved mountains to make it happen. Amy decided not to be left behind.

Fourteen days later, Steve and Amy flew to Los Angeles. Ten days later they flew home. What Steve experienced changed his life. He was on fire.

If Steve believes in something, he shares. When Steve really believes in something, he shares big. Over the course of the next two years, Steve put on three events in Phoenix and one in Salt Lake City, Utah, where Katie came and did The Work. These were not fireside chats, but major events. Each required months of organizing, coordinating, and sharing. Steve was a whirlwind of energy.

On the morning of September 16, 2006, Steve arrived early at the Phoenix Civic Plaza. He stood in front of the stage and took it all in. Steve was emotional. Katie's personal assistant tapped him on his elbow and brought him out of his reverie. She guided him to the green room where Katie and her husband, Stephen Mitchell, were waiting. Soon, like a bride with her father, Katie put her arm into Steve's, and he escorted her to the stage.

The morning session broke early for lunch, thanks to an errant fire alarm. Steve and Katie snuck away to a small, local eatery where they found a quiet corner in the back.

"What would you like to talk about?" she began.

"Katie, I don't need to talk about anything. I just like being with you. You don't need to entertain me. We don't need to talk at all."

She smiled. She touched him on the arm and said, "Oh, sweetheart, we both know we both love to talk. Let's talk. What do you want to talk about?"

Two great minds, two great hearts, an ordinary lunch, a magnificent hour.

Steve has shared Katie's work with hundreds, probably thousands, of people. He has enrolled many of his clients into Katie's nine-day School of You. He, himself, has attended it twice. Steve and Amy have frequently participated in the New Year's Cleanses. They do The Work.

Little wonder that one day Steve received a phone call. A formal voice on the other end of the line, said "Do you have a moment?"

"Sure."

There was a *click*. A new voice came on the phone.

"Hello, sweetheart. How are you?" Steve knew immediately it was Katie.

"I love the story you have of me," she said. "And I love the story I have of you."

For Katie, that is the most accurate way possible to express love.

Part Two

The Ultimate Coach

Chapter 22

The Office

For a couple of years, Steve had been coaching at his dining room table. It worked. By 8:00 a.m., the kids had left for school and Amy was ensconced in her office. It was private enough, but not ideal.

One day in late 1993, Steve was puttering around his property and stepped into the storage room on the west end of his house. The kids' bicycles stood clustered, propped on their kickstands, like dominoes tempting fate. The lawnmower was parked to their side, flecked with grass bits. Tools were scattered on the work bench. It smelled like gasoline and paint. Steve saw possibility. In a few months, with the help of Gary Gietz, a client and general contractor, glass-panel doors replaced the heavy utility doors. Lush cherrywood cabinetry displaced plywood storage shelves. A couch and leather chair sat where the bicycles and lawnmower had been. The transformation was extensive. How apropos.

When Steve was young, he envisioned wearing suits and flying around the world doing business. It's common enough today, if you substitute business casual for suits. It wasn't so common in 1965. In 2021, Steve still loves wearing suits, but not to work. He often walks into a coaching session wearing shorts and flip flops, or maybe loafers. One of the perks of living in Arizona is that such attire is weather-appropriate year-round. When he wants to gussy up for a session, he dons long pants and one of his sixty pairs of shoes, perhaps his favorite: patent leather magenta oxfords. He does not fly around the world to coach. His clients fly or drive to him. No exceptions.

Lisa Hale, executive coach and former president of the board of the Colorado chapter of the International Coach Federation, says of Steve's no-travel mandate:

> That is a really tough transition that most coaches never make. A beginning coach that gets a big-shot CEO as a client typically thinks, "I have to make it easy for him. I have to go to his office. After all, he's paying me a lot of money. I better be available for him at all times." Most coaches operate that way. I've operated that way. What Hardison models for us is really, really important. He doesn't go to his clients. He doesn't upend his life. He loves, respects, and serves his clients—and he has boundaries.

Why is Steve so adamant about his clients traveling to him? There are several reasons. Steve had enough travel during his Rodel years to last him for a lifetime. Steve loves his current commute. Even with a strong headwind or heavy traffic (crickets on the sidewalk? leaves to step over?), it's no more than one minute at the most. This dovetails into another reason. Yayati Desai, a personal coach based in India, observes, "He doesn't travel because he loves Amy. He wants to spend more time with her." Yayati muses, "Like, wow, who does that?" He also notes, "I'm going from this city to that city. I am speaking to a thousand people here and two thousand there to generate future clients. He doesn't need that kind of marketing. He always has lots of clients of fantastic caliber."

There are other reasons. Steve wants clients to have skin in the game. The greater the commitment, the greater the results. Hardison charges a lot for his coaching. For some clients, that creates a sell-your-firstborn kind of commitment. For some clients, any fee at any price would be immaterial, but arranging their schedule to regularly be in Hardison's office requires colossal commitment. Norma Bachoura, a doctor living in Southern California, had a ten-hour agreement with Steve. She relates:

> By the end of the fifth session, I had changed so much that I couldn't imagine not being with him for one year. I wondered what more I would get if I extended my coaching. Of course, I hesitated, partly because of the amount of money, but also because each session required one whole day of travel. I made the decision to continue with the coaching. Every time we met, I had personal breakthroughs and learned so much about human nature. He changed my life drastically, like really drastically. I started teaching what I learned during my coaching sessions at my church. At first, I had only two or three students, but they recruited others. I ended up teaching ten people for eight months. And they changed drastically because I just copied Steve.

Many coaches offer coaching via Skype, FaceTime, Zoom, or some other video conferencing. It would be so much easier, so much more convenient. No long lines at airport security. No hours in the sky. But it wouldn't be the same. Steve knows this. So do his clients. One potential client from Argentina asked Steve if he would be willing to coach her through Skype.

His response was immediate. "No." So was hers. She promptly wired money. She knew she had found the coach she was looking for.

Preparation

Steve's office is not simply a meeting place where coach A meets client B—a more private Starbucks. It is a sacred place. Succinctly stated, the word "sacred" means to take something from common use and dedicate it to a sacred use. At all levels and in all domains, sacredness does not just happen. It is intentional.

In the Hebrew Bible, God commanded the Israelite people to wash their clothes and to refrain from sexual relations for three days prior to the Sinai experience. They were not to casually waltz into the presence of God. He demanded preparation. In secular terms, "preparation precedes power," as Charles Lindbergh said. But preparation not only precedes power—it *creates* power. Both Steve and his clients intentionally prepare for their time together, creating the power of their sessions before stepping into his office.

In being interviewed for this book, Stephen McGhee said, "Write about how Hardison rakes the carpet between meetings. Have you heard that? Who does that?" Perhaps the same person who brushed his carpet when he was fourteen. But *why* does he do it? The office has pearl-grey shag carpet. (Hardison has a soft spot for anything that reminds him of the 1970s.) Before any client enters, Steve himself rakes the carpet, starting at the far corner and walking backwards to the door. The effect is renewal. Each client steps into a fresh space. Stephen McGhee says, "Anytime I walked in that office, mine were the first footprints on that freshly raked carpet. I don't even think I realized it at first. I just knew that there was something different going on, like 'I'm breaking ground here.'"

Without fail, when a client arrives, his or her flag is flying. Many clients start scanning for their flag while they are still on the freeway, approaching the exit that will take them to Steve's house. When they see their flag, they get a little jolt of bliss. They are royals in residence, at least for the next two hours.

There are two flagpoles at Steve's house, one by the front entrance and one in the backyard, near his office. Each client has a flag. It may be the flag of his university, state, or country. It may

*Philip
Weech,
2021*

have a logo of his business or something he loves or something that characterizes the client. It may represent the client's vision or the essence of the work he or she is doing with Steve. There are flags of Italy, India, and Ireland and flags of Florida, Texas, and Hawaii. There are flags with unicorns and flags with hearts. There are flags with golf balls, horses, and doves. And there are custom-made flags designed by clients. When long-term clients complete their coaching agreement, Steve and the client hold a sacred ceremony. They lower the flag, sign and date it with a marker, and carefully fold it. Steve then gives the flag to the client.

Everyone who knows anything about Steve, knows about the flags. Even clients who show up for a one-time, two-hour *Be With* session have a flag. At the end of the *Be With* session, Amy takes pictures of Steve and the client standing beneath the flag. If Amy isn't home, Steve recruits a neighbor to be the photographer. It's that important. The client is that important.

Lisa Berkovitz relates, "I arrived at his house and he had two flags flying for me, a Canadian flag and a 528 flag. I had shared with him that 528Hz is the frequency of love. It's the heart of my life's work. I coach clients to thrive by doing more of what they love. Also, I am working on a global "528 project" that is about love-based businesses worldwide. It is my biggest vision." What was the impact of seeing the flag of her country and the flag of her passion? Lisa says, "I've never had an ally like him. I feel he has my back in a way that I've never experienced, and he's holding me to my highest in a way that no one ever has."

Steve's preparation is not solely external: flying flags, raking carpet, getting the office at the right temperature, and setting out snacks and fruit. He prepares internally. Lisa Hale shares what she learned from Steve and how she adapted it into her coaching:

> Steve prepares himself to be one hundred percent present with his clients. If I was going to say the one thing that has impacted me the most about Steve Hardison, it is that he spends four hours every day preparing for his clients. His preparation looks like spending time with his wife. It looks like exercise. It looks like eating well. It looks like meditation and writing and journaling. It looks like deeply immersing himself in a book, not just reading, but studying to the point of absorption. And he does that with his clients too. From the moment I got that, I began to cultivate that practice.
>
> I record my sessions with my clients, and even my prospects. I keep my recordings completely private. I listen to them and I take notes and I listen for the things I didn't hear the first time around. I listen to the patterns and then I'll listen again for the content. When we meet again, I'm really prepared. I'm meditating. I'm up early and exercising and journaling and clearing my head and clearing my mind and coming into a place of presence and service. I do that because I learned from Steve Hardison the value of being one hundred percent present and the importance of preparation. It has made me an extraordinary coach and, frankly, an extraordinarily well-paid one.

The preparation is mutual. Steve's clients have invested significant funds for the opportunity of sitting in his office with him. They have arranged their lives and their schedules to be there, sometimes flying across the country, sometimes flying from other countries. Some fly into Phoenix a day or two before their session to prepare, and some stay a few hours or a few days afterwards to digest their experience. Even if they are just driving across the valley, too much is at stake to just show up.

Steve Chandler says, "I used to be at Hardison's house thirty minutes before our sessions." He wanted to make sure he wasn't late. Jason Jaggard says, "Getting ready to work with Steve Hardison is like preparing myself for travelling to Mecca. I set everything up. I have a special pen. I have a special notebook. There are all these things that I do to treat the process with the sacredness that it deserves."

That is the preparation once you have laid down money. You don't even get in the door without a considerable, upfront investment of time and effort. Jason shares his experience:

> I reached out to a couple people whom I really admired for coaching. We talked for a little bit and they said, "We would love to work with you, but we think that you would really, really enjoy working with this guy Steve Hardison." When I started talking to people about Hardison, I realized you say his name and it's like a hush falls over the crowd. So, I went to his website and checked him out.
>
> I sent him a nice little email and said I would like to work with him. He said, "Great." Then he gave me a bunch of shit to do. He sent me two books, not written by him, and said, "I want you to read these first. And I want you to read everything on my website. And I want you to watch these three hours of videos. And I want you to think about what it would be like for us to work together. Then get back to me."
>
> It took me a month to do all these things. And then I reached back out to him and we set up a time. Initially I thought he was creating hoops for me to jump through to see

if I really wanted it. What I didn't realize until later was that he started serving me from the second that I reached out to him. I hired him two months after he and I initially talked. At my first actual session, I felt like I had already been working with him for two months for free.

There is more. Steve doesn't invite just anyone into his office. Gina Carlson says, "Working with Steve is to go big or go home." Iyanla Vanzant put it this way: "Steve Hardison is not for the faint of heart, or the hopers, the wishers, the tryers. He's not for the dreamers. He's not for the wannabes. When you step into that experience, you've got to be ready. You've got to be ready to take your A-game and throw it the hell out the window. Because in the presence of Steve Hardison, your A-game ain't going to get you to first base."

True, but as long as you come in swinging for the fence, it will be a great game.

The Gatekeeper

The first time someone comes to meet with Steve, he does not take them straight to his office. First, they come into his home. He offers them water. They visit for a bit. He asks a few probing questions. When they are ready, Steve says something like he recently said to Joseph Rabin: "Fitz, we can go out into my office now. It is the most sacred and holy place on Earth for me. It is a place that has no -isms. It is not a place for chit-chatting. It is a place of pure creation. It is a place for healing marriages, for building companies, for creating movies and books. I ask you to respect and honor it. Is that something you can do?"

Jason Jaggard recalls, "In my very first session, before going to his office, Steve said, 'Jason, I want you to understand something. Here is my religion.' And he held his hand up at chest height. Then he raised his hand to head height, 'And here is my office.' I'd never heard anyone talk like that before. He invited people into his office with total clarity and a powerful commitment."

Devon Bandison was part of an elite group of coaches Steve Chandler created. Inviting associations with the British intelligence agency MI6, Chandler named this group "M6." During one of the weekends when the M6 team had flown to Arizona, Chandler arranged a visit to the Hardisons. Bandison was excited to see Hardison *in situ,* as a regular guy. Bandison relates:

We go into the Hardison's backyard and Steve Chandler, who has written about Hardison in so many books, and goes back years with him, and is a lifetime coaching client, asks Hardison very respectfully if he can take me into the office. Hardison says, "Absolutely." So, we go in and Chandler shows me several things in the office and tells me stories about them. Then I look up at the bookshelf and Hardison has my book, the book I had written and sent him, on the shelf. I'm like, "Holy shit."

We leave the office, and two other members of our group start walking into the office. Hardison is sitting on the bench over by the wall and is in a conversation with Karen Davis. Out of the corner of his eye, he sees these two heading into his office. He stops mid-conversation and makes a beeline to the door. He says, "Excuse me. I need you to know that this is a sacred place. I don't let just anyone go in here." They assumed that because Steve Chandler and I went in that they could go in next. Hardison stops them and says, "I'll allow one of you to go in at a time. But I need you to know it's a sacred place." To me that was a small but powerful moment.

A lot of people might have thought, "Well, these are Steve Chandler's people, so they can go in," or "Just this time," or "I'm in the middle of this conversation . . ." But Hardison has always said that his office is a special place. He coaches people on integrity. In a world where a lot of people are wishy-washy, it is very refreshing when someone actually means what they say. Their word creates their world. To me, that was the most powerful moment of our time there that evening.

The preparation, the gatekeeping, and the work that goes on in the office yield tangible results. Most who cross the threshold of the office feel something. Brandon Green wrote, "I found the office to be serene and peaceful. It definitely had a special energy to it. And I could tell, even without any additional information from Steve, that special work had happened in that room. It definitely had that feel."

Kai Jordan says:

I walked into his office and I was brought to tears. I could literally sense the miracles created in that room. This space is an infinite field of possibility. I have had the privilege of being with Sadhguru, an enlightened master, for four years. I'm very familiar with yoga practices and spiritual masters and the quality of energy. But this was a different kind of energy. I could literally feel it. It was like I was hearing the whispers of the conversations that had happened in that room with Steve. It was moving.

Dr. Daniel Harner had heard about Steve, mostly by reading Steve Chandler's books. He wasn't sure if he was ever going to meet him. He recognized that Hardison doesn't give speeches, make video courses, or do public appearances. The only connection Daniel had with him was through Facebook. To his surprise, one day

Steve posted on Facebook that he was speaking at a church in the Phoenix area. Daniel cleared his schedule and attended. Afterwards, he went to Steve's home for a casual gathering. The highlight of the day was speaking with Steve for a few minutes. He relates, "As I talked to Steve, he was totally present; not one percent of his mind wandered. I told him that I didn't have anything specific to say or to share with him. I just wanted to express my gratitude." At the end of their conversation, Steve asked Daniel if there was anything he could do for him. Daniel hesitated to request the one thing he craved. After a few moments he said, "The only thing that could possibly make me happier is to see and sit in your office for a few minutes."

Steve considered Daniel, pondered his request, and agreed—with the caveat, "Just remember where you are when you sit in there."

"I felt honored that he trusted me," said Daniel. "At the end of the day, I said to myself, 'This was one of the best days in my life.'"

Gifts

The most striking things in Steve's office are the gifts his clients have given him. These are not off-the-shelf gifts. They are unique and beautiful, but they were not chosen for their beauty. Some are prized possessions a client has given to Steve, like a Tibetan bowl the Dalai Lama had given to Dr. Alison Arnold. After working with Steve, she knew it belonged in his office.

All the gifts mean something. For instance, John and Jody Vehr gave Steve a sculpture called *Metamorphose* by Maria-Luise Bodirsky. It shows a new face breaking out of an older face. Bodirksy's website states, "The process of shedding a skin and opening up is painful, yet also releasing; it challenges us to let go of the old and open up to the new." It is a fitting description of Steve's work.

Metamorphose sits right next to a small brass telescope, also given to Steve by Jody Vehr. Steve distinguished for Jody that she habitually looked through the minimizing end of a telescope when it came to looking at her strengths and the maximizing end when she looked at her weaknesses. She bought a telescope for herself to remind her to reverse the order, and one for Steve to thank him for the distinction.

John Cutrone's *Silent Prayer* also sits in Steve's office. This sculpture has two hands pressed together in prayer in front of a face which appears to be suspended in nothingness. This is an apt gift for a coach who steps into his office with nothing and creates miracles out of the words a client speaks.

On a small table next to the client couch sits a red crystal heart from Tiffany's, given to Steve from Iyanla Vanzant. Steve cherishes it. It not only reminds Steve of Iyanla, it became his designated object to teach people that they are as powerful and capable as he is. It is a principle he has taught to many. Steve Chandler vividly remembers sitting in his office when Steve said, "Anything I do, you could do. If I take this glass heart and throw it at the window, the window will break. If you pick up this glass heart and throw it at the window, the window will break."

Chandler relates, "He was holding the heart. I thought, 'He's going to throw it at that window right now.' So I said, 'I really see that. Please put it down.' I knew he wouldn't hesitate to throw it at the window if he thought I wasn't getting the point." Chandler didn't want to be responsible for the carnage.

The Office

Some gifts typify the client's home, like a boomerang from a client who lives in Australia or a feather from one of the peacocks that lives on Daniel Harner's property. Some gifts have been personally made, like the artwork of Nadine Larder and Greg Olsen. Some gifts aren't in the office because they are consumable, like a favorite treat from a client's country of origin. There are so many gifts, too many to mention. They are generously given. They are definitely not expected or required.

Each of these gifts is so much more than a gift. It is a piece of the client. It is a token of their work. Sometimes the work was done through soul-trembling labor, like natural childbirth. Sometimes clients stood at major crossroads. Sometimes clients needed help to reach their dreams. Sometimes they yearned for peace. Always there was transformation. Always there was creation. Always Steve gave all he had to help his client see possibility. No wonder the office is sacred.

Chapter 23

Fasten Your Seat Belt

"On his webpage, Steve says his coaching is not for the 'faint of heart.' That is a gross understatement. Bring a seat belt."

— Scott Parker

Dave Orton first heard of Steve in 2011. Two years later, he was driving up to his house to meet him for the first time. Recognizing that Steve was "a pretty important person," he had taken extra care in dressing. He hadn't brought a seat belt. He relates his experience:

I came to this meeting wearing a suit and tie. I had polished my shoes and made sure that I looked really good. I walked into Steve's house and he offered me a piece of fruit. I had eaten recently, so I declined. We talked for a few minutes and then he looked at me with his piercing look and said, "Dave, you're the most pretentious son of a bitch I've ever seen in my entire life."

What am I supposed to do with that?

The crazy thing about it was it was a statement of being, not a judgment. He wasn't saying, "Hey Dave, you're really bad because you're fake." He was acknowledging the importance that I had placed on my appearance and in showing up the way that I thought he thought I should show up, which was two times divorced from my reality.

Then we went to his office and talked for about three hours. We cut through the layers of bullshit that I had used to protect myself from the reality of life. I realized that I am as fake as can be with my wife. We created who I am now. That three-hour talk changed my life.

Karan Rai has also had seat-belt-wearing experiences with Steve. He says:

I had gone to Yale business school. I started on Wall Street. I was a CEO of a big company and a president of a second company. I was flying around in my own little plane. I had a house on the beach. I had a beautiful wife. I had a healthy child. I didn't go to Steve because I didn't know how to be successful. I went to Steve because I had done the things that I thought would make me successful and I was miserable. My reason for going to him was to help me redefine success. I knew how to play this game called success. I had played it. I had won it. And I had lost. Obviously, I was playing the wrong game.

I told Steve that I had a really lucrative job and the only thing I was struggling with was trying to find a bit of happiness. I figured he would tweak a few things on the margins of my life and things would be good. Steve helped me see that part of the reason I wasn't happy is because I had traded who I really am for money. I wasn't doing it consciously, but I was doing it all the time.

I distinctly recall sitting with him one day and saying, "Steve, I think I'm in too deep. I think I'm making too much money. I'm too vested. I've been doing this for too long. I see my path. Another ten or fifteen years of doing this and I'm all set. I think I'm stuck."

Without blinking, he said, "Just burn it all down and build it again, this time the way you want to."

I said, "What are you talking about, old man?"

He was deadly serious.

"Doing more of what you're already doing is a waste of your time and a waste of my time. So, we have to figure out what we can do within you so you get to a place of joy and happiness in this situation. If you can't do that, then you have no choice but to burn it down and start over."

My homework assignment for the next month was to sit in solitude and silence and do the work to figure out if I was going to make the internal adjustments or build something from scratch on an ethos that I believe in. After a month of deep introspection, I knew what I had to do. I burned it down. That was the genesis of Asgard.

We're three years in and our company [Asgard] is doing great. We have two portfolio companies that we own directly, a third one that we own in partnership, and a fourth one that we're just getting ready to buy right now. All the businesses are doing well.

We're here on this planet for a very short time, a very, very short time. I spend six, eight, ten, twelve hours a day at work and they are completely integral to who I am. I don't have that mental bifurcation of "this is why I'm at work" and "this is why I'm at home." Now I just roll from one to the other seamlessly because my value set is exactly the same. The same accountability I have for myself as a father is the same accountability I have for myself as a boss or as a partner in my business. Most people don't get that. And they don't realize what a superpower that really is. It has been a beautiful journey, and Steve gets all the credit for that.

Life-altering coaching doesn't have to be grand. It might even show up as ordinary. Lisa Haisha had known Steve for almost two decades when the time was right to hire him as her coach. She writes:

I have a strong coaching and speaking practice, but I was downsizing because I was feeling drained. I was working too much. I was taking whatever speaking gig or client came to me because they were all exciting to me. I had a lot going on in my personal life. It seemed that within a year, many of my acquaintances needed help or a temporary place to stay. I obliged, even though they weren't besties or family.

Steve showed me that I was getting tired because I had been collecting 'broken people' that I felt needed rescuing. That was preventing me from being there, one hundred percent, for myself, my family and my clients. I learned from Steve that no one needs my rescuing, and everyone needs my love. Loving others does not mean I should allow their drama to dominate my world. Rather, I need to love them unconditionally and allow them to find their way.

I learned that my energy was being drained by not setting proper boundaries. Now, my boundaries are strong. That shifted my whole world. I can think, listen and create from my higher self again. I feel I have control of each day and that I'm not a pull-toy anymore, dropping everything anytime my phone rings. I have time to take action on the things that bring me joy. My creativity has skyrocketed and I'm out of my slump.

One of the things that contributes to the sense of a wild ride, the cinch-the-seat belt experience of Steve's coaching, is that he does not have a pre-set program. He does not have five or six different coaching plans, one for business, one for personal, one for relationships, one for dreams. Scott Parker says, "Steve doesn't have a boilerplate template from which he works. He creates each session for each individual on the spot, as it happens. That is his genius."

James Malinousky discovered this for himself. James lives in Vancouver, Canada. He attended Werner Erhardt's leadership course in Cancun. While there, he became good friends with another participant, Martine Cannon. She kept talking about her coach, Steve Hardison, and encouraging James to visit him. Eventually, James saw "this YouTube thing about an NFL player that Steve worked with." James was curious, so he picked up the phone and called Steve. He relates:

That first, live conversation was when he really grabbed me. I don't know what it was. He just had this real pure, straight talk. It was like it was coming in me, or right through me. It was coming from his heart to mine. So, I hopped on a plane and flew to Phoenix for the day.

I went to his house and we got started. He didn't mess around. He just got right into it, right there. There was no beating around the bush. I thought, "This guy is wild." The way he was talking was really intense too. When you're sitting on the couch across from him, there's no hiding. He's reading right through you. There's no bullshit. It's like he's peeling you apart within ten minutes. He was so intense.

We were at the end of the session and he said, "Come with me." While we walked across the street, he explained he was going to introduce me to his neighbor [Ruth Collins, the founder and president of Arizona Brain Foods]. Steve told me to donate whatever I wanted, a little bit or whatever. It was up to me. I have a feeling that this was completely spontaneous. No script. I get the sense that when something comes to his mind, he has no hesitation. He just goes with it. When the woman opened the door, he said, "I have a guy that might like to donate to your charity."

She explained to me that some kids in the city don't eat on weekends. They get one free meal a day at school, but they don't get any help on the weekends. She and her husband set up this program to help. It really moved me and the next thing I know, I was reaching into my pocket and handing her all the money I had. She was shocked. I remember the one thing Steve said to her was, "Now you know what I do." It wasn't about him being a coach, but more like, "Now you get what I'm about." We ended our session and I drove away. I was almost dizzy. My mind was spinning with everything that had happened. He rolls with the universe, right?

I'm so grateful that he introduced me to this woman and her charity. Helping these kids made me feel amazing. I think it was enough money to feed them lunches for quite a long time. It really taught me that people get too caught up in the grind and in possessions and they miss opportunities for helping people. It was a pretty unbelievable day.

From start to finish, James' coaching experience was not what he expected. He walked away on a high. Mandy Lehto didn't experience what she expected either. She wasn't quite so excited. She writes:

As a kid, I learned that getting love in my family came through winning and getting gold stars. My dad pushed me relentlessly to achieve. When I did, I was a good girl. He would pick me up and spin me around. And when I didn't, I got the message that I was a disappointment. To say we had a challenging relationship is putting it mildly.

Being a super-achiever actually served me in many ways. I moved from Canada to the UK to get my PhD at Cambridge University. After that, I went into investment banking in London and had a successful career. Then everything started falling apart. I blew through two marriages. I was a single mom in this crazy job with a young son. My body refused to continue with my punishing work schedule and eventually I was diagnosed with severe adrenal fatigue and fibromyalgia. I was in bed for about a year, unable to do much. All the while, my sense of worth was rapidly diminishing. If I couldn't be the over-achiever, what was even the point of me?

Alongside my medical support, I hired a coach who suggested that I needed to change my relationship with achieving. I wouldn't heal if I kept overworking every time I felt a bit better. All the subsequent coaches, healers and helpers I hired said the same thing: do less, be more. *Great*, I thought. *Give me a ten-step plan on how to achieve that.* I went to expert after expert seeking insight. I did naked dancing. I went to a Wild Woman retreat. I conversed with my vagina. I sat on a mountainside with a shaman. I had tantric healing. I read hundreds of books. I journaled, meditated, and chanted mantras. And though I did these things as perfectly as I could, the old me was nowhere to be seen. At the end of my tether, I sought out the ultimate coach. He'd know the answer.

I flew twelve hours to sit in Steve Hardison's presence. Would this finally work? To calm my nerves, I wrote some notes and questions on the plane, things I wanted an action plan for. I hoped Steve would clap his hands and say, "Here's what we're going to do . . ."

Instead he listened (and listened and listened) as I explained how my body had abandoned me, and how all these jagged memories and messy emotions were bubbling up. Not convenient *at all*. Worst of all, I felt weak and pathetic. I didn't know who I was anymore. I was desperate. Could he help get the old me back, STAT?

Steve sat there looking radiant, holding my gaze with his swimming-pool-blue eyes. He was silent for a while. Pensive. Finally, he smiled and leaned forward. This was going to be *it*, the wisdom I'd come for. I thought to take out my notepad.

"Nobody's coming, Mandy. We save ourselves."

I deflated, then screamed inside my head: *Isn't that what I'm doing?* He talked some more, but there was no ten-step plan, just encouragement to forgive my dead father and be self-compassionate. That was my takeaway. Totally disappointing. But ever the good girl, I smiled and said, "Thank you."

On the plane home, I mulled over our conversation. What would be possible for me if I didn't have to be so darn angry with my dead father anymore? What if I stopped looking for someone to fix me and trusted that I had everything I needed within? What if I didn't have to work myself to death to earn my worth as a human? What if I was enough, just being me?

My big AHA in the weeks after seeing Steve was that I didn't trust myself—not to heal, not to be with my emotions, not to be loveable if I wasn't perfect. I thought of something Steve had said, "If you line me up with everyone else in a room, I'm not the smartest guy. I might even be the dumbest one." It occurred to me that his *being* was what made him such a joy to be around. It was the quality of his presence. His radiance. His deep listening. It was about the connection that his being makes possible. He was so lovingly acceptant of his own limitations. There are no diplomas or gold stars for that.

Let's try this, I thought. I had nothing to lose.

I stopped looking for people to fix me. I trusted that I had everything that I needed within, even if I felt wobbly and uncertain. Courage, I discovered, doesn't always roar. I stopped hustling to try to impress people. I was less of a jerk to myself. I wrote a letter of forgiveness to myself from my dead dad. Then I wrote one to him. I cried till I felt empty. I took walks in the forest. Slept. Cooked good food. Read for pleasure. Did nothing.

Steve Hardison made me realize that no one was coming—especially not the old me. She was gone for good. I could be softer now, more fun. I could ask for help, or say no, or let somebody else win. I didn't have to be the best. I could just BE, which was best for me. And funny enough, work still gets done. Thank you, Steve, for lovingly refusing to give me what I wanted. Thank you for not saving me, because the exquisiteness of saving myself was precisely the growth I needed.

When Dr. Alan D. Thompson interviewed Iyanla Vanzant for this book, she shared her seat-belt moment. Because Alan is from Australia, Iyanla included some background information that might elude global readers. She says:

> Let me say something so that we can be very clear. I am a black woman out of the belly of Brooklyn. I don't know if you know about Brooklyn. If you're black, Brooklyn is the place you want to come from. Either Brooklyn or Chicago. They got black people all over, but Brooklyn, Harlem, Chicago—these are the places to come from.
>
> Steve Hardison is a very tall white man. I think you may have noticed that. My encounters with him caused the slave chains of my ancestors to rattle in me because he represents everything that I was taught to be afraid of. He's male. He's white. He's big. He looks you in your eyes when he's speaking to you. You have to understand, my grandmother was a Native American raised in the South. Even though I had a college degree and a law degree, I was not to look at a white man. And I was terrified that Steve Hardison wouldn't let me speak to him unless I looked him in his eyes. So, when I met Steve Hardison, I was very clear we were going to heal something.
>
> One of the things I'm sure you know is that Steve is masterful at affirming people. He is also authentic. Steve Hardison would say to me, "You are powerful," "You are masterful," "You are gifted." Every time this big, white man would say something to me like "You are powerful," it would take me about three weeks to process that because my ancestral slave chain and my Native American bloodline could not receive that from a white man. As smart as I was, as accomplished as I was, he was accessing a cellular

memory. He helped me move from that. It changed who I am as a person.

Changing your life often means digging deep, deep into your ancestral past, deep into the troubled relationships that shaped and wounded you, deep into the you you barely admit is there. It may mean burning it all down and starting again. Hardison is gifted at guiding you through the journey.

But bring a seat belt.

Chapter 24

The Coaching Experience

"The first time I went to Steve Hardison's house I was with Steve Chandler's ACS (Advanced Client Systems) group. As much as I wanted to be present, I was in my mind about meeting this $200,000 coach. I'm going to walk into his house and I'm going to levitate, right?" So mused Devon Bandison.

What is it like to coach with Steve Hardison? There's talk on the street: He yells. He is intense. He throws people into his swimming pool. He will see into your soul. You will be transformed. He is like no other human being on the planet. Of course, people exaggerate. He has never thrown a client into his swimming pool, and you won't levitate.

In considering the coaching experience, it is well to keep Iyanla's words in mind: "Nothing that anyone has said, can say, or would say can describe the experience of coaching with Steve Hardison. Every experience is unique and authentic to who you are and what your spirit needs—not your mind, your heart, not even your soul, but your spirit." Consequently, Steve's coaching is the proverbial elephant with the blind men. Your experience depends on what part of the elephant you touch. Some clients get the tail, some get the ear, and some get the tusk.

Coachable clients usually touch the soft ear of the elephant. Jered Schager says, "I don't think he has an angry bone in his body." Norma Bachoura says, "I don't see Steve as that intense. I see him as a very soft guy. He is very sharp, but he is primarily gentle, as far as I'm concerned. My experience with him is that he's the gentlest person I have ever been with."

Sometimes Steve and his clients hit a sticky spot. The harder Steve has to work to get a client to hear him, the more he ratchets up. The resistance changes his delivery. Jason Jaggard says, "Steve's the only guy I know who can yell at you and be in love with you at the same time." Sometimes there is so much love that Amy can hear the ruckus at the other end of the house. It's the tusk.

Shanti Zimmerman has heard from many people that Hardison yells. She is okay with that. She observes, "He might have yelled in my presence, but I never felt like he was yelling at me. He's just really committed. There's no filter. He lays it out there. That *is* care, whether you get the blazing side or the softer side."

In spite of the fact that each person's experience is unique, there are some constants in coaching with Hardison. It is those constants that comprise this chapter. Some things, however, are too fundamental and too ample to share chapter space. They get their own chapters, which follow.

The Experience

Sitting with Steve in his office is not just a coaching session. It is an experience. Teresa Walding says, "When I met Steve, I was taken by his intensity and his directness. He leaned in and said, 'I want you to remember these words.' As it's turned out, I don't specifically remember the words he said, but I remember the energy with which he said them. The experience was seared into my person—or my spirit, if you want to call it that." When it stopped sizzling, Teresa was left with "this extra-loving presence."

Allison Watts first heard of Steve Hardison from Steve Chandler and Jason Goldberg. She was intrigued. She says:

After watching some videos and checking Steve out, I said to myself, "I want to have a *Be With* session one day, just to have an experience with this guy." A *Be With* session is the first meeting with Steve, where for two hours he is with you and you are with him to explore who you are, why you are with him, and how he might be able to serve you.

About three years later as my birthday approached, my family asked me several times what I wanted for my fiftieth. Birthdays are not usually a big thing in my house, but because it was my fiftieth, my family was relentless in asking what I wanted, thank goodness. And then it came to me. I knew what I wanted: A *Be With* session with Steve Hardison! Happy Birthday to me! Best birthday gift ever.

I traveled from Costa Rica, where I live, to Mesa, Arizona for my *Be With* session. It was indeed powerful. It was powerful because of who Steve is, not anything he did. I remember my husband asking about it afterwards and I couldn't really tell him anything that had happened, just that I saw, heard, and felt pure mastery that day. During those two hours, I shared space with a man who is so clear about who he is and so clear about who I am that it affected me. Just being in the presence of that level of clarity changed me, and I wanted more of that.

Coach Devon Bandison uses a basketball metaphor to describe his experience. "If Kobe Bryant was going to go sit with Jerry West or Michael Jordan, he wouldn't say, 'Hey Michael, hey Jerry, tell me how you do this move or that move.' He would just be in their presence and absorb them. I wanted to sit in the essence of who Steve Hardison is and experience that."

Michael Serwa, one of the elite coaches in the United Kingdom, says, "My coaching style has never been just sitting there. I do move around, but not as much as Steve. I remember having a session with him. He's sitting in his chair, talking to me, and the next thing I know he is right in my face. I thought, 'I love this.'" Michael recounts his experience of being in Rome and going to a performance of Mozart's Requiem. Everyone was crammed into the back rows of this beautiful church while the first row was completely open, so Michael sat front and center. He had the single most profound musical experience of his life. Sitting with Steve was a similar experience. It was the most profound coaching experience of his life, and it was like having a front-row seat "while watching one of the greats perform in front of me. I would argue that an individual could be more impacted by spending just ten minutes with Steve than by having a whole coaching program with most of the coaches on the planet. His presence and his state of being are on another level."

A Visceral Experience

Many people have strong, visceral responses when meeting or working with Steve. Greg Hiller, a pro golfer, met Steve in 2003 on a golf course in Tempe, Arizona. He says, "Steve and I met through fate. I was traveling through Phoenix and met Steve at the ASU [Arizona State University] Karsten golf course. I had never heard of a personal coach before. After being around Steve for a very short time, I knew I needed to spend time with him. I will never forget the first session, the sight, the smell, the emotion . . . everything."

Dr. Aaron Benes says, "My first session sitting with Steve was what Luke Skywalker must have felt like when sitting with Yoda for the first time. There was something about him that touched a very deep place within me. It was so powerful that it rattled my soul while pulling me forward at the same time."

Tom McGovern became aware of Steve through Dusan Djukich. Tom traveled from California to meet Steve. After having sandwiches in Steve's kitchen, Steve invited Tom into his office. Tom says:

> We sat down and he started talking. Within two to five minutes, I'm crying my eyes out. I don't know why. Well, I do know why. It touched me in a way that I hadn't been touched in a really long time. Within a half hour, I left, and I called Dusan.
>
> He said, "What do you think?"
> I said, "I got to do it."
> "Do what?"
> "I got to coach with that guy. I just got to do it."
> Before I met with Steve, I had no intention of flying from California to Arizona on a weekly basis. I wouldn't even

consider it. After our first meeting, I signed up and went to see him for two years.

In London, Martine Cannon learned of Steve Hardison from her husband (now ex-husband). She relates:

My ex-husband is a coach and he knew of Steve Hardison through Steve Chandler. One day, he was looking at Steve Hardison's website and he said, "Hey, listen to these testimonials," and then he read them out.

I said to him, "I'm going to give him a call and have a conversation."

He said, "You can't just call him up. This is Steve Hardison. This guy has a waiting list for coaching, and he charges X, Y, and Zed."

"What do you mean? Of course, I can call him up," I said. I sent him a message saying I'd like to talk to him. Within fifteen minutes, I got a message back saying he could talk to me the next afternoon at 2:00. I called him at the allocated time.

On that phone call I couldn't work out why he was so special. He didn't appear special. There was nothing in the way that he communicated with me, apart from what appeared to be on the surface an overly confident, bordering on arrogant, sense of self. That had me think, "Whoa, either he is a complete salesman or I'm missing something here. Other people are seeing something in him that I haven't yet seen." And that's what took me over for a *Be With* session. I was in Arizona eleven days later.

As I sat in my *Be With* session, I was thinking, "I have no idea why people say all these things about you." But my heart was engaged in a completely different experience. My heart wanted to sob a million tears.

After that session, I straightaway sent him a message saying I would like to be a client. I didn't know how I was going to pay for it, but I made the commitment. I was willing to sell my house or do whatever it took because of what I was experiencing in my heart. Over time, my head caught up with my heart.

Presence

One of the hallmarks of the coaching experience is Steve's laser focus. Michael Schantz says, "I felt somehow that his strong light had singed a hole in me. For those two hours I was given his undivided attention, heartfelt listening, and unconditional support. In short, I was engulfed with love. There are very few places on this earth where that level of intimacy and trust are available." Michael signed up for one hundred hours of coaching and found that Steve brought that same vigor to each and every coaching session.

Lisa Berkovitz had a similar experience. "He is so present it feels like there is literally no one else on the planet. He said, 'So tell me everything. Who are you?' I started to tell him my story and he was fascinated. He was alive and present, with those piercing eyes." Tom McGovern says, "There is that feeling that people talk about, the feeling that you're the only one in the room. All that is true. All his attention was focused on me. He was one hundred percent committed to me. That's quite a feeling."

This intense focus goes both ways. For Steve, it is his way of being. For his clients, it is their way to suck the marrow out of their sessions. Teresa Walding says, "It goes fast. Two hours is like a blink and you're done. You want to take in every single moment of it." John Patrick Morgan explains, "Steve doesn't allow anyone to record a session. I hate it and I love it. I wish that I had the recordings and I love that I don't because it demanded a presence of me that had me get so much more out of the work when we were together."

Clients can take notes, but it's optional. Steve is very clear that the most important thing going on is the experience. It is about having a shift in being that changes how the client sees and then acts in the world. It is not about consulting notes and remembering what Steve said. Clients get that, in time. At the beginning of their coaching, about seventy percent of Steve's clients take notes. At the end of their coaching, only ten percent do. Tom McGovern lost the notebook that contained the majority of his notes from his two years of coaching with Steve. It was okay. "What I was left with is life is about who you're being, not what you're doing. If I am getting off track, I go back to 'Who am I being in this situation?' or 'Who do I need to be in this situation?' I can be anybody I need to be. I am not a fixed identity. That is one of the most valuable things I got from my coaching."

The Heart of the Matter

"Steve has a very unique ability to get right to the heart of the issue," says Scott Parker. That is well and good when Steve is working with your spouse or your friend or your business partner. When it is your heart and your issue, it can be disconcerting, especially when you experience the speed with which he can do it. Steve Chandler says, "For an average coach, or even a good coach, it takes a year or two to really uncover your client's limiting beliefs, because clients don't reveal them very easily. They're insecure about them to begin with. But Hardison sees them immediately." That is why Iyanla talks about showing up naked. That is why Scott Parker says, "You can't bullshit Steve to save your life. You might think you are, but you're not."

Steve has no problem calling someone on their stuff—none whatsoever, as Carla Rotering found out. She says:

Steve knows if you're getting slippery. I had something happen with my partner in my practice. My partner had done something that was actually pretty unethical. I was terrified of confronting him. I'm not sure why because I am the one who founded the practice, but there was something that was creating a lot of fear for me about confronting him with this. I made an agreement with Steve that I would talk to him. In my very first session with Steve, he had said, "Look, I keep agreements, I expect you to keep agreements. If the Queen of England called and said, 'I want to see you at 11:00 on Thursday morning,' I would say to her, 'Sorry, I have a commitment with Carla.'"

So, I made this agreement with Steve that I would talk to my partner. I went back to my next session and Steve said, "How did the conversation go?"

I said, "I couldn't figure out a time to sit down with him. I was so busy. So, I sent him this letter instead."

Steve leaned over and looked at me and said, "That is not the truth." Of course, it wasn't the truth. It absolutely wasn't the truth. We worked in the same office. We worked in the same hospital. We were partners. But all my excuses felt very real to me until that moment when he said, "That is not the truth." He continued, "That's not even believable, not even close to believable." And he was right.

That was the only time I ever remember getting really

squirmy with him. I was uncomfortable. I couldn't get comfortable in the chair. I felt like I needed to fix the moment, and fixing was not available. There was just being in it for that period of time. I still have that tendency to want to skirt around something that I don't want to do face-to-face. In those moments, I remember Steve's words: "That's not the truth. That's not even believable, not even close to believable." That has been powerful for me.

Self-Discovery

Steve works with amazing people. They are successful, capable, enlightened, and intelligent. It would be easy to walk into a coaching session thinking that all they needed was a little tweaking. But Steve doesn't tweak. Stephen McGhee relates:

After our USM connection, I reached out to Steve. We had a couple of conversations by phone. You know how that is. It's just profound. Steve would say something like, "Tell me who you are." Now, I'm a pretty conscious guy. I've been around the block a few times. I have degrees in spiritual psychology and consciousness, health and healing, and I've been an ecumenical minister forever. I feel pretty present. So, when Steve asked me to tell him who I am, I launched into some automatic dialogue. And he said, "No. I want to know who you are." The layers that we would explore in these conversations were so profound.

Diving deep into the essence of a person's being often goes deeper than his or her awareness. Gary Gietz, one of Steve's early clients, writes:

The most profound gift Steve gave me was to shine a light on a way of being that had formed everything about me since childhood. The crazy thing is that I didn't even know it was there.

Wanting people to think highly of me secretly drove every part of who I was, what I did, and the daily choices I made. It caused me to place acceptance over integrity, appearance over substance, and illusion over authenticity. It ran everything. I didn't even know it existed until Steve woke me up. He allowed me to see it and choose another way of being. We created a new game, one that I could actually win.

When signing up to work with Steve, self-discovery is always on the agenda. Rich Litvin recalls his experience:

Before I began working with Steve, I got clear that I didn't want to spend a year working on how to create more money. I'll be honest. That wasn't easy. But I didn't want to pay a lot of money to my coach only to learn how to make it back.

So Steve coached me around the deepest stuff—why I've lacked confidence for so much of my life, why I struggled around money no matter how much I earned, why I had a constant need for approval, why I couldn't even hear people's acknowledgments, why I showed up as powerless, why I was afraid to be a leader.

Excavating your identity is not always easy. "Sometimes the things you work on are scary or not so pretty," says Greg Hiller, "but Steve will help you through all of it and love you through all of it." The result may be profound peace or freedom or pure exhilaration. Ollie Trew says of his *Be With* session, "The result of being with

Steve is more love, more power, more Ollieness! I have upgraded my clients, my business, and my life. I have a deeper sense of who I really am." Aaron Benes observes, "For so long, I felt uncomfortable being me, being in my own skin. No matter how much work I did, there were still parts of me that didn't feel comfortable, didn't feel safe, didn't feel okay being out in the world. The biggest blessing Steve has given me is getting me to see myself and to finally feel comfortable standing in the space of who I really am."

When Steve asked Daniel Harner what he would like to work on in their time together, Daniel thought of Michelangelo standing before a block of marble and seeing David. He told Steve he wanted to be his true self, the God-created self that exists when the wounds, the baggage, the fear, and the pain have been chipped away. "I don't want anything else in my life, because if I had that, I would have everything." Steve specializes in that kind of work.

Openness

"You know that Steve's human, right?" said Carla Rotering. "It's foolish to think that Steve has been spared the experience of being human. It would be a mistake to believe that he hasn't bumped into hard times and grief and loss and pain and sorrow and fear and suffering and all of the things that contribute to what it is to be on the planet as a human being. What is extraordinary is that he doesn't hide that experience from anyone."

John Vehr remembers beginning one session by asking Steve how he was doing. Steve said, "Man, I just got in this crazy argument with my wife and it's really wearing on me." Was John disappointed that his coach had feet of clay? On the contrary, John thought it was really cool. He reflects, "Most people do the 'I'm brilliant. I'm awesome. I'm amazing' thing. They wouldn't disclose 'I just got in an argument with my wife.'" Such candor creates a space for the client to be fearlessly authentic.

In *Creating Great Relationships,* Steve Chandler writes:

> When I first started working with Steve Hardison, I remember trying to get up the courage to tell him about some of the messes I had made of my life during my younger days when I was drinking and causing trouble everywhere I went.
>
> He could see that it was hard for me to talk about these things, so he stopped me.
>
> "Okay, I understand. Is it okay if I talk about something else for a minute?" he asked.
>
> "Sure," I said, glad to be changing the subject.
>
> And then Steve launched into a series of stories that stood my hair on end. Stories from his own life about ways he had strayed from the straight and narrow as a wild youth. I was stunned. Because here he was, a business consultant, impeccably dressed and respected by top CEOs across the world, and he was describing a past that sounded like the script to *Rebel Without A Cause.* By the time he was finished, I was liberated! I was free to talk, and, boy, did I want to. Because here was a person who would understand.
>
> "There isn't anything you could tell me about yourself that would cause me to think poorly of you," Steve laughed. "There isn't anything you've ever done or thought about doing that would ever reduce my commitment to you, my love for you, and my promise to help you become as great as you can be. Nothing would shock me. Nothing would be a negative to me. Ever."
>
> And it was at that moment that I opened up and became more or less teachable.

Extreme Coaching

"It is very relaxing to be with Steve Chandler," says Daniel Harner. "He is like the wise grandfather that is mellow and laid back. He's very wise. He's slow and deliberate and communicates with such delicate and skillful expression. I wouldn't call being with Steve Hardison relaxing. His mind works so fast. It's very energizing, but you are also aware that you might just get your head cut off—in a loving way."

Billy Woodmansee put it this way, "Steve Hardison is a lot like a wolverine, which is, pound for pound, one of the most ferocious animals on the planet." What happens when you take a wolverine and put him in a cage—or an office? Ask Daniel Harner. He relates: "Steve's coaching is not just formal, professional dialogue. He gets animated. He walks around. He paces. He screams, not at me, but just out there, at his bookshelf or the universe. You feel, 'Okay, he's stepping into his energy right now and it's really strong.' And then he sits down, and we keep talking."

No doubt Steve generates an energy field—and sometimes it is high voltage. That doesn't work for some people. Others thrive. John Patrick Morgan says, "Intensity is familiar to me. I can relate to it. When Steve got fired up and started shouting, I had no fear. My mom's family is Italian and my holidays are everybody yelling at each other, so I thought it was fun." It was more than fun. In the middle of one experience, when Steve's yelling hit high decibels, John Patrick thought, "I don't think I've ever felt this loved or cared for. It was an awesome experience."

Carla Rotering says, "I have witnessed Steve's fierceness. I've not experienced it personally with him. I've never had that. I've also never had a fear of that. If I encountered Steve with that fierceness, it would absolutely call me. It would absolutely draw me forward into the flame, because fire is not a bad thing!"

Sacred Moments

Steve is a whirlwind of passion and power. He is brash, bold, and big. But underneath all that power and energy lies a tender heart. He falls in love with every client. He is deeply moved by their magnificence and courage. His awe triggers tears. The trust, the love, the baring of souls, and the shared commitment all work together to create transcendent moments. Carla Rotering shares one of hers:

> I remember a time when the depth of my work with Steve had gone beyond what I had ever anticipated. Such moments are holy. Ordinary moments with Steve can also be holy, but there are some very profound moments. And the truth is, I don't really recall what this one was about. But I remember the words he said right before the experience. He said to me, "If you could see how close you are. All you have to do is tilt forward an immeasurable amount, and you would be there, because you're already there." And then he put this music on. He got out of his chair and he held my hands and he knelt in front of me. And he wept for the whole duration of this piece of music by Kirtana. That was one of the most profound experiences of my life because of the level of connection, sacredness, and love.

The Post Game

People process their experiences with Steve differently. John Patrick Morgan shares his method:

The way I approached my hundred hours with Steve was like I had just gotten into a PhD program at Harvard or onto a top football team with the best coach in the league. My session was my opportunity to gain extremely valuable insight. To get the most out of it, I trained the shit out of it before my next session.

Steve wouldn't let me record the sessions, so I scribbled as many notes as I could, trying not to break eye contact. Something powerful was transmitted in that eye contact. When I left his office, I went to the airport. I made sure I was a couple of hours early for my flight. I used that time to type up my written notes, remembering as much as I could. Then I expanded them. On the flight home, I added more.

The next morning, I read my notes. I tidied them up. I rearranged them. And I added more. I tried to remember the stories. My few pages of written notes became twenty pages of typed notes.

Throughout the next week or two, I read my notes every morning. I was getting them into me. I took all the exercises that Steve asked me to do and all the challenges he gave me and put them on a list. I worked the list. I did the work. That helped me create the immense value I got from my work with Steve.

Jason Jaggard involved his company in his post-game. He says:

There are about thirty-six people in our firm on three different continents. We have a Wednesday morning meeting. Often, after a session with Steve, the whole focus of that meeting was me talking about my experience. What did I learn? What did I see him do? What am I seeing now? It was like story time with Jason, as if I had gone away to a faraway land and I came back with Asian spices. And they were excited to hear. Coaches all over the world gathered to hear me tell stories about working with Steve.

I extended an invitation to anyone in our firm to meet me at the airport and fly with me to and from Arizona. They had to pay for their own flight, but I paid for Uber and the meals while we were there. The flight to Arizona was like a pregame, what I wanted to get from my coaching. Then afterwards, they could be with me and experience "the glow." After you work with Steve, there is this radioactive glow.

Sometimes people really loved being with me post-Steve, and sometimes they really hated it. I came out of my session like a bat out of hell. I came out more decisive and raising the bar. It was like Red Bull. I have often been in meetings when people said, "What's gotten into Jason?" Someone would say, "He had Steve yesterday" or "He is having a Steve day." I always created results on those days, but it was sometimes an adjustment for the people in my life.

In their book, *Decisive*, Chip and Dan Heath write about a tool for making good decisions called 10/10/10. The idea is to ask yourself how you will feel about your decision in ten minutes, ten months, and ten years. The framework is appropriate in considering the coaching experience. What do clients feel, do, and experience in the hours, days, months, and years after sitting with Steve Hardison, the Ultimate Coach?

Hours and days. It's not unusual for a client to walk away from Steve's office a bit dazed, wondering, "Who is this guy?" Jaya Lalita relates, "I just had an enthralling two hours. It felt like I had just made a pilgrimage to this sage in the desert. And nope, I did not see him as a sage before that meeting. It was the content, the heightened quality of our time together, the import of those two hours, and all that I walked away with."

Most people experience a noticeable shift in their way of being. John Patrick Morgan says, "I left his office walking on a cloud, feeling so confident in myself, so happy, so peaceful, so certain." Gary Mahler says, "The thing my wife loves about my work with Steve is every time I come home, something is different. I'm not the same. She says, 'You transform every time you come back. You're more loving. You're more kind.'"

Steve's coaching is dense. Often it takes time and thought to grasp all that occurred. Aaron Benes says, "Steve is able to look into my soul and know exactly what needs to be done. It's like he goes in, turns a couple gears, twists a couple things, and I come out saying, 'Oh!' And then a day or two later, it all settles, and it's like I'm a different person. And that's every session with him. Sometimes it would take me days to recover from a session, just for everything to settle down inside."

Months. As the hours and days lengthen into months, clients lose the shell-shocked look. Possibilities have substance. New ways of being have traction. Matt Laughlin says:

One of the most telling things about my time with Steve Hardison has been to observe the influence the two or three hours of my *Be With* session has had on my life a year after being with him. It's remarkable how many distinctions and crystal-clear memories I have from our time together. Over a dozen stories or pivotal moments have come to my mind repeatedly. How many people leave you with so much after such a short encounter? He's just that powerful. I am not referring to the personality of Steve. He is a unique character, to be sure, and his personality is a delight, but as much as I appreciate that aspect of him, I am referring more deeply to his quality of beingness, to the quality of his consciousness.

Allison Watts shared some of the specific ways in which working with Steve has impacted her life:

All of my relationships have improved. My relationship with my husband is significantly better because of who I am being and the loving actions that come from that. My husband and I are consciously creating our relationship together. We are working together to transform unhelpful patterns into helpful patterns. I am less defensive and more unoffendable in every relationship. I love that. I have significantly improved as a listener in every way. Specifically, as a coach, I show up even more loving and non-judgmental. I more powerfully invite people to see and step into their greatness.

Years. Finally, the long perspective. Daniel Harner says, "It is going to take the rest of my life to unpack everything I have learned while coaching with Steve." And Dave Orton states, "It was an amazing experience over which I have not gotten, over which I will never get."

Through Steve's Eyes

When asked, "If I spend the day with you, how would my life be different?" Steve responded:

For starters:

You would experience aspects of yourself that prior to our meeting you were unaware of.

You would feel heard in a way that you may have never felt heard before.

You would see things that you had never seen before, about you, your life, others, their lives, and life itself.

You would feel a sense of immense love and gratitude for yourself and for me.

You would experience the distinction "presence," yours and mine.

You would want to spend another day together.

As you walked away and got in your car and drove home or flew home, you would think, and rethink, and ponder on what it is we created together, and you would say, "What happened? How did it happen? How can I keep that alive in my life?"

Loving you. Be Blessed. SFH.

Steve, 2013

Authors' Note

Vignettes are people's experiences with Steve written in their own words. They correspond with the preceding chapter.

Vignette

Heidi Boyd

I was pulled to this man. I knew I had to work with him. At this point I had just enough money in my account for a *Be With* session, and I knew that was exactly where this money was meant to go. I sent him an email letting him know that come Monday I would send him a check, and if he would let me know his first available time and day, I would be there.

On Friday, with my nerves in a bundle, I awaited Steve's call to set up my *Be With* session. The phone rang in the evening.

"Heidi." I heard the kindest, sing-songy voice, which I'll never forget.

I felt I had known Steve my whole life. I felt at ease immediately. The conversation was quick and to the point. We agreed to the upcoming Monday at 2:00 p.m. Perfect. I was informed that this was my time with Steve, no matter what. If I didn't show up, my investment would be forfeited. Got it. This man meant business, and I was on board!

I thought about flying to Arizona, but as my account was dwindling, I decided to drive. I would get up and leave at 5:00 a.m.

to give myself seven-and-a-half hours to get there (it's a six- hour drive), and I would leave about 4:00 p.m., getting back home around 11:00 p.m. I was excited about my road trip. It would give me time to think, process, and reflect.

Monday morning, at 5:00 a.m. I was ready for my adventure. I had my car checked out, gas tank full, and all of my courage in my hands. "I am going to meet Steve Hardison. And my life will be forever changed." Period.

With *The Greatest Showman* soundtrack on play, I headed out. It was dark and the roads were quiet. That was soothing. Sipping on my coffee with coconut milk, I enjoyed the ride and the sunrise which soon followed. Everything was going smoothly.

In the back of my mind, thoughts whirled about. "What will he be like? What will happen? What does his house look like? What am I doing with my life?!"

There was a quiet and steady knowing that this was exactly what I was to be doing right then. My heart was brimming with hopeful exhilaration. I pulled out my breakfast, with the sun rising steadily ahead. This is the Greatest Show!

I went through a terrifying ordeal of running out of gas in the middle of the desert, and then rescuing myself. I was so glad to have an extra buffer of time; there was no way I was going to miss this appointment!

At last, I pulled up to Steve's house. I parked my car and saw a text from Steve. It said if I arrived early, I could sit on his front porch under his umbrella. I allowed my emotions to settle. All the chaos was a distant memory. I was there. I was ready for what was in store for me. I had already decided the meeting with Steve Hardison would change my life. Did I mention that? The "change my life" part? I'm just saying, it was important. I felt an eerie calm and excitement at the same time. I knew without a shadow of a doubt that I was meant to be right there at that moment in time.

The door opened. I looked to my right, and the sweetest 6'4" man walked out to greet me with arms outstretched.

"Okay, destiny," I thought. "Here I am."

The session was a whirlwind, and I can't really remember what happened. It would be impossible to put it into words. I only know that I went through a transition over the next two years. I believe this sweet force of a man was the catalyst, as well as a support for it. My intention was to love my life. I never expected the experience of revelation and unsurpassed state of inner peace that would follow.

Meeting Steve is like an explosion of love. He puts rockets on your heart's dreams. He is a dynamic, unbridled force of energy. He has the ability to take your heart and put it on paper and to form it into language so you can use it as a tool to recreate your life, the life of your dreams.

Vignette

Jody Vehr

Steve called me a day or two before my Thursday session. "We're going to produce a miracle," he said.

"Another one?" I asked.

"This one will make last week's miracle look like small stuff."

Last week's miracle had opened my eyes to the fact that as soon as I wake up, I feel all this heaviness and negativity. As soon as my feet hit the ground, I am constantly judging and complaining.

When I shared this breakthrough with my writing coach, Lydia Nibley, Lydia suggested I get a counter and click every time I had a critical or non-useful thought. I found a clicker on Amazon that I could wear around my neck. After just two days of wearing it, I took it off and threw it across the room. I was exhausted from clicking it all day long. It was then I realized I am a complain-aholic.

I had done the University of Santa Monica, MeRT therapy for my brain, *A Course in Miracles*, *The Way of Mastery*, and so much work with Steve. Sometimes I had a foot in heaven, but the next thing I knew, I was faceplanting into old patterns.

At my coaching session, Steve told me that my desire to catch myself was beyond anyone he had ever worked with.

"I feel like I am going to be clicking this thing forever," I said. "I feel like I will never, ever get to the bottom of this." Click. Click.

"I promise you," said Steve. "It will get less and less and less."

I needed to hear that. I needed to remember how far I had come. Currently, I don't drink and I devote every day to God and to my path. How big that is only makes sense with some background.

Nobody knew I had a drinking problem, not even my husband John. But when I drank a lot, fights would break out. Let's just say they were worse for John than for me. I sort of blanked them out. On July 4, 2018, John and I had a big, blow-out fight. This time, I literally blacked out. When I woke up, John was not next to me. I had a sinking feeling. What had happened?

I realized John had locked himself in another bedroom. I knew better than to engage with him that day. But I did something stupid. I continued to drink. It got ugly. I was suicidal. I felt possessed. I was in a really bad place.

When we went to bed that night, John fell asleep. For him, it was just Jody freaking out again. I stayed up all night panicking. Had I ruined my marriage? I was tormented. I cried out, "God, I can't do this anymore. I CANNOT do this."

I heard words. "Tell everybody everything."

The first person I contacted was Steve. I texted him. At that point, I was hypercritical of my texts. I wanted every word to be perfect. But this time it was like, "F that. Just send it. Hurry. Send it."

Then I sat on the edge of our bed, staring at John, waiting for him to wake up. As soon as he did, I said, "I have a drinking problem." I told him everything. John and Steve were the two men in my life who had loved me unconditionally. Both were now enrolled in my healing.

At my next coaching session, I walked in and said, "I'm done. I am going cold turkey." I didn't stop drinking. I chose a path with God. Some people can decide to stop drinking and have enough willpower to stop. I chose a path with God. That is why it's inappropriate to complain. God doesn't complain.

I had come so far. Still, I was discouraged at how much I was still complaining, if only in my mind. Steve helped me see the missing piece. "What if," said Steve, "every time you clicked, you said, 'I forgive myself for that judgment.' Imagine yourself as the person you have created in your document, not from 'this is going to take so long.' Have fun catching yourself in your judgments. Don't be devastated. As long as you have a mind, you will judge. Delight in being human."

I started coaching with Steve in 2012. I look at who I was then and who I am now. I am not the same woman. I love that woman. I have compassion for her. But I am so glad that is not who I am today. It is so cool to love myself. I got to this point by doing the work. Steve didn't do it for me, but he did help me see what was possible. His gift is to help people see themselves.

Early in my first year of coaching, Steve said, "Jody, I want to talk to you about Byron Katie, Werner Erhard, and you."

I told him I couldn't believe he included me in that distinguished group.

"I knew that would shock you," Steve said. "But you are a powerhouse, just like they are."

At the time, I was still coming from IDM—"I don't matter." I believed that was true. Steve saw who I really was. He saw my greatness and he didn't let it go.

Chapter 25

The Sky's the Limit

The feeling "the sky is the limit—and here are your wings" is one of the constants of coaching with Steve.

For thirty years, Luna Viva Ananda has been a psychiatrist and a psychoanalyst. She loves that her career has given her the opportunity to serve people and make a difference for those with debilitating mental illnesses. Still, something was missing. She says, "I didn't think I was sharing everything I have to offer. I was sixty-four years old and my calling had not been fulfilled."

Luna felt compelled to bring spirituality into the medical world, the business world, and the marketplace. She explains her vision with a metaphor. "I can go to the River Ganges and drink of the sacred water and feel blessed. But not everyone can go to the River Ganges. So how do I bottle Ganges water and put it at Starbucks? Spiritual transformation is a critical need in our world today." While her vision was clear, how to get there was not. "Who was going to help me see the bridge from my medical profession to the work I really wanted to do for the next ten or twenty years of my life?"

Luna found her answer during the COVID pandemic of 2020. Grounded by the quarantine, Luna was getting her exercise by walking around her property in Scottsdale, Arizona. She was accompanied by her daughter Meera, who was aware of her struggle. Standing under a palm tree, Meera said, "Mom, there is this coach named Steve Hardison."

Steve's name sat in Luna's brain. She couldn't dislodge it, so she started searching the internet. She found that "people come from all over the world to see him and he is basically in my back yard." She knew she needed to meet him. As soon as the quarantine was lifted, she took Steve's first available appointment.

When she drove up to Steve's house, her flag was flying. As is typical, they visited in the living room for a little while. Steve then prepared her to enter into the sacred space of his office, also typical. Not so typical, they first took a walk in Steve's Zen garden. Luna relates:

> We were walking and Steve showed me where he meditates every day. We walked some more, and we saw rows and rows of names written on his wall. These are the names of people Steve has met and worked with. And there was "Luna Viva Ananda." I can't describe the feeling. I had been struggling so much with identity—the professional, medical identity and the identity of somebody who's got more to offer. This struggle is reflected in my name. I have two names: Dr. Purnima Mehta and Luna Viva Ananda. Luna Viva Ananda was given to me in a shamanic ceremony a few years ago. In Sanskrit, *ananda* means joy, bliss and the highest state of being. When I saw Luna Viva Ananda on the wall, it was almost like he gave life to Luna Viva Ananda in

that moment. My name had meaning and purpose. I felt a new sense of hope and optimism. I thought, "Okay, I'm at the right place." It felt like a confirmation.

When they stepped into the office, Luna expressed the desire to sit on the floor instead of the couch. In her tradition, "it's very common to sit on the floor when you are doing deep work. Whether it's meditation or talking to your guru, you always sit on the floor. I can't imagine sitting on a sofa trying to do a work that serves the spirit and the soul. Sitting on a sofa just feels like it is not in alignment with the whole vibrational process." So, Steve and Luna sat on cushions on the floor.

Luna shared her conundrum with Steve. "I don't want to be locked away in this medical field. It has purpose. It has meaning. It has something to give humanity, but I feel that's not what I'm here for. I'm here for something bigger and greater and more meaningful. I would be so happy to be able to practice *and* bring about that kind of spiritual work in the world."

Steve was moved. He said, "If it weren't COVID time, I would have given you a hug. But since it is, we are going to do a COVID hug." He then kissed Luna's feet and said, "I want to acknowledge the work you've done."

It was a startling reversal. A student kisses the feet of the guru. Tears streamed from Luna's eyes. "It was the most precious thing that could have ever happened. It was a moment of reverence and acknowledgement." In the brief two hours of Luna's *Be With* session, she realized that "Steve is my bridge. And he guarantees he is my bridge, so I'm good."

How is Steve the bridge to living the life of one's dreams? First and foremost, Steve does not believe in limits. He sees no obstacles. He is a pit bull for possibility. When clients share their dreams, Steve never reels them in. Melanie Waite says, "Steve says, 'Tell me what you want, and we will get it. We will create it. I don't care what it is.'" He can do that for his clients because that is how he thinks and how he lives.

In *Through the Looking Glass*, Lewis Carroll's sequel to *Alice in Wonderland*, Alice exclaims a person can't believe impossible things. The queen responds, "I daresay you haven't had much practice. When I was your age, I always did it for half-an-hour a day. Why, sometimes I've believed as many as six impossible things before breakfast." Steve eats impossible things for breakfast, lunch, and dinner. He breathes impossible things. He swims in impossible water. None of it looks impossible.

Nicholas Smith remembers sitting in the parking lot outside of a church-run commodity resource center. He and his wife had just picked up groceries because they couldn't afford to buy them. Nicholas relates:

> I got on the phone with Steve, and he spoke to me in a way no other human has ever spoken to me. Even now, I get emotional as I think about it. I asked him, "Can you—?"
>
> He said yes before I finished the question.
>
> I asked, "How can you say yes if you don't even know what I'm going to ask?"
>
> "There is nothing you can ask that's bigger than me."
>
> That response impacted me. It became the foundation of my book, *The Giants and the Smalls*.

When Carla Rotering sat in Steve's office, she mentioned that she had just read something by Bruce Lipton, a stem cell biologist and the author of the bestselling book *The Biology of Belief.* He is the recipient of the 2009 Goi Peace Award. Carla mentioned to Steve that she had incredible respect for Bruce Lipton. Steve responded, "So let's call him up."

"What?" said Carla. Someone that famous? Someone that busy? Someone that important? Isn't talking to your hero a little bit scary? Even intimidating?

The next thing Carla knew, Steve had Bruce Lipton on the phone and Steve was handing the phone to her. Carla thanked Bruce for his book and his work and then handed the phone back to Steve. Steve thanked him for taking his call and for making Carla's day. Before hanging up, Steve told Bruce how amazing Carla is.

"So, that's that," said Steve. "Now you've talked to Bruce Lipton." Nothing about connecting with Bruce Lipton looked insurmountable, or even difficult, to Steve. It was just a set of actions to take, like picking up a gallon of milk at the grocery store.

When Steve served his mission in London at nineteen, one of his companions was Paul Waite. They baptized the Dixon family. At the time, Melanie Dixon was eight years old. Fast forward twenty-four years. Both Paul and Melanie were single. Steve told Melanie that she and Paul were perfect for each other.

Melanie wasn't sure. "Paul was twelve years older than I. He was divorced. He had four kids. We lived in different countries."

Steve's response was: "And . . ."

Melanie was used to thinking outside the box. She got her degree in education, but when she realized teaching wasn't for her, she left a secure profession and became an entrepreneur. She created businesses. She saw possibilities. But Steve took her to the next level of no limit thinking. Paul and Melanie were married in 2005.

Steve performed the ceremony.

Steve also revamped Michael Neill's thinking about limits and possibility. Michael writes:

> On the first day of our coaching together in 2009, I was going through my goals for the year with Steve and I got to the seventh item on my list. I hesitated when I saw it, as it had been on nearly every goal list I'd written for the business since we began more than a decade earlier. While our income had certainly crept up each year, we had never really even come close to what seemed like a mythical target. It felt like a waste of time to even speak it, like a New Year's resolution to "read the fifty greatest novels of all time" or "learn Italian" that would make the list every year without ever making it out of my head and into the world.
>
> I said to him, "Well, I was going to say, 'Make over a million dollars in my business,' but I put that on the list every year so we can just ignore that one." While he didn't speak anything out loud, I noticed his left eyebrow arch as if to say, "We can leave it off the list if you like, but it would be just as easy to create it."
>
> Somehow that raised eyebrow did more for me than any piece of coaching I could imagine. The legendary Steve Hardison didn't think it was silly or stupid or childish for me to make a million dollars. Maybe not having done it for so many years in the past didn't mean it couldn't happen this year. Maybe it didn't mean I was a bad person to want it. Maybe even a loser like me could make it happen.
>
> Maybe, just maybe, it was really possible.
>
> When we crossed the million-dollar income threshold just over eleven months later, I remember thinking, "I

wonder if that raised eyebrow was deliberate."

The next time I saw Steve I asked him about it. He had no memory of any of it, not my hesitation and doubt in speaking about it or his lifting of an eyebrow. Which led me to two conclusions that have influenced my coaching to this day:

1. Things look impossible to us because we can't imagine doing them, not because they can't be done.
2. The impact of a coach comes far more from their being than their doing.

Had making a million dollars looked like a big deal in Steve's world, no amount of positive encouragement would have dented the sides of my already made up mind. But since he was living in a world where pretty much anything was possible, no amount of negative storytelling on my side could dent his.

Steve's attitude is contagious. Clate Mask notes, "Steve doesn't have any limits on what's possible, so he changes the way you think about limits. I don't know anybody that sees possibility like he sees possibility. He just sees stuff, and you can't help but start to see possibility when you work with him."

The Paradox

The paradox about Steve is that he is masterful at seeing both people's limiting beliefs and their limitless possibilities. Billy Woodmansee says of being with Steve, "It was like he jumped inside of me and saw the part of me I don't show anyone. Then he put up a mirror and showed me how these things limit me." Jordan Dangelo says of his sessions with Steve, "Time stopped as we dove into everything that I had created in my mind that was limiting me."

Once clients see their limiting beliefs, Steve helps them understand that the only limits that exist are those structured by their own thinking. Then the real fun begins: bringing untethered possibility into existence.

For Steve, the line between possibility and reality is gossamer thin. Possibility is inchoate reality. Only time differentiates the two. And Steve holds time like Einstein did. It is illusory and relative. Possibility exists in the present for Steve. For some, that puts him in Steve Jobs' camp, a creator of reality distortion fields. For others, it makes Hardison the consummate vision holder. Clate Mask notes, "He's your greatest cheerleader." Undeniably, he speaks your possibility to, for, and around you. He slathers you with your possibility.

Melanie Waite says, "Steve would describe me in a way that is phenomenal. I don't always see that and that's really moving to me. It is very empowering." As a teenager, Sebastian Hidalgo worked for Steve, taking care of his yard. Sebastian relates:

> My workdays at Steve's house quickly became one of my favorite parts of my week. There were times when Steve would bring his clients outside to meet me, or Steve would invite me into his office to present myself to his clients. On one occasion, Steve invited me to his office. He was meeting with a client who was the head of a multi-million dollar corporation. He told this client that if he had the work ethic of this fourteen-year-old landscaper, his corporation would be producing at a much higher level. That is one of Steve's gifts. Steve sees people's gifts regardless of age or experience.

Brandon Sulser is a survivor of four different traumas: a brain injury, a broken neck, freezing to death (and being revived), and a head-on auto collision. He has a master's degree in social work. He is also paralyzed from the waist down and author of the book *We Are All Paralyzed.* Brandon says, "Steve loves you more than you, at times, love yourself. He sees more in you than you see in yourself. He sees a future that I've always wanted, but never thought I could achieve." John Vehr says, "The reason I keep coming back to Steve is because he keeps helping me see new possibilities for how I can live my life."

Steve sees impossible futures, at least six before breakfast. He eats impossible things for breakfast, lunch, and dinner.

And he invites you to the table.

Vignette

Lisa Haisha

Two years ago, my husband Lee and I were in Sedona, Arizona, for Thanksgiving. I said, "We should go see Steve before flying out. He's close to the airport. I'd like you to meet him."

He said, "Well, you can't spend a hundred grand to work with Steve."

"Lee, we are probably going to break up and chances are it's going to be ugly. At the end of the day, you'll be happy if I work with Steve."

We went to Steve's house on Thanksgiving evening. We socialized with him and Amy for an hour and then Lee, Steve, and I went to his office. Lee really liked Steve. After spending that time with him he said, "Okay. It's worth it. Go see Steve. Maybe I'll come with you." He never did.

The thing that changed Lee's mind, and the thing that was so powerful, was that Steve saw both our sides. He really listened. When we asked him whether we should stay together or not, he said, "I don't know. It depends on what you want." He listened to us and then stated our options. He asked, "How can you both win?"

I started working with Steve in February of 2018. He walked with me through the process of consciously uncoupling with my husband. It went so well. When Lee would say something mean to me, which is easy to do when you are dealing with finances and separating, I didn't argue with him, like I used to. I would just say, "I love you. Let's talk later." Steve didn't tell me to do that. It came from being with Steve and seeing how he deals with situations and the coaching he gave me. It came from creating who I am and writing it down.

Steve helped me to have peace but also to stand in my power. When I backed down from a difficult exchange, it wasn't from "I'm not worthy, so do whatever you want" or "I'm not up for a fight, so do whatever you want." Rather, it was, "This feels right to me. I want it to also feel right to you. I want you to be happy. How can we make this a win-win?"

When I talk to my daughter, I say, "Your dad is amazing. Our uncoupling is for you to have a better life. We're both soaring, both living our passions, and both doing what's right for us." Lee and I both talk to her that way. There is no blaming. There is no drama. We haven't had one argument in a year.

Lee is really happy that I worked with Steve.

Chapter 26

Listening

Tom McGovern is a commercial real estate broker in California. He worked with Steve from 2010-2012. He reflects:

People work with Steve for all reasons. I sense this almost spiritual following that is around Steve. I don't have that so much. I'm a business guy. I went to Steve because I wanted to get some results. What I like is he walks the walk and talks the talk. It's pretty impressive.

There are a lot of people who hold themselves out to be business coaches and they are struggling to make $100,000 a year. Now, to me, that's kind of BS. How can somebody coach you to make a $1,000,000 a year if all they have been able to do themselves is make $100,000? But Steve, he's the real deal. He's doing it, and he has a background of running a company and the whole bit. I asked him during one session, "Okay, what makes you special? What makes you worth $1,500 dollars an hour when most coaches are $100 an hour?"

He said, "I am a master at listening."

That is definitely true. It is what I experienced. He creates a space to listen that is unmatched by anybody in the world.

Steve doesn't have a set program or curriculum. Instead, he listens. He listens intensely. He listens with laser focus. He listens to what is said between the words and in the silences. He listens to what is not said. He listens in a way that people ask, "How do you know that? Did you call my mother?" Greg Hiller says, "He has the ability to listen within your speaking and literally look into your soul . . . That is where your work with him begins."

"At the beginning of any *Be With* session," says Steve, "I talk to my clients. I might ask them to tell me who they are, what brought them to me, or what they want to get out of our time together. Within fifteen minutes I know enough that I could work with them for a year." The client doesn't think he has bared his soul. He has simply talked. He is shocked that Steve has discerned so much. Steve is shocked that "people think it's just words."

Patrick Provost recalls a conversation when Steve said, "I listen to people as if their words were hardwood."

"What do you mean 'hardwood'?" Patrick asked.

"People reveal themselves in their speech. Do you remember the old wooden blocks that toddlers would play with that had letters on them? It is like those blocks fall out of people's mouths as they speak." Each block tells a story. Each block reveals how the person sees himself, others, and the world.

"Listening" is the simplest way to describe what Steve is doing when he sits with a client. But "listening" also includes taking in visual cues, asking the right questions, and sensing what is going on. "Steve has an incredible power of discernment," says Scott Parker. "He can see it in your eyes if you're in front of him and he can hear it in your voice if you're talking on the phone." Scott has experienced times when Steve has called him and Scott has said something as basic as, "Hey, I'm about to check out at a store. Can I call you back in five or ten minutes?" When Scott calls back, Steve's first words are, "What's wrong?" He had heard something in Scott's voice.

Steve can even "listen" to a picture. Oren Harris has never met Steve in person. Their encounters are limited to a couple of phone calls, a few texts, and an internet connection. Nevertheless, Steve has impacted his life. Oren relates:

> We first connected when he saw my picture. He commented on the picture, describing my essence in a way that was so precise and so clear that I felt instantly seen. I know exactly what he said because I took a picture of it. He wrote, "Oren—spiritual fusion, incarnate swag, and perfect, brilliant stillness." It's like he saw into my deepest, most inner place, and then expressed it in a way that was beyond what I could articulate. I thought, "I know this soul and this soul knows me. He's seeing beyond the physical."

How does Steve do it? He says, "Just as a person has a voice print, a fingerprint, and a specific DNA structure, they have a unique way in which they view the world. I access that."

But *how* does he do that? He says, "I will be in a conversation with a person and I stop them and ask, 'Did you hear what you just said?' They almost always say that they didn't. So, I grab the words, go back into their throat and into their thinking."

It's colorful, but not enlightening. We are left to speculate.

Steve was born with acute senses. It's a family thing. Amy relates:

Every Sunday, Steve's mom Maurine and her husband Ted (whom she married in 1978) would come over and visit. We would ask Maurine how she was doing. Most of the time she would say something like, "Oh, I'm not feeling well. They are spraying the fields." We could get she had a hard time with the chemicals—but the fields were ten miles away from her house. Maurine had adverse reactions to so many things: jewelry, leather, new carpet, paint, and especially perfume. For a long time, we thought she leaned towards hypochondria. With time, I realized she was a highly sensitive person. Had her senses been much higher, she might have needed to live in a bubble.

Steve inherited her acute senses, but not the same sensitivities. He definitely doesn't have an issue with cologne. Steve gives himself a good dousing each morning, plus several refresher squirts throughout the day—and night. Amy notes, "Even when I am swimming my laps, I can smell when Steve walks by, even with my head under the water."

Steve has acute visual awareness. He jokes that he can see if someone's teeth are crooked from fifty feet away. He notices the tilt of the head, the dilation of the eyes, the fleeting curl of the mouth. He hears with the same precision. He can hear meaning in an "an" or a "the."

Another thing that contributes to Steve's exceptional listening ability is his intensity. When people describe Steve, "intense" always makes the short list. Several years ago, the parents and brother of a girl Steve dated in high school were in Arizona. Steve had been close to the family and was delighted to have them come by for a visit. As they chatted, Amy asked the brother what he remembered about Steve from those teen-age years. Immediately he replied, "He was intense!" His intensity was obvious by the time he was in high school, but we can see it much earlier, like when he rode his bike through the glass door of the doughnut shop, in how he played sports, in his frustration, and in his ability to enroll numerous kids into his adventures—or misadventures. Intensity is in his blood and bones.

It is only natural that Steve listens intensely. In those moments, nothing exists for Steve but you. He "looks through your eyes to your soul. He is totally present in the moment," says friend and neighbor Stephen Pothier. The result of Steve's focused intensity is presence. Devon Bandison says:

> I've never seen Steve in a rush. In my experience, it seems the only time that matters to that man is here and now. It reminds me of the greatest of athletes. If you watch the Michael Jordan documentary, *Last Dance,* that's Steve Hardison. I'll tell you why. There's a moment where a guy says, "What made Michael Jordan the greatest of all time wasn't that he could jump high and it wasn't that he could shoot jump shots. What made Michael Jordan the greatest of all time was he was always present in that moment. He was never somewhere else." The guy goes on to say that people go years hanging out in ashrams to get to that level of presence. Michael Jordan was never anywhere but here. And I think that is Steve Hardison. He is never anywhere but right here. As quick as his mind works, and as intense as he is, he's always right here.

Acute sensitivities. Intensity. Presence. There is something else, something more elusive. When asked to explain how he listens, Steve says, "It is seeing, feeling, hearing, and also something else I can't put into words. I am a huge receptor." Iyanla says, "Steve hears, not with his ears, but with his being."

Several years and a few thousand books ago, Amy read an account of a woman who had been deaf since birth. As a child, she thought her mother had special powers. Every time her mother opened the door, someone appeared. When the girl opened the door, no one was there. It was many years before she understood that her mother heard the doorbell ring. She did not. In trying to describe what gives Steve the ability to listen the way he does, perhaps we should simply say that Steve hears the doorbell; most people do not.

Chapter 27

Creation

S teve likes his cars. And he likes his personalized license plates.
He is intentional in choosing just the right word for his license
plate, one that captures who he is or what he is currently focusing
on. He tinkers with the seven allotted spaces. He plays with the
possibilities. Finally, he chooses his favorite. After a couple of
years, he starts the process again. He likes change. But he is also
nostalgic. He keeps his old license plates on a wall in his garage. A
partial list includes:

MASTERY	AMYSGUY
LTGO2LV	INOVATE
SFH	COACHIN
BEBLSSED	CR8IVE
LUVINGU	

He wanted CREATE, but it was taken. He came up with CR8IVE. Both words describe him. He zigs when others zag, creating ways to get things done that are so far out of the box that the box is a speck in the rearview mirror. He creates possibilities for his clients that are non-linear. He creates space for people to step into their magnificence. He creates his life. It's a good license plate.

Creation in Coaching

"My office is a place of pure creation," Steve says frequently.

Steve Chandler agrees. "I would bring a problem from my life to our coaching session. Steve would never say, 'How are we going to solve this?' or 'How do you want to communicate with your creditor?' or 'How do you want to repair that relationship?' He would say, 'Given this situation, what do you want to create?'"

Carla Rotering says:

Steve always said to me, "So given this, what do you want to create? . . . And *now* what do you want to create? . . . And *now* what do you want to create?" That is the world according to Hardison, right? He takes things that don't exist and makes them exist.

My dream was to create a home on Anguilla, a Caribbean island that I was in love with. I had absolutely no idea how to do that. No idea. I'm a fifty-year-old single woman who practices medicine ninety hours a week. Steve helped me turn that dream into reality. In the time I coached with Steve, I actually purchased a piece of land on Anguilla and started building the house. I now have this beautiful 4,500 square foot house in the Caribbean. I have had it for twenty years. I love that he flew the Anguilla flag when I came to my coaching sessions.

Taking things that don't exist and making them exist is second nature to Steve. John Patrick Morgan says, "One of Steve's clients once said Steve has pathological certainty. I love that. Pathological certainty. He has absolute certainty that everything that you speak can and will be created." It doesn't look so simple to the rest of us. There are practical realities we have to work with, right?

Karan Rai relates his experience:

We had sessions where Steve would say, "What do you want to talk about?" If I didn't have anything specific, he would say, "Well, let's just be present." We would sit in meditation and then we would go with whatever came up for me. And then there were sessions where I went in knowing I needed a complete strategy. At one coaching session, I was in the middle of a deal and my backers fell out. I had to raise seventy or eighty million bucks to get the deal closed.

Steve casually said, "Okay, well, let's create some new backers."

"Steve, that's not how it works in the real world. You can't just create new backers."

"Of course you can," he said. "That's exactly how it works."

And we did.

Creating Possibility

Mary Turner is a registered nurse in Houston, Texas. She belongs to the Black Nurses Association. When Iyanla Vanzant was speaking in Arizona, Mary flew to Phoenix to attend the event. It also gave her the chance to meet Steve, whom she knew about through two of Steve's clients, Teresa Walding and Lyn McCright. Teresa and Lyn are principle-based coaches and teachers in

Advancing Nurse Coaching.

When Mary met Steve at the Iyanla event, she learned that Steve and Amy had passes to go backstage after the event and meet up with Iyanla. She asked, "Hey, Steve, is there any way I can go backstage?"

Steve asked her if she had a pass. She didn't. "You see that door over there?" said Steve. "That is the door we will be going out. If I were you, I would hightail it over there as soon as this is over."

Mary followed Steve's suggestion, but she was told that only people with passes could go backstage. She told the security guard that she didn't have a pass, but she did have an email from Iyanla where Iyanla wrote she couldn't wait to see her. The guard was skeptical, especially when Mary couldn't produce the email on her phone. But Mary was confident and tenacious enough that he asked Iyanla. Mary got in. She relates:

> When Steve saw me in the room, he said, "Well, I see you're very resourceful. You made your way up here." We both cracked up, and then he whispered in my ear, "I think Iyanla is going to be the keynote speaker at the Black Nurses Association. She just doesn't know it yet." That planted the seed for me to reach out to the National Black Nurses Association and see if we could actually bring Iyanla in to be the keynote. I will never forget the power of Steve's words and how they created life. He planted the seed and I thought, "Whoa, that is a possibility."

Gina Carlson relates how Steve helped her create possibility. She writes:

> Early on in our coaching work, Steve took me on a field trip to Infusionsoft, a company where he coached the CEO and

other executives. We pulled up in front of the Infusionsoft headquarters in Chandler, Arizona, in Steve's really fast car. Before going in, we sat and discussed what it is that I love to do. At the end of the conversation Steve said, "So, you are a CEO."

I had no desire to be a CEO and told Steve so. It was in that moment that I realized what my passion was. I described it to Steve, and he said, "Okay, so you are a CCO."

"What is a CCO?"

"Chief Culture Officer," said Steve.

"Steve, there is no such thing."

"Well, speak it into the world and watch it occur."

"What do you mean?"

"Speak about it wherever you are and with everyone you're with. When people ask you who you are, tell them you are a Chief Culture Officer. Start speaking it and watch what happens."

Four months later, a recruiter called me and asked me if I would meet with the CEO of a company who was interested in talking with me about leading his sales organization. I wasn't interested in leading sales for a company, but I am always interested in talking with CEOs about their vision. I agreed to the meeting. It was supposed to be over a drink, but it turned into a four-hour dinner.

I shared with Ken, the CEO, my journey through the corporate ranks. Because I had nothing to lose and wasn't interviewing for a position with his company, when he asked me to say more about myself, I told him the truth of who I am and how my success was less about being strategic and more about being loving.

I gave Ken the real version. I had started my sales career

afraid of my own shadow and it was a wonder anyone even hired me. But, by embracing that part of me and not making it wrong, I became a heart of listening for clients, which seemed to correlate to lots and lots of sales. I held the number one or two slot in my sales organization year after year. Management and sales colleagues, especially the extroverted go-getters, were scratching their heads at my success—while losing their side bets that I wouldn't last in the highly competitive corporate sales environment.

I told Ken how the CEO of the company I worked for, along with CEOs of other companies, tapped me to assist them in creating a better culture for their companies based on the fact that my results were consistently great and that I had a reputation for being nice to work with.

In my head, the voice of prudence was shouting, "This is career suicide! Shut up!" But I couldn't. As I spoke from my heart, I felt a sense of peace and authenticity. It felt so good to take off the corporate mask and be real.

When I finished, Ken was quiet. I sat there while he looked at me and rubbed his chin. All of a sudden, Ken slapped his hands together and said, "Actually, I don't want you to run my sales division. I want you to join my C-Level team as my Chief Culture Officer."

I had never mentioned those words to Ken, but I had been speaking those words into the world, in me and around me and to anyone who would listen—even to my dogs—for four months. I stared back at Ken. Before our evening ended, I excused myself to the bathroom and from a bathroom stall I called Steve and left a message, "You are never going to believe what happened . . ."

Creating Being

"For Steve, creativity doesn't belong solely to certain fields like music and art," says Steve Chandler, "but to everything, and especially to being. He creates who he wants to be in the world and then lives from that creation. It's divine creativity. It flows through him from moment to moment, not just once in a while. He taught me that's possible for anyone."

Steve begins creating who he is the moment he wakes up. It is the last thing he does before he goes to sleep. And he does it in every conversation and every thought. Constant creation. He speaks who he is loudly and boldly everywhere he goes. The person he creates himself to be is also big and bold. His personal declaration begins, "I am the universe."

He has been accused of arrogance, but it isn't arrogance to Steve. Every time he declares who he is, Steve is creating himself to himself, to others, and to the universe. Every time he creates himself, he is making it more real. The idea of a person burying his magnificence is offensive to Steve. He believes false humility is pernicious. He refuses to go there—social conventions be damned. Jeff Dinsdale comments, "No one loves Steve like Steve, and that's how it should be. Steve's self-love is not narcissistic. If it were, he wouldn't serve the way he does, but the dude serves twenty-four seven." Steve seizes every opportunity to create himself, but he is as committed to creating others.

Cherryl Vernon, Amy's niece, writes:

Over twenty years ago, when I was a young adult, I asked Steve what he did for a living. He sat me down at a table and started talking to me. He asked me questions and I remember how intensely interested he was in my answers. It wasn't a very long conversation, but I will always remember it because he told me that I was a genius. I could tell he really meant it. Knowing what a successful person he was, it affected me. How could that not increase your confidence and self-esteem to know someone thinks so highly of you? One of Steve's great gifts is seeing greatness in others. He sees their potential and strengths and gifts and builds people up so that they see those things in themselves.

Natalia Smith experienced how Steve creates Amy. It was impactful. She says:

I first met Steve when his wife was speaking at a church, a church that I was kind of looking into. Steve got up and introduced his wife. I couldn't tell you the words he used, but the feeling I had was, "Holy smokes. Not only do I want my future forever person to introduce me that way, I want to be a person that is introduced that way." What he said was full of honor and love. It was complete adoration. I remember feeling very present. And he didn't even say anything significant. He was just introducing his wife, but I remember thinking, "This is important. Pay attention."

Steve also creates through expressing appreciation. Steve met Jered Schager when he was the general manager of the Porsche dealership in Chandler, Arizona. Jered says:

Steve had an issue with the clear bra on his Porsche. We took care of it. When he came and picked the vehicle up, he had me take him to the back to where our detailers and the clear bra guys are so he could thank them. I've been in the car business twenty-six years, and that had never happened. Those guys are one of the more underappreciated positions in the business. I know. I started my career in their position. For a customer to go back there and thank them . . . Well, they were floored.

Steve routinely thanks the cooks at restaurants and the housekeeping staff at hotels. But he doesn't just thank. He creates. Steve lets them know that their work is valued and that they are important. When Steve walks away, people are smiling and standing a little bit taller.

Since Steve is constantly creating himself and others, it is not surprising that creation is the heart of Steve's coaching. He helps every client create a deliberately chosen and powerful way of being. Every client discards ways of being that do not serve him. Ward Andrews recounts his experience:

> I came from very little. There was no one giving me money. I had to earn everything. There was a point earlier in my life where I was down to a few hundred dollars. I had a mortgage and kids and I didn't have a job. Experiences like that have a way of lingering. So, I can be very frugal. It is where I naturally come from.
>
> I've been successful, so I don't *need* to be so frugal, but it was hard to break old habits. One time I showed Steve a picture of my trash can outside my house. It was overflowing with trash, piles upon piles of trash. I told him that I needed to get a second trash can. He agreed. But it cost five dollars more a month. My mindset was such that I didn't want to pay for the extra trash can. Steve worked with me on my scarcity mentality. I remember him telling me that I was the poorest wealthy guy he had ever sat with. I was a pauper— not on paper, but in my head. He helped me come from abundance.

Steve and I used that story to look at other places in my life. Where can I spend a little bit more to gain a much greater capacity so that we can do more and be more comfortable? That's been really effective for me. We always laugh about the trash.

Steve on Creation

If you ask Steve to talk about creation, he has plenty to say. His passion will start revving. His volume goes up. His intensity spikes. It is slightly terrifying if you are unaccustomed to his power surges. Steve will point out that "create" and "react" have the same letters, except create has an extra "e." The "e" stands for energy. Reacting doesn't take energy. Creating does. Steve roams the room and gesticulates with his arms as he describes the energy involved in creation. He is his own object lesson.

The following is what Steve said when asked to talk about creation in his life. To experience it the way it was delivered, imagine the letters are sizzling.

Steve Hardison on Creating

I am creating every single day. I am never not creating. That is why I'm so good at it. I am always creating. Most of the time people step over the opportunity to create. It takes time. It takes energy. But it yields miracles.

For example, just the other day, I was doing my sun therapy when Martine Cannon texted me from England. It was a fun, light text. She finished by texting, "When are you going to get some gorgeous UK clients to send my way? Can you convince some eligible bachelor that London is the place to be?" Most people would send back a smiling emoji. Perhaps some would reach out to a friend in the UK and say, "Hey, do you know anyone. . ." After all, there isn't even a request in Martine's text. But there is an opening to create.

I texted Raghav Parkash in London. Raghav and I have only met in person once. He came to the open house I had in London. We are Facebook friends. I know from his postings that he is committed to serve in extraordinary ways. I texted Raghav and said, "Raghav, this is Steve Hardison. Call me or text me your phone number so I can call you." He texted me his number at 1:55 p.m. (Arizona time). I had Jody Vehr in my office at 2:00. I walked into my office and asked Jody, "How would you like to create a miracle today?" She jumped all over it. I showed her the communications from Martine and Raghav.

You have to understand that part of creation is seeing the end. I see the end. I feel the experience. Then I do what comes to me. The minute I saw Martine's text, I responded, "I'm on it." As soon as I texted that, it was already done inside of me. I knew the next thing to do was to call Raghav, so I did. I knew I couldn't just jump straight to my request. In order to create a miracle with him, there was groundwork to be laid.

When Raghav answered his phone, I said, "Raghav, how would you like to participate in a miracle with me?" He was enthusiastic with his yes.

"You know about TBOLITNFL? [TBOLITNFL stands for The Best Offensive Lineman In the NFL. The story of TBOLITNFL is told in Chapter 34.] Let me give you some background that most people don't know." I spent the next thirty minutes telling him how the TBOLITNFL event came about and the creation that occurred with Julie Blake, Chris Dorris, the venue, the filming—everything.

After that, I spent ten minutes creating Martine. I told him, "This is not just some gal. She is a woman committed to mastery and to personal growth. She flew from London to Arizona to meet with me every other week for two years. She is talented, intelligent, beautiful and fun." After creating Martine, I again asked him if he would like to participate in creating a miracle. He was quiet for about twenty seconds. Twenty seconds of silence on a phone call feels like three days. Jody whispered to me, "Did he get cut off?" I put my finger to my mouth in the universal "shhhhh" sign.

Finally, Raghav said, "This is big, isn't it?"

"Yes. This isn't a weekend assignment. Do you want to take this on?"

"I do."

His commitment allowed me to make big promises to him. "I promise you there will be miracles all over in your world. You are going to have great things happen in your relationships and your business. Miracles will come to you from everywhere, but this is going to stretch you."

Raghav said, "I'm in. I'm in. I'm in."

"So Raghav, here is what I am requesting you do. I am not requesting you meet Martine. I'm requesting that you get a relationship with her so that you understand her. Then, because you know Martine and because she is a part of you, you can—and will—actually connect her with someone."

Raghav responded, "Great!"

I told him I would send him her contact information. He said he would contact her the next day. (By this time, it was pretty late in England.) He finished by saying, "I get it. I will do this until I take it all the way up."

But I wasn't finished yet. I texted Martine three words:

"Consider it done." She called me and I continued to create. "Let me tell you who Raghav is . . ." I then created with Martine who Raghav is. If I hadn't, Raghav shows up and she just sees him as some guy, not a miracle worker. I made her promises. I said, "Can you see what this guy is willing to do? Now, you create a miracle in his life from him knowing you."

These calls took forty-five minutes of Jody's coaching time. We spend the rest of the time coaching Jody on creation, which was another creation.

Here's another experience. My phone rang. A total stranger said, "Hi. My name is Erin Donovan. My coach says I should work with you."

"Who is your coach?" I asked. She tells me and I said, "I don't know your coach. Tell me what you want." She started talking and I began creating.

She said, "I want to take ideas and principles like you teach and take them to young people in the world."

"If that is what you want to do," I said, "you are talking to the right person. How committed are you?"

"I want to do a hundred-hour agreement with you."

"The only way I will do that," I said, "is if we meet every week. Given what you are up to, we can't meet every other week. Are you married? Single?"

She responded, "I live with someone."

"You better make sure this works with him."

"Oh, it will," she said. "I know it."

"How do you know it?"

"Because if I need to move there, I will."

"You should."

"I will."

Nobody else is even going to have this conversation with this lady. They aren't going to even hear her. They are going to answer the questions she has. What we were doing was a creation.

"If you are serious about working with me, you will need to send me $200,000 by a date we agree on."

She said, "I will have it to you by my thirty-fifth birthday."

I share with people that there is nothing inherently urgent, critical, or important. There are things that are urgent, critical, or important, but they aren't sitting there like that. They must be *created* as urgent, critical, or important. I told Erin (and I say to all my clients), "If you want to work with me, you need to create that our time together is the most important thing in your world. And that's not about me. It's because we are working on your life." When I meet with my clients, we deal with their identity, their relationships, their future—everything. If they let something that important get bumped off by a board meeting or a last-minute invitation to golf at a premier resort, they aren't ready to work with me. I will give them my life and my blood, but they have to match my commitment. If they do, there is no end to the miracles we can create.

Let me give you one more. I was working out with my trainer Billy Woodmansee. He was working with me on my legs at the gym. He shared with me a business idea he had. It was barely an idea, just a seed. Between reps, I helped him see what to do next. That went on for several weeks. Then Billy said, "You are brilliant at what you do. I would like to hire you as a coach."

"Why don't you create a way to do that?" I said. "You know that idea you told me about? You could sell that idea." Shortly after that, Billy emailed me and said he had someone who was going to buy his idea and ten percent of his company. He had the money to hire me.

Fast forward a few weeks. I have deposited his check. We have scheduled our dates. It was five days before our first meeting. He called me up to confirm. I said, "I have a couple of things you need to do before Friday." I gave him some things to do, including rereading Jody Vehr's book, *Just Hit Send*. I already had his money, but I was still creating with him. Create. Create. Create.

He said, "I don't read very fast." So, I created an alternative where he called and spoke with Jody. Three days later, he texted me:

Steve, after watching all the stuff and reading most of the website (I still have a few more), I decided that I was playing really small when I told you I don't read well. In fact, I do not. That was not a lie. But in the name of being committed to excellence and building a multi-million-dollar foundation for my family, I need to read *Just Hit Send*. I'm not going to get better unless I create a way to get better. Reps and consistency in reading are the only ways I can improve and make the water level rise. I can't wait to blow the top off the wellness business world!

Two days later, we had our session. It was as good as any two-hour session I have had. We distinguished that Billy sees in grey, not in color. In other words, he looks out into his world and everything he sees is mediocre and lackluster. Grey scale doesn't give a person much to work with when creating. Billy sent me this text the day after our session: "Today I saw some new colors in life. I am able to see that changing my listening alters how I see everything. My previous listening muted color. Today I had to have my sunglasses on all day because all I see is color. Thanks Steve."

Too Much or Just Right?

Not everyone sees Steve's creation the way Steve does. For some, it veers too far from reality, too far from what exists in the here and now. For some, Steve's creation of himself is over the top. For some, Steve is too Steve Jobs-ish, creating his own reality distortion field. Brandon Craig notes:

His heart is good. He's sincere. He is enlightened. He's done a lot of really extraordinary good in the world. He's a masterful creator. And he sometimes uses that talent in ways that aren't totally authentic. For instance, he takes a special card or letter and then he shares it in a way to create more acknowledgment . . . There is a certain kind of satisfaction that comes from being acknowledged. It can be healthy, or it can be unhealthy. I think Steve has to balance that. The irony, or maybe the contradiction, is that the guy has probably made more of a difference for people than anybody on the planet as a single human being.

Lisa Hale also measures for authenticity. She writes:

I finally got to meet Steve at Steve Chandler's Advanced Client Systems program. We were in Scottsdale. On this particular weekend, Steve and Amy came really dressed up because they had just come from a funeral. They sat in the front of the room. There were a number of things that I was looking for. First and foremost was how authentic is Steve? I have a very keen sensor for authenticity. So, how real does he strike me?

It made sense to me that Werner and Hardison and other people who are well known would be negatively talked about in some ways, and what I wanted to see is what was really there. I don't want to have an assessment based on what I hear. I wanted to know what his energy is like and what is real about him. I am really good at hearing inconsistency. If a person said something on day one and something different on day six, I'd be the first to step up and say, "Hey, I don't lose track of that stuff." So, I was tuned in. I was listening with my skeptical mind. I was listening with my open heart. I was listening with my growth, openness—all of that.

What struck me about Steve Hardison is how authentic he really can be when he slows right down. I don't think he's ever inauthentic. He can be bigger than life. And it can strike like he's not authentic. But boy, when you slow him down and get a feel for his real heart, it's all aligned in there. And that impresses me. That earns something from me.

How you see Steve and his creating depends on so many things: your personality, your past experiences, your value system, your listening. The list is infinite. Most people who work with Steve will take a bullet for him. Most will send texts and letters similar to this one from John Vehr:

Steve,

I want you to know that I dearly love you and truly appreciate your impact on my life. Meeting Blake and then you has created so many openings in my life. I have no words to explain the profound shift that has occurred since then. I really appreciate your honesty, openness, and the lack of any judgment that has helped me understand what truly loving myself actually means. In short, I love, respect and admire you.

Love,

JV

Many would write something like what Allison Watts wrote when asked about her experience of coaching with Steve:

Before meeting Steve, I had done a lot of spiritual, psychological, and personal development work, and I thought I was pretty conscious and aware of who I was. I knew that we create our reality with our thoughts, but Steve helped me see I still had old ideas and stories about myself, even with all the work I had done.

Steve helped me see that my ideas are creating all the time, that I created those ideas in the first place (mostly unconsciously) and therefore, I could choose new ideas that would create a new reality for me. This was profound.

I love intentionally creating myself and I can honestly say, if I had to pick one thing I am most grateful to Steve for, it would be that he has given me the gift of knowing and experiencing myself as the creator of my life. This is a gift that will keep giving for the rest of my life. This realization is the thing I've ultimately been searching for my entire adult life. For the first time, I really know this in my bones . . . and it's deepening every day.

How does Steve teach his clients to be the creators of their lives? It all begins with the document.

Chapter 28

The Document

Erin Donovan walked out of Steve's office after her first official coaching session. She had a new identity. As Steve walked her out to her car, Dustin Venekamp happened to drive by. Dustin is Steve's neighbor and also a client. Dustin stopped to say hi. Steve said, "Dustin, let me introduce you to Erin. She has the smile of the universe."

"Hi. I'm Dustin. I exist to serve."

At some point in their work together, Steve helps every client create a deliberately chosen, powerful way of being. It is a significant part of the creation that goes on in his office. It is so significant that it can become a client's moniker. It is so significant that Daniel Harner says, "It is the whole experience with Steve. It is the ultimate empowerment. If you have that, you have access to everything."

Creating a new way of being begins by creating a list of declarations that are collectively known by Steve and his clients as "the document." Some clients refer to them as their "declarations" or their "I am statements." The statements in the document manifest the highest, noblest essence of who you are. They are you at your inner core, the you without baggage, the you without wounds, damage, or fear. They are you without the need to impress or the struggle to be good enough. They are the you you know you are in your gut when you have moments of clarity. They are the you that soars.

These statements are not goals or affirmations. Goals are great. Affirmations are powerful—as far as they go, but too often, goals and affirmations are short-sheeted by underlying beliefs. For instance, one of Steve's male clients had the underlying belief that "women are a pain in the ass." It is challenging to build a good relationship on top of that. Another client had an underlying thought, "I'm not respected. I am always dismissed." When that is your dominant thought, it is hard to step into your power. Creating goals and affirmations without first examining your underlying beliefs is what Steve calls "putting frosting on dog poop." That is why creating a new way of being begins with digging deep and doing internal work.

John Vehr says, "Since I was nineteen years old, I have known how to talk to myself to create a future that is awesome, but I didn't pay attention to the thoughts that are below the surface, the thoughts that *really* run me. I didn't know how to access those." Most people are unaware of the thoughts that run their lives. These thoughts exist like water to a fish. But just because you are unaware of them, it doesn't mean you aren't wet. So, Steve's first assignment when you create your document is to notice the thoughts you currently have about yourself and your world.

John describes his experience:

In one of our coaching sessions, Steve mentioned this amazing woman he had worked with. I told him I would like to meet her. Steve didn't respond, so I said more forcefully, "Steve, I would really, *really* like to meet her."

Steve looked at me and said, "Uh . . . no." At the time, I was a womanizer. Later I could see that he was protecting her from me. That night, I was thinking about her and a thought came to me, "Why would a woman like that be with a guy like you?" I was shocked. Where did that come from? That's not how I talked to myself. Once I zeroed in on that thought, I started hearing all kinds of thoughts that didn't serve me at all. I saw the spin I was putting on my life, and it was covering up the mess that was down below.

I spent about six weeks getting all these thoughts on paper. Then Steve said, "You have written enough down. Let's create a new reality."

"So, I just take 'I'm not powerful' and turn it into, 'I'm powerful'?"

Steve laughed. "It's not that easy. Your ego is too powerful to be tricked. We can't just put a positive thought on top of a negative one. It would be like putting a crown on a tooth without getting rid of the underlying decay. You have to exercise radical self-forgiveness on those judgments. Once you do, you are in a clear world. Then you create your declarations."

Steve taught John to forgive himself. Self-forgiveness is easy in theory, but it's hard to actually do. For some, self-flagellation feels more just than self-forgiveness. But it hurts. Steve has created a process for self-forgiveness that is accessible and effective. He is hesitant to describe it, lest the reader turn it into a formula and emasculate it. The reader must remember that when Steve works with his clients, so much of the power comes from being present in the moment, knowing where to go and what to say based on what the client has just said. By analogy, the explanation of the self-forgiveness process is like a tiger in the zoo. The intuitive, in-the-moment coaching is like a tiger in the wild. One is more accessible. The other has raw power that sends shivers down your spine. The tigers in this book are at the zoo.

Self-Forgiveness

Steve's first step in teaching self-forgiveness is to distinguish the concept "self." Philosophers, psychologists, and sociologists all have their own working definitions of "self." When Steve refers to "self," he is primarily referring to the you that thinks, the command center that directs your actions. More specifically, he is speaking of the inner voice that offers a running commentary about you and your life. It is this internal monologue that determines how you see yourself. For instance, if you drop something and break it, your self might say, "You are so clumsy." Or it might say, "Accidents happen. I'll just clean it up." The self has an opinion about everything. It is constantly judging whether you are brilliant or stupid, bold or afraid, good enough or inadequate.

Once a client understands the concept of self, he can see that the thoughts he has identified and written down are actually self-judgments. Steve explains, "If you can't see that it is you who judged yourself as these things, then we need to go and find the person who did. He is the person I should be talking to." It doesn't matter if someone else—parent, teacher, or sibling—originally said these things to you. If you didn't buy into them, they would not have adhered. *You* glued them into your self-concept. *You* made them true.

Steve helps his clients understand self-forgiveness with metaphors. One metaphor is that the mind is the consummate GPS. With a traditional GPS, if you type in "1010 Arthur Street," it takes you to 1010 Arthur Street. If you type in "Disneyland," it takes you to Disneyland. Occasionally, there is a fail, but GPSs are exceptionally accurate. Your mind is flawless. If you input "I'm amazing," you get amazing. If you input "I'm afraid," you get fear. If you input "I have extraordinary decision-making abilities," that is what you get. Most people have plenty of crippling thoughts stored in their GPS. However, they are not etched in stone.

Another metaphor Steve uses comes from the world of word processing. Those who grew up with typewriters appreciate the miracle of correcting errors, reformatting, and cutting and pasting with a few keystrokes. The find-and-replace feature allows you to find and replace every occurrence of a specific word with a different word in seconds, no matter how long your document. The mind has the same amazing ability to replace a destructive thought with an empowering one.

A third metaphor comes from the power the United States Constitution grants a president to issue pardons. The president can issue pardons throughout his term, but many have issued them in their final day(s) as president. George H. W. Bush issued 75 pardons. Presidents Reagan, Carter, and Clinton each issued between 383 and 534 pardons. One of the more controversial pardons was the one Bill Clinton issued to Marc Rich, who had fled the U.S. and was living in Switzerland. He owed $48,000,000 in taxes and was charged with sixty-five criminal counts, including tax evasion, wire fraud, racketeering and trading with Iran during the oil embargo. Had he been found guilty on all the charges, he could have been sentenced to more than three hundred years in prison.

Often people have indicted themselves by their harsh and negative thoughts and feel like there is no way out. It feels like a three-hundred-year sentence. But we can give ourselves presidential pardons through self-forgiveness. Steve says, "If I can get people to step into a presidential pardon, we can clean the slate and create anything."

Legal presidential pardons have their limitations. They do not erase the record of the conviction. They do not apply to state or local offenses. If Marc Rich embezzles after his pardon, he will not get another one. This is where personal presidential pardons outstrip legal ones. You can use and re-use a personal presidential pardon daily, hourly. You will need that. Your judgments are bolted into your thinking through years of repetition. But every time you catch yourself judging yourself, you can forgive yourself. Each time you do, you loosen the bolt.

John Vehr mastered self-forgiveness, which brought him to a place of ultimate clarity. From there, his declarations emerged. John recounts, "'I'm not powerful' became 'I am an extension of the one true God and I am powerful beyond measure.' But I didn't create that. I don't talk like that. It came through me." Tapping into the Divine, "I was able to create a manifesto that is truer than who I was."

Norma Bachoura describes her experience:

I take a lot of Christian courses, especially on how to help people through prayers and through declarations. People say you need to declare, "I am a child of God. I'm loved by God. I'm this. I'm that." But these declarations never worked when I did them. It felt like I was lying to myself. I could never figure out why they didn't work. In my first session with Steve, he helped me write down all the negative thoughts I told myself about myself. I forgave myself, and then I spoke the truth. Those declarations worked like a charm because they were born out of me. In about two to three weeks, the thoughts that had played like a broken record—devastating thoughts like "you're ugly"—no longer existed.

In about two months, what naturally came into my brain was, "You're loved by God. God is going to take care of you. You're such a beautiful woman. You're very smart. You can do anything that you set your mind to." These thoughts popped up automatically. Before, I could never figure out how to change the negative record in my brain to a positive record. That was done the easiest way with Steve.

This inner work, rigorously done, is essential. Marina Lazaris learned that first hand. She was impressed with Steve's document and wanted to have one of her own. After she created her document, she shared it with Steve. When he read it, he was stunned. It was his document, with a few tweaks. He called her. "You can't use that," he said. "Those are my statements." Was Steve bristling with proprietary pique? Not at all. Steve explained to Marina, "You can't take my statements and start using them like they are your own. It won't work. You have to do the work that generated them. I created 'I am extraordinarily patient, loving, and kind to all living things, especially to Amy Blake Hardison,' because I wasn't always nice to my wife. I wasn't always loving. It took soul searching and forgiveness, from myself and Amy. That statement is my prayer."

Marina got it. She created a document based on her life, her story, her vision, and her name. Marina was born on Valentine's Day, so she created "I'm here to spread more love in this world." Her surname is "Lazaris." It was bestowed on her great, great grandfather who, with fortuitous timing, awoke at his funeral— shocking family and friends.

Marina said, "Steve woke me up. He reminded me that one of the reasons I'm here is to help people wake up from the dead and live a life of passion and purpose." The first person Marina helped live a life of passion was herself. After meeting with Steve, she resumed a career in acting, something she had put on hold years earlier when her father was diagnosed with cancer.

Once a client has created his document, Steve has him commit the document to memory.

Steve encourages—even pushes—his clients to speak their documents loudly, frequently, and boldly. First and foremost, that means speaking your document to yourself every morning and every night. Why? Because what creates your reality is what you think about and what you talk about each day. Simple enough. But for some, the cognitive dissonance between the document and current reality is a challenge.

Daniel Harner says, "Saying some of those statements is uncomfortable for me. Steve will say, 'Just say it twenty-five times. It doesn't matter how you feel, or how much you don't believe it. Just do it. The doing of it will create it.'" It is well to remember that the document faces forward, not backward. It is not a report on the past but a future to live into. As Dave Orton says, "This is a living document through which I constitute myself in my life. It's aspirational, meaning it is possibility. I am not the fulfilment of these things yet. It's where I come from."

You can get creative in how you speak your document. Many

clients record themselves saying their document. Steve has recorded one version where he says his document in the first person (I am . . .) and one where Amy reads it to him in the second person (You are . . .). He listens to both daily. Recently, at an endodontist appointment, Dr. Christopherson asked Steve if he would like to listen to music while he worked on his teeth. Steve said he had something better. He set his phone on the counter, clicked on his document in his phone's voice memo app, hit repeat, and opened his mouth.

When it comes to saying your document, there is speaking and there is *speaking*. If you want your document to have the power of transformation, you energize it. Steve says, "When I say, 'I am the universe,' I am going into my mind and picturing the universe. I see it expanding. I have a visceral connection with the expansion. Like the universe, I am constantly expanding who I am, what I know, and what I see. I am the universe. I dance with my document. I feel it. I experience it."

Steve encourages his clients to seize every opening to declare who they are.

And if there isn't an opening? Make it. Dave Orton learned this lesson well. When being interviewed for this book, Dave said, "My document is not engraved in stone like the tablets Moses carried through the desert. It is a living document. May I share it with you right now?"

Steve lives what he teaches. He speaks his document to himself and to the world, and he brings it into being. It is a singular experience to hear him speak it. Chris Dorris says, "You can read Steve's document. Reading it is one thing, but hearing him articulate those statements with the vibe and the energy—it is a whole other thing."

Dr. Alisha Das recalls her experience:

Steve looked right into my eyes—he couldn't have been more than a foot or two from me—and he started saying his declarations. It was extraordinary. There was a power and a confidence with it, but also a humility. I'm at a bit of a loss for words to describe the power of it, because there was a definite power. I don't know that I will ever forget that. It went on for a while—I don't know how long because with that sort of experience time kind of stops—but anywhere between five and ten minutes of this very intense looking into my eyes and telling me who he was. That struck me in a way that I will never forget.

In September 2017, Steve and fourteen of his clients attended a Byron Katie event at Big Sur, California. Their attendance fee included meals at a cafeteria on site. During one break, Steve and his clients gathered at the cafeteria. Many of these clients knew about each other but had never met. Karan Rai suggested each person share who they were. Each spoke their document.

Afterwards, a stranger approached Steve and said, "Wow, I only heard part of that, but what I heard was amazing. Who are you?"

"Do you want to know my name or who I am?" asked Steve. She wanted the latter. Steve stood inches from her. "I am the universe. Love is. I am That. . . ."

Flowing in your Blood

Speaking your document to yourself and to others is essential, but it is just the beginning. Daniel Harner says, "Steve wants you to be the embodiment of your document. It is to be so much a part of you that it is second nature, like muscle memory. Steve says, 'If I cut your arm open, I want to see your document flowing in your blood.'" It is no surprise that Steve has little patience for those clients who are casual about their document, as A.J. Richards found out. He relates:

> I'd been running the gym for a while when I was hired by Chris Powell from the TV show *Extreme Makeover* to be a weight-loss coach. Having worked with Steve and done many of the Landmark programs, I had started to unfold a level of consciousness and awareness that I'd never understood before. I knew that was what people needed in weight loss. The act of losing weight has everything to do with who they know themselves to be. If I believe I'm fat, I'm going to do things fat people do, right? Athletes don't stop for fast food because in their head they're an athlete, and athletes don't do that. This was the direction I wanted to go with these people.
>
> I contacted Steve and said, "Would it be okay with you if I taught the process of forgiving yourself, not judging yourself, and creating a document?"
>
> He said, "Why don't you come and see me?"
>
> Now, keep in mind, I wasn't actually doing this process when I asked him. I'd dropped my twice-daily declarations after a few months. In hindsight, it wasn't a smart move.
>
> The way I recall it, I went to his office and sat down. Steve asked one simple question: "Who are you?"
>
> I hadn't committed my document to memory enough that I could tell him who I was. Steve turned his head to the side, and he spit on his floor.
>
> "You asked me if you could teach what I teach and you're not even doing it. That is like spitting in my face."
>
> And he spit on his floor again.
>
> Steve is a father figure to me. He is beyond a father

figure. I owe a big part of my life to who he is for me. When he spit on his floor, it shook me to my core. It was the wakeup call I needed.

Then he said, "Can you hear me? I love you."

That was a year ago, and I have been committed to speaking my document since then.

The Difference

What difference do the documents make in the lives of the people who have created them? The document is not magic. It is a declaration and a commitment. Daniel Harner says, "Steve encourages the speaking, being, and *doing* of your document." Steve is crystal clear on this. He says, "You are the one responsible to go out and make your document happen." The document pulls you into action. It invites you to step into opportunities you might have passed up pre-document. It is your partner as you dance with possibility. But you still have to dance.

Those who put on their dancing shoes find the document's impact is considerable. John Vehr says that the moment his actions aren't aligned with his statements, bells and whistles go off to signal him that it is time to course correct. Daniel Harner says, "Life can throw so many things at you. But I can always go to my document. It is the one place to come from. It reminds me of the only things worth doing. It gives me ultimate simplicity."

Jeff Dinsdale was having a bad day. He doesn't have many. He is pretty balanced. But this day, he was in a funk. He was coaching with Steve at the time and he reached out to him. He recalls, "I called and left a message. I said, 'Hey, I'm having a bad day. Do you have any advice? Blah, blah, blah . . .' I guess I was kind of dramatic about it. All he texted back was 'Read your declarations and get in action.' That was it. It was just that simple."

Karan Rai shares his experience:

I knew it was going to be damn hard. It was my first marathon. It was in Antarctica. We were running on a glacier wearing crampons. It was fifty below. I'm not a runner. I do CrossFit. I stay fairly fit, but I'm not a runner. I wasn't even halfway through the marathon and everything was hurting. I had a shin splint. It felt like I was getting frostbite on my face. I remember thinking, "What am I doing out here?"

It was at that moment that I remembered Steve saying, "When you get into a place where you start questioning yourself, just be quiet and create yourself."

I was maybe ten miles into the marathon, in the middle of a glacier, on an open track. There were only forty-two people running this race, so there was no one else around, just me and my misery.

I clearly remember getting in a zone and starting to chant my "I am" statements. They became my mantra. "I am a powerful creator and I speak my world into existence. I am an unstoppable force of nature and accomplish the improbable and the impossible with ease . . ." That really helped me get centered and focused, and it gave me my second, third, and fourth wind.

The fact that my document came up for me was not accidental. It's in my mind. It's in my bones. It naturally comes up whenever I need it. I have used it so many times. I'm in private equity. I'm in the business of buying companies. It's an industry with a lot of big personalities. Everybody's smarter than everybody else. There are a whole bunch of egos in the room. There have been so many times when in the middle of shit going sideways, I have excused myself and gone to the bathroom to compose myself. I literally recreated the guy that walked back into that room. And it has shifted meetings.

When you are feeling distress or you're feeling anxious, it is because you're off your center. Your document is who you truly are. When that guy shows up, everything is easy. The question is, how do you get him to show up at the right time? And I think that's what my work with Steve has given me. That's the superpower that I have gained working with him.

Abigail and Edward Olaya are parents of triplets. They are also former clients of Steve, which means they each have a document. Their documents have been an invaluable asset in their personal lives and their business. One day, Abigail and Edward were discussing what they wanted for their daughters. If they could give them anything, what would it be? The answer was easy: the document. So together, Abigail, Edward, and six-year-old Audrey, Ava, and Adelina created a document. The triplets were not silent partners. This is what they came up with:

Audrey, Ava, and Adelina's Document

I am enough.

I am in control of my power—my thoughts, my feelings, and my actions.

I am so brave.

I have peace inside of me.

I am kind, loving, and grateful.

I am so loved.

I am loving to my family.

I am so cute.

I respect my body.

I can learn anything I want to.

I am so beautiful.

I am loving to myself.

That is a formidable foundation for six-year-olds. But do they get it? Abigail says:

It may seem like a lot for young children to grasp, but they get it. They really do. Their eyes sparkle when they say their declarations. They speak them to each other in the day, saying, "You are such a loving sister" or "You are so beautiful." And when they say their declarations, they throw in new ones based on whatever they are feeling at the moment. That is how "I am so cute" got on the list. In some ways it is easier for six-year-olds to get declarations than adults. They have far less programming to undo.

The triplets say their document once a day, sometimes in the morning, sometimes in the car. They also say it if they are struggling, if they need an energizing pick-me-up, or even if they just encounter a routine snag. The Olayas live in a house with a split floor plan. Abigail says, "Sometimes when I ask one of the girls to go get something, she will say, 'I don't want to go to the other side of the house by myself. Can someone go with me?' I will say, 'You are so brave.' It gives them something to live in to." The document gives them tools to handle things. For instance, if someone at school says they don't like their hair, "it just rolls off of them because we have our declarations. They can recognize their power. They are intentional at a very young age."

An Uninvited Visitor

Steve had walked 6.75 miles of his 7-mile morning walk when his phone rang. It was Amy.

"How far away are you?" she asked.

"I'm close, just a block or two."

"I don't feel safe. Get home as soon as possible." This was not typical Amy, affectionately known in the family as the "flatliner." She is, in her own words, a chronic underreactor.

"What happened?" asked Steve.

"The doorbell rang, and I answered it. A strange guy was there. He handed me a package that was on the porch, one of our Amazon packages. He pointed to the label and said, 'Is this you?' After talking to him for about ten seconds, I realized he was either high or not all there. I shut the door, locked it, then ran around and locked all the doors. But he's still there. Actually, he's lying on the front porch, right in front of the door, twirling his hat in the air."

By the time Amy finished, Steve had turned the corner and could see his house. Steve can get charged when it comes to protecting his woman, but he had been saying his document ever since Amy called. He was calm, yet alert as he approached the man sprawled on his front porch.

"Who are you? What do you want?" Steve asked.

The stranger babbled. The only phrase that made sense was, "I escaped from prison."

Steve dialed 9-1-1.

A woman answered, "9-1-1, is this an emergency?"

"I think it is." Steve related what had occurred.

"Is he armed?" the operator asked.

"I don't know. Let me ask him . . . Are you armed?"

The man got up slowly, then started running down the street. It's a dead end. There was nowhere to go unless he jumped a block wall. A car was parked at the end of the cul-de-sac, one that didn't belong in the neighborhood. In minutes, the stranger was driving away in it.

A watching neighbor stood at the ready, sensing something was not right. Steve briefed him on the bizarre events of the morning and then hurried to his office just in time to meet Josué, a client from Miami.

"Hi coach. How are you doing?"

Steve told him about his morning. Josué's eyes widened. He fidgeted. Steve concluded by saying, "You know, I actually feel sorry for him. If this happened again, I would sit down and talk with him, calm him down. I would let him know that I care about him. He needs help." Josué let out a low whistle. They began their coaching.

An hour later, Steve saw Amy approaching the glass-paned door of his office. Amy *never* interrupts Steve while he is coaching, not even when she fell and hit her head, leaving a three-inch gash that needed stitches.

"Steve, our neighbor is on the phone. The guy is back. He is in a car—in our driveway. He's right outside your office. I thought you should know."

As Steve headed to the driveway, the car bolted backwards. In seconds, that morning's visitor was driving in frenzied circles in the nearby vacant lot. Rocks were flying like bullets. Dust blurred the scene. He tore out of the neighborhood. He was gone, again.

Steve and Josué sat in the office, again. Thirty minutes passed. Steve glanced out the window. "Josué, we have a little problem. The guy is in the driveway, again. Go into the house, get Amy and have her call the police again. I'm going to talk to him."

Steve and the stranger were eye-to-eye at the wrought iron gate that stands between the driveway and Steve's back yard. The stranger was almost as tall as Steve, but he carried about thirty more pounds, all in muscle. He looked like a middle linebacker. His eyes were the greenest Steve had ever seen.

"Who are you? What do you want?"

"I need to deliver the package to the lady."

"No, that's my wife. She doesn't need the package. We've already taken care of that. Who are you and what do you want?"

"I need to take a shower."

"That won't be possible," replied Steve.

"I need to get in your swimming pool."

"That's not going to happen. How can I help you?"

The man rambled, making no sense. Finally, he said, "I need somebody to talk to."

"Are you planning on hurting me?" asked Steve.

"No. I won't hurt you. I trust you."

"Then I can talk to you," said Steve. "First, who are you?"

The man reached into his pocket, pulled out a driver's license and handed it to Steve. His name was Dominique. He was 6'2", 230 pounds, and twenty-nine years old. He was a veteran. He said to Steve, "Call me Domo."

"Domo, I am going to get us some water. Go to the front yard. Sit by the mailbox and I will be right there. Don't leave."

Steve went in the house and asked Amy to make a copy of the

license. She was on the phone with the police. She made a copy and relayed the information on the driver's license to the operator. Amy and Josué stood in the living room, watching through the window. The 9-1-1 operator kept Amy on the phone.

"What's going on now?" she asked Amy.

"They are sitting on the grass . . . talking." Actually, they were laughing. They looked like two friends, shooting the breeze.

"We have patrol cars arriving. The police officers will approach on foot. Please stay on the line."

Steve was telling stories to Domo. Steve saw four policemen creeping up, two across the street along the neighbor's property, two on the edge of Steve's property, behind Domo. It was surreal, like a TV show.

"Domo, remember I said I want to help you? I am going to help you right now, but you need to be calm."

Two policemen grabbed Domo from behind. Domo thrashed and shouted.

"Steve, don't let them take me! They will say I did it. I didn't do it. They will say I have drugs. I don't."

The policemen pulled drugs out of Domo's pocket.

"Domo, you need to be calm. These policemen are going to help you."

"Steve! *When*? When do I need to be calm?"

"Right now, Domo. You need to be calm right now."

Domo hollered to the police, "Let me shake Steve's hand! Let me shake Steve's hand!" The officers weren't inclined to do so. Steve reached out. They shook. Domo's body relaxed. He stood, like a child. The police officers cuffed him.

"Please be gentle with him," said Steve. "I love this man."

The arresting officers left with Domo. The supervisor remained behind, taking statements from the neighbors and Steve. He said,

"We've arrested him before. He's strong. Before, it took four officers to subdue him. I can tell you, when you have someone who has escaped from jail, this isn't how things go down. What you just did was amazing."

"Do you need me for anything else?" asked Steve.

"I only have one more question. Who the hell are you?"

"I am the universe. Love is. I am that . . ."

The 11:11 Masterpiece

Before it was *The 11:11 Masterpiece*, it was an ordinary block wall. For many years, it was hidden by six flourishing ficus trees. They were pretty. They were green, a highly desirable feature in Arizona. But they also hurled their leaves and berries onto the deck, into the ornamental rocks, and most foully into the pool. They did it daily. Hourly. Finally, enough was enough. Out they came. But the treeless space was harsh. Clint dubbed it "the prison yard."

After much discussion, the idea for an extensive wall mural was born and Nadine Larder was engaged. The wall was sealed and painted with an undercoat. Before Nadine began painting, Steve had his clients write their documents on the wall.

Every day, two or three clients penned their document in black marker on the white wall. It took each client at least an hour, sometimes two, occasionally three. Sometimes they were still writing when night fell, and Steve took out a flood light. Amy, ever the pragmatist, questioned spending all that time writing on the wall when it would be covered up in a few weeks. Steve never wondered. He was crystal clear.

From a distance, the wall looked like an enormous newspaper.

Close up, it read like a manifesto to change the world. Here is a sampling, taken from several clients' declarations:

My very breath is enough. I am love. I serve all humanity.

I am a lighthouse.

I am an inspirational leader who brings out the best in others.

I am excellence personified. I am profound wisdom. I am unconditional love.

My life is contribution. I use my time and money to bless others.

I love me for who I am and I love me for whom I am not.

I am Abraham Lincoln leadership.

I live a life I love with those I love, and I love it.

I bring out the best in others.

I run towards scary things.

I am unconditional happiness.

I am consciously kind. I am deliberately patient.

I am a warrior of the heart.

I am a Christian, a family man, and a billion-dollar company

CEO. I know my priorities and I enjoy the journey.

I am a powerhouse. I am that there are no problems, just solutions. I am that I take actions to produce extraordinary results. I am that people light up and are their best self when I am around. I create for my family a home full of love, understanding, and fun.

Each evening, Amy and Steve stood in front of the wall, reading the latest edition. They took in the declarations. They felt their power. They experienced the magnificence of humankind. One evening, a week before Nadine was slated to begin, Amy turned to Steve and said, "Are you sure you want to paint over them?"

Today, vibrant art covers the documents. Six different paintings cover six panels of the block wall. Each reflects people finding their power, illuminating their soul, and transforming their lives. The documents are still there, under the beauty. They are an essential part of the masterpiece. Dozens of clients left something of their magnificence, vision, and commitment. There is power in the wall. And there is power in the clients. As Karan Rai says, "When you have your document inside of you, you get to the point where you are no longer arguing with yourself for your limitations. You start arguing with yourself for your greatness. It changes how you view the world, and that by extension changes how the world interacts with you."

Steve's Document

I am the Universe.

Love is. I am That.

Be still and know that I AM God.

I am a disciple of Jesus Christ.

I am deeply moved by Spirit, the power of all Creation.

I am consciously aware of other people's points of view and I honor their right to have a different point of view.

I am Lovingkindness.

I am that no one is worthy of my judgement and that everyone is worthy of my Love.

I am graciously authentic.

I am strong, healthy, and attractive.

I am happy and peaceful.

I am that my heart is filled with peace.

I am Divine Intuition.

I am connected to Infinite Intelligence.

I experience extraordinary discernment and decision-making powers.

I dedicate all thought to Union.

I am that I do not sweat the small stuff, and it is all small stuff, including death and dying.

I am that I have no complaints.

I distinctly remember forgetting that—and the "that" is my past. I never use my past to victimize myself or others. I do not wallow in it. I use my past to lead, build, inspire, teach and love.

I am madly in Love with my intelligent, gorgeous, brilliant and vivacious wife, Amy Blake Hardison.

I am that I am extraordinarily patient, loving, and kind to all living things, especially Amy Blake Hardison.

I am that I live, I love, I learn, and I serve, profoundly and extraordinarily.

This is who I am, and my mother named me Steve.

Vignette

Nadine Larder

from Conquering Fears to Create Masterpieces

I decided it was time to hire myself a coach. A life coach. I'm a huge fan of coaching. I've experienced tremendous growth in the past when working with coaches.

I'm very spiritual, so I decided the best way to find a coach was to simply ask God to send me one. I stepped into the courtyard outside my office, lifted my hands up and asked God to send me a coach. My faith and my ability to manifest thoughts into things is tremendous, so I knew I needed to be VERY specific in what I wanted. I told Him that I didn't want just any coach. I wanted the best one on the planet! It was a tall order, but I knew if anyone could help me find the coach meant for me, it was Him.

I put the request out and didn't give it much thought after that.

It wasn't two weeks later that a man named Steve Hardison walked up to me in a parking garage and introduced himself . . .

His energy was different than anything I had ever felt before. There was something about him that was unexplainable, something that felt pure and authentic. His aura was so light and bright white, it was almost blinding. Electric . . . yet so calm, centered, authentic and beautiful . . .

When Steve and I met, we were both attending a business conference in Phoenix put on by Infusionsoft. I was headed to my car with my team, and he was headed to his . . .

Steve was a VIP guest of Clate Mask, the CEO of Infusionsoft. He was Clate's coach. I was there to accept a marketing award and as one of the conference speakers. I was also releasing my first book that very day, a business book called *The Secrets I Share with My Friends: Everything I Know About Building A Small Business.*

We spoke briefly in the parking garage, mostly small talk. I invited him to my session the following day, and he left. He returned a few moments later, pulling up alongside us in his car. He had come back to share gifts! He hopped out of his car, opened his trunk and proceeded to give each of us a book written by Steve Chandler. His only request was that we not take a book we wouldn't read. I was excited and appreciative. I love to read, and these titles were right up my alley! Steve Chandler is a brilliant author!

Because I was releasing my book that day, I asked if I could reciprocate and give him my new book. Before he accepted it, he asked what it was about. He wanted to make sure it was something he would actually read. Me being me, I jokingly said to him, "Don't take what you're not going to read." We laughed and he promised he'd read it. He said, "I am my word and I will definitely read it. You have my word." I knew he was sincere, and I knew he was telling me the truth. I could feel it . . .

It took a year of praying, meditating, focusing and manifesting great miracles to become one of Steve's clients . . . My coaching with Steve was as miraculous as our meeting in the parking garage, and it was only the beginning of what we would create together . . .

In November of 2016, I began manifesting and praying, asking God to help me once again. I put my request out into the world via my journal, declaring and owning the fact that "I am an artist who is paid well for the art I create."

[The following comes from Nadine's journal.]

12-6-2016

Today my life took a turn when I received a message from Steve Hardison at 11:00 p.m. asking if I was awake and able to call. I was awake . . . so I called.

It was on this day he told me he'd been paying attention to me and my art on Facebook. He told me how much he loved my art, that it spoke to him. He invited me to paint a mural of my art in his back yard on a wall he described as large. Large doesn't begin to describe its size!

He posed this question to me at precisely 11:11 p.m.

The 11:11 Masterpiece Wall was born on December 6, 2016, at 11:11 p.m.

I didn't sleep that night . . . I couldn't believe it was real! Was this really happening???

12-7-2016

I responded at precisely 11:11 a.m. saying I wanted to accept the job and discuss it further.

12-9-2016

I was hired!!! Today I met with Steve at *The 11:11 Masterpiece*

Wall. It's HUGE!!!

I accepted the project. I'm being compensated nicely, and I have the greatest boss ever!

I am feeling both excited and completely overwhelmed!

What have I gotten myself into? I've never painted anything larger than a canvas of 30 x 40 inches [76 x102 cm]! This entire wall is 600 square feet [55 sqm]!

Steve chose what he wanted on the wall from several canvases I brought with me as samples of my work. And so the journey begins . . .

As an intuitive artist, I don't ever know what I'm painting or what will happen when I sit down in front of my easel and begin applying paint to my canvas. I follow the paint and the canvas to wherever it takes me. The outcome is a surprise and the creating of it a journey.

I always infuse energy into my art by painting inspiring words and messages on the base layer of each canvas. I like to begin with good energy to help move my art in the right direction. With *The 11:11 Masterpiece Wall*, I suggested to Steve that we do something similar to his wall . . . but that I wouldn't be the one to write the words. I suggested that this time my "canvas" could have energy infused into it with words put there by his clients, friends and family.

I was thinking about simple words like "love, happiness, gratitude, dream, God, achievement, family," and so on. Steve had something completely different in mind. It blew my mind! He planned to have all of his clients and family write the declarations of who they are and what they stand for on the wall. He would reserve the wall where The Tree of Life was to be painted for his family, and only his family would write there.

1-6-2017

When I received a text from Steve with his declarations on the wall, I cried. I was so moved to see it on the wall. He's shared the declaration of who he is with me many times when I was coaching with him. This time was different. I cried because this is the man I'm working for.

It's an absolute representation of him as I've always experienced him. How can I not continue to grow being in his presence?

Trust me . . . Steve Hardison rubs off on you!!!!!

1-14-2017

I continue to feel overwhelmed by all that is happening. I receive texts every day with photos attached from Steve. Photos of his clients and family writing their declarations on the wall . . . The people writing on the wall have created something far more meaningful, magical and miraculous than I could have ever dreamed myself. I had no expectation, but it far exceeds my vision in ways I don't have words to describe.

Nadine's Declaration

I am an artist that touches people around the world with my story, my art and my expression. I am the best at what I do. My light shines so bright it's almost blinding, as does my authenticity and my brilliance. I show people the light that is God and I live the greatest expression of the life gifted to me by God. I treasure every moment and I remain present. I am Nadine . . . I am Hope.

Nadine and Steve, 2017

Chapter 29

Being Your Word, Commitment, and Integrity

Sitting in the jury assembly room with two hundred prospective jurors was pure pleasure for Steve, whose version of the quote "So many books, so little time" is "So many conversations, so little time." He met a fascinating woman. Of course, it could have been a man, a banker, an auto mechanic, a grizzled hippie, a Harley enthusiast, a transvestite, an exotic dancer, a grandma, ad infinitum. People fascinate Steve. But this time, it was a woman.

She was interested in what Steve did. He said he had a book in his car that he would give her. Steve was chosen to be on the jury; she was dismissed. She left hours before he did. Some people would say, "Oh well. That's how it goes." That's not how it goes for Steve. "Anything that comes out of my lips," says Steve, "I take action on." At the end of a long day in court, he drove an hour out of his way to deliver the book to her. Her words were predictable. "You didn't need to do this."

Steve's words were less predictable. "I needed to do it for me."

Why? Because if Steve says he is going to do something, he does it. It is his cardinal principle. He lives it. He breathes it. He has taught it to his kids. As adults, they have each said, "Do you realize that most people don't do what they say? It is so frustrating!" This is something that has always confounded Steve. One of his earliest memories is of his father saying he would take Steve to the mountains—and not doing it.

Doing what you say you will do—being your word—imparts power. Things get done. Efficiency soars. Frustration falls. It's so obvious. It is surprising how frequently people don't do what they say they will do. It is shocking how unaware people are of the discrepancy. When Steve asks a group of people how many of them keep their word, almost everyone raises his hand. When he asks clients how often they do what they say they will do, most estimate high. Clate Mask projected ninety percent. Then Steve sent Clate off with an assignment to keep count of every time he did and didn't do what he said. When he came back to his next coaching session, Clate's estimate had plunged to twenty percent. And Clate is a high-producing, effective CEO.

Steve explains:

Many people say, "Let's get lunch on Tuesday," knowing it isn't going to happen. They don't even have an intention of making it happen. Sometimes people will make two lunch commitments for the same day and then cancel both if a better offer comes along. They live in a world of "doing what I want when I want to" and then use their speaking to justify the mess. That is shutting the barn door after the horse has bolted. For me, it's about honoring myself as my word. That starts at the moment of speaking.

We live in a world that isn't rigorous about being your

word. We let each other off for not being our word. When someone comes along who actually does what he says and holds others accountable for what they say, that person looks crazy, demanding, and excessive. But if you can't count on yourself, who can you count on?

Steve uses an analogy to distinguish the principle of "being your word" for his clients. When a country's government starts printing money to pay for its spending, it causes inflation and reduces the purchasing power of the printed money. Alternatively, a government can limit the money it prints to what is backed by an equal amount of gold in their reserves. This is called the gold standard. It was widely used in the nineteenth and early twentieth centuries. It worked because gold is a real, physical asset and tends to hold its value. Most people speak like they are printing paper money. They throw out words like they don't mean anything. The more they speak, the less valuable their word becomes because they are flooding the market with words with no backing. We live in a verbally inflationary world. Being your word is talking like gold bars are coming out of your mouth. If you are your word, people can count on your words like they are real.

One of the consequences of verbal inflation, explains Steve, is that we are forced to implement fudge factors. When certain people say they will do something, you know there is a slim chance that what they say will happen. You'd better have a solid backup plan, a fudge factor. With others, there is a fifty percent chance they will do what they say. You may or may not need a fudge factor. And there are a few people you know you can count on like their life depends on it.

Steve asks: "How can you become one of the few?"

"What I speak *matters*—meaning my words materialize

something," says Steve. "They literally 'matter'—or create mass. No one is one hundred percent, but if I say something, the odds are really high that I am going to do it. If I don't, I clean it up. What I notice is that when people honor their word like it really means something, their lives work better." Steve teaches and trains his clients on this principle.

Brandon Craig was working at TimeMax, selling courses taught by Steve Chandler and Dennis Deaton to corporations. He relates:

> I had a meeting with Steve, and I was probably two minutes late, at the most. Steve seized the opportunity to teach me about the power of being your word, in this case the power of being where you said you would be when you said you would be there. I was two minutes late and we spent about an hour and a half on this distinction. That meeting really opened my eyes. I saw the impact of not being your word and I saw the power of being your word. I was inspired. I was young, about twenty-three, and looking to build a career. I saw that being your word is the opening act for success. That meeting impacted my life.

Byron Applegate speaks for all Steve's clients when he says, "If you know Steve, then you know that your word is all you have, and commitment is how you know what to do next."

Commitment

Steve was picking up a few things from the grocery store when his phone rang. The caller introduced himself. We will call him William. William said, "I want you to be my coach."

"You'll have to get in line," replied Steve.

It was not the response William expected.

Steve asked William what prompted him to call. William knew one of Steve's clients. He had seen his transformation. William wanted some of that. Again, he asked Steve to be his coach, upping the ante. He would fly him to Las Vegas in his personal jet so Steve could coach him in his home. He would pay triple Steve's usual fee.

"Sorry, I can't be your coach."

"Why?"

"First of all, I only coach in my office at my house. Second, because you want to own me. I am not ownable."

William was intrigued. He saw enough of what was possible in working with Steve that he made a commitment to be in Steve's office on a specific date, at a specific time, with a check for $150,000. For Steve, it wasn't a done deal. He needed to make sure William's commitment was big enough to produce results.

On the agreed-upon date, at the agreed-upon time, in Steve's office, Steve outlined for William what he would need to commit to if they were to work together:

1. Their work together must be the most important thing in William's world, not because he was working with Steve, but because they were working on William's life.
2. He must be in Steve's office when he said he would be. They would agree on their schedule at the beginning of their coaching, allowing for vacations, conferences, etc. After that, their sessions had absolute priority over things that came up.
3. He must be open to what Steve said—very likely it would not be what William wanted to hear.
4. He must be willing to learn to love.

When William hedged, Steve picked up the $150,000 check and

tore it into pieces. William's jaw dropped. William was a billionaire. No one talked to him like that. No one disregarded his money like that. It got his attention. He committed. He pulled out his checkbook and started to write another check.

"And cut off your left testicle and your right pinkie finger and give them to me with your check."

William's head jerked up. Steve was smiling—but he was also serious. Not about the testicle and pinkie finger, but about the importance of commitment. For Steve, commitment is fundamental. Like being your word, it is something he works on with every client.

One of the analogies Steve uses to teach commitment is what he calls "a mother's commitment." Steve says to his clients, especially his clients who are mothers, that he is going to show them the model of commitment. "I'm going to ask you a question. Don't think about it for a long time. Just answer the question. Are your kids going to starve?" The mothers belt out an instant, unequivocal "No!"

"They don't ask for any clarification," says Steve. "It doesn't matter who the president is. It doesn't matter if there is a trucking strike. It doesn't matter if there is a quarantine and the shelves in the grocery store are depleted. They will do whatever it takes so their kids don't starve. That is commitment."

Before Tom McGovern committed to work with Steve, Steve had a conversation with him about commitment. It wasn't a one-and-done. They periodically circled back to commitment during their coaching. Steve used an analogy that Tom has frequently shared and still uses to this day.

Imagine you are with a group of fifty people. These are your people. It could be a church group, your local Rotary club, whatever. You ask who can help you set up chairs for a meeting next Saturday at 8:00 a.m. Ten people raise their hands. Saturday morning comes and not everybody who committed to be there at 8:00 is there.

"Name some reasons people might give for not showing up," says Steve.

"I had a flat tire."

"I ran out of gas."

"I overslept."

"I forgot."

Steve continues, "If you were to list these reasons on the left side of a piece of ledger paper, how long would the list be? How many possibilities are there?"

Dozens. Hundreds.

Now, on the right side of the ledger paper, write how you know if someone has honored his commitment? How long is this list? How many possibilities are there?

The list is short. There is one possibility. He showed up at 8:00. He did what he said he would do.

Then, pointing to the right-hand side of the paper, Steve says, "That's me. That's my life. I am commitment."

Tom reflects, "I certainly get that about Steve. If he says he's going to do something, you can bank on it. It is a very, very, very powerful way of living."

It is how Steve lives, even in extreme circumstances. Martine Canon relates how she learned this:

When I coached with Steve, I was flying back and forth from London to see him. I flew for fourteen hours, arrived in Phoenix, stayed at one of his client's apartments, woke up the first thing in the morning, drove to his house, coached for two hours, went straight to the airport and flew back home. I did that every fourteen days. So, it was a big commitment. Steve always said that it was not a commitment to him; it was a commitment to myself.

I had a year and a half of flights booked in advance. Just a few days before our first coaching session, Steve emailed me and said, "I'm really sorry, but my wife's mother has passed away. The funeral is set for the day we are meeting." I fully expected to read a bit further and he would say, "I won't be able to see you." I would lose money canceling my flight, but that was irrelevant. This was an unforeseeable, very personal circumstance.

He went on to say, "I can't meet at our normal time because that is the exact time of the funeral service. Can we move it a few hours later? I will make sure that it's the best session that you've ever had." I remember reading that and feeling really emotional about the extraordinary level of commitment that he had for me, but even more, for his word. He talks about "I am my word" and "whatever words come out of my mouth is what exists." He really lives it. That completely changed my life in terms of being aware of what I say.

Then he said, "I'd like you to come to the funeral."

I didn't want to intrude into his family's space at a time like this, but he assured me that I was very welcome. It turned out his father-in-law passed away a couple of days later. Amy's parents had a beautiful love story, a love like no other. They ended up having a double funeral.

I went to his house on the day of the funeral and spent time with him and Amy. I could clearly see the level of emotion both of them had. Then Amy left for the church. A little later, Steve and I drove there.

I met quite a few people, family members, people who had known his father- and mother-in-law. I felt like I was part of the family. I sat at the family table. I ate with them afterwards. It was a mind-blowing experience to be welcomed into somebody's world in such an intimate way, but never feeling like an accessory. It was like, "You're going to be here because you were part of a commitment that was made. Things happened. It doesn't change the commitment."

After that extraordinary experience of being with his family and hearing the profound love story of his mother- and father-in-law, and being touched by hearing Amy and her sisters speak about the love and respect they have for their parents, he then drove me home and we had a normal session together. But the session wasn't essential. I had learned so much already.

The passing of your mother-in-law and father-in-law is a pretty good reason to renegotiate a commitment. But Steve doesn't look for reasons that are good enough for people to buy. He looks for ways he can keep his commitments. His commitments aren't burdens. "They are access to freedom and power," says Steve. "People who understand commitment and live from it produce amazing results."

Integrity

"Steve is an amazing coach," says Van Dunham. "He has the ability to identify when an individual is out of balance and out of integrity. Then he guides you to become balanced and back in integrity." Sometimes "guide" isn't quite the right word. Sometimes it feels a little more like a shove. Just ask Jeff Dinsdale.

I was twenty-two years old. I was working at University of

Phoenix in sales. I had just hired Steve to be my coach and my first session was at 9:00 a.m. I was supposed to be at work at 8:00. My boss was this ex-hockey player. He was a big, macho guy, not this transformed guy. I was pretty sure that telling him I was going to meet with a life coach was not going to fly. So, I called in and let them know I would be running a little bit late because my grandma had had a heart attack and was in the hospital. Why did I say that? Because no one's going to come back and try to pin you on that.

I showed up at Steve's and we started talking about what brought me there. I told him, "Man, I've done so much to get here and to have this session with you. I even told my boss this morning that my grandma's in the hospital. I was willing to do whatever it takes to be here." I didn't even realize how out of integrity I was. I was so blind to it.

Steve said, "I want to show you something." We went into his family room and he turned on the TV. He showed me a *60 Minutes* segment about Bernie Madoff, whose one little white lie led to the biggest Ponzi scheme in history. He turned to me and said, "That is what out-of-integrity behaviour looks like."

When I went to my work, I said to my ex-NHL, big, manly-guy manager, "Hey, bro, can we go on a walk?" On the walk I said, "I just want to clean something up with you. My grandma wasn't in the hospital this morning. I just said that because I went to meet with this coach. And to be honest, I felt embarrassed and I felt nervous. I didn't know what to say. And I wanted an out."

He said, "Jeff, thanks so much for sharing that. Do you know how many of these other people I manage bullshit me every day about this sick person or that sick person and I know they're lying?"

So that was my first session with Steve. He smashed me over the head with integrity. That conversation changed the course of my life.

Jeff's experience fits into the typical definition of integrity. Often, when Steve talks about integrity, he is using it as Michael C. Jensen, Werner Erhard, and Steve Zaffron use it, as "ontological integrity." Simply stated, ontological integrity is honoring your word as you speak it to yourself and to others. It is not only doing what you said you would do, but also being the same person in the world that you are at your core. It is consistency of being. It is a lesson Steve taught Chris Dorris. Chris relates:

I've been a social worker, a licensed therapist, and a coach. I thought I got integrity. Steve had me see straightaway that I don't know shit about integrity. I don't remember what the context was. I know that I wasn't late for my coaching. I would never have been late. Steve made the importance of being on time abundantly clear. I was definitely early for every appointment. I probably was acting arrogant, like I knew what was going on. He challenged me. He said, "You're a liar. And I don't mean that in a harsh way. I mean that you're living in a lot of lies." I didn't comprehend that at first, until he explained that he was talking about me pretending to be different than I really was. He challenged me to pay attention to all the times when that showed up.

"All right. Let's do that. Cool." I actually thought it sounded pretty fun.

That very week, I was hosting a Halloween party at my house. How much safer can you get? You're at your own home with all your friends. We were on the back patio, drinking and standing in a circle. Everyone was talking about some movie. It was pretty clear that I was the only person who hadn't seen the movie. They were all dropping lines from it. I'm laughing and acting as if I had seen the movie. I don't know what I was thinking. Somehow, I was convinced that I couldn't let them know that I hadn't seen the movie. I'm not sure what would have been the problem with me saying, "I haven't seen this movie, but I'm sure as hell going to go see it now. It sounds like a great movie."

It was the perfect wake-up call. I discovered I had a problem with what's real. I could also see all the extra work I do because of that. That alone has profoundly changed my life.

The other thing I took from that experience is how unbelievably dialed in Steve is and how fast he picks up on what is running you. It is instant, as soon as you open your mouth and say something. There has not been a day that has passed since he assigned me that exercise that I haven't practiced being at peace with what is and eliminating the lie that "this should be different." That is easily one of the biggest takeaways from my work with Steve.

In his paper "Integrity: Without It Nothing Works," Michael Jensen writes: "People tend to view integrity as a virtue that is 'nice to have', but not as something that is directly related to performance . . . But the increases in performance that are possible by focusing on integrity are huge: I'm not talking about a 10 [percent] increase in output or productivity—it's more like 100 to 500 [percent]." Steve falls in the 500 percent category. Integrity, being his word, and commitment are the warp and woof of Steve's life. People notice.

Coach Oren Harris recalls:

One day Steve calls me up out of the blue. Oprah invited Iyanla to invite someone powerful and influential in Iyanla's life to appear on the show. Steve said, "She invited me, but I declined. I don't do things like *Oprah*. I do this. I don't do that." That was expansive for me. In the moment, I was like, "Wow, here's a man who's so true, and so aligned, and so impeccable with who he is, what he does, and what he says, that he is able to be continually aligned with his power."

Vignette

Cathy (M. Catherine) Thomas

It was February 2010. Steve had just finished reading a book I'd written (*Light in the Wilderness*). Synchronistically, that weekend I'd traveled from Provo to give some firesides in the Mesa area. On Sunday, at my last fireside, Steve and Amy came and sat in the left front row of this chapel. I didn't know anything about him or who he was. As I stood at the podium, I sensed a pretty intense energy coming from where he sat. He seemed really engaged. A day or so later, out of the blue, he phoned me. He said he was a coach. He pointed out some things he'd picked up on, said he knew what was important to me and what hurt me. He invited me to come work with him in Mesa—at least to try it out and see if we liked each other. He told me he could sit with a person and sense many things; he could feel what was needed. I gathered he had some kind of intuitional gift. Perhaps he could see into my mysteries and move me to greater clarity.

I flew to Mesa, four times I think, to work with him in his little office by the pool. He asked me what kind of flag he should raise when I came to visit. Apparently, each client had his own flag. I chose the yin yang symbol, which thereafter was always flying when

I came.

I sat on the little couch and he sat in his office chair. High energy. Intense. Ruthless. But also loving, which I interpreted then as over the top. But I got over my resistance and began to see into his genuinely loving and perceptive heart.

For myself, I thought I looked like I had it all together—I was a professor in Ancient Scripture at BYU, a published author, a wife and mother of six, an active member of my church. But I told him the truth, even though it sounded so trite—I just wasn't good enough.

But he wouldn't accept that I wasn't good enough and introduced me to a truer way of being. He taught me to excavate for inner "I am's" to activate my own real power. He also taught me to have power in my word. I could see from the stories he told of his own experiences that the Heavens responded to his decision to be his word. He seems to harness the powers of the Universe to bring good things to pass. He loves creating miracles. He has created many. I began to see a bigger world of much greater, even magical, possibilities. I was never quite the same afterwards. I had a new vision.

After working with Steve, I finished another book, *The God Seed*, in which I wrote:

"We can wake up from the dream of hell . . . And when we wake up, we realize that our words are the instrument of creation. Let us become conscious of speaking as though God Himself were speaking—because if not, we may create chaos. Let us make the decision to be our word, and that what we say we mean, and that what we say we do, because we said it, and that's who we are."

Pure Steve. That's how you move Heaven and Earth.

Chapter 30

Steve on Thought and Action

"**O**ther coaches deal with their clients' stuff by going outside," says Steve. "If a client says he has a problem with his wife, most coaches start working on the problem; perhaps it is communication. I go in—every single time. What creates our problems, what creates our whole lives, is our thoughts."

Going in. Working with thoughts. That is Steve's work.

The following are Steve's thoughts regarding thoughts and action, in his own words.

Principle 1: Action

Sometimes when I am talking to clients, I will ask them what they think the most important traits are in order to create a desired outcome. The desired outcome can be in any area, from becoming a company president to losing weight to writing a screenplay.

Some people say desire. "Desire is good," I respond, "but do you know people who have desire who can't produce?" Of course they do.

Some people say passion. "Passion is important. It is better to have passion than to not have passion, but there are passionate people who have no results."

Other answers include a good college degree, perseverance, vision, belief, and attitude. These are all important, but they aren't the determining factor. Only one person, Holly Profitt-Venekamp, hit the bullseye.

The key factor to creating a desired outcome is action.

Principle 2: How We See the World

If there is one secret to life, it is this: All actions are directly correlated to how we see the world. I teach this to all my clients through a variety of metaphors. Before we get to the metaphors, notice that I didn't say, "All actions are directly correlated to how the world is." The world is not a fixed reality, seen by everyone the same way. For instance, I'm color blind. For the first fifteen years of our marriage, I thought we had green plates. Eventually, I said something to Amy about the green plates. She had no idea what I was talking about. To her, they were wheat-colored. The plates looked different to me than they did to Amy. The world we experience is a personal experience, not a universal one.

To show my clients that every action is directly correlated to how they see the world, I pick up a pillow from the couch and start to hit them. Inevitably, they hold up their arms to deflect the pillow. I point out that if we were having a quiet conversation, they wouldn't throw their arms up into the air all of a sudden. That would be crazy. Only when they perceive a reason to put their arms up in the air do they raise their arms.

Sometimes I use an apple to demonstrate this principle. I toss them an apple and they catch it. We throw it back and forth a few times. I say, "Notice that when you were sitting on the couch ten minutes ago, you weren't reaching up as if to catch something. Only when the apple comes at you do you reach out."

"Notice, right now you are just sitting here. You aren't dropping to the floor and crawling to the corner of the room. That would be bizarre. But if a bullet came through the window, that is exactly what you would do, and it would make perfect sense. Every single behavior we take is based on how we see the world."

Pillows, apples, and bullets are obvious things. It gets more fun when we see how this plays out in real life. In one coaching session, Clate Mask [the CEO of Keap] and I were talking about his company's sales. I told him that his top salesperson and his lowest-producing salesperson are not taking the same actions. If he could get the lowest-producing salesperson to take the same actions as the top salesperson, he or she would get the same results.

Clate asked, "How do I get him to do that?"

I said, "Every action we take—or do not take—is directly correlated with how we see the world. I can guarantee that your top salesperson sees Keap as a great place to work and loves the people, the company, and the compensation plan. The lowest-performing salesperson says, 'I hate this job. When are they going to improve the product? I am stuck at this place.'"

"So," said Clate, "what creates how we see the world?"

That brings us to our third principle.

Principle 3: Thinking, Speaking, Writing, and Doing

Our world is created by what we say to ourselves (our thoughts), what we say to others (our speaking), the things we write, and the things we do. Thinking, speaking, and writing are obvious; "the things we do" needs an explanation. If someone says that he can get anything done, but when an opportunity presents itself he shrivels up in fear and doesn't try, then his doing language is speaking louder than his spoken language. Doing is language in action.

People say things to us all the time. We can accept or reject what they say. How much power it has is completely up to us. If someone says, "I think you are a jerk," we can believe it and take that into our identity as truth. Or, we can think, "I can see how you think that, but that is not who I am for myself." On the other side of the spectrum, someone could say, "Wow, you are so amazing," and we could dismiss that as nonsense. We are the ultimate gatekeeper. Many people let in what is crippling and keep out what is empowering.

The document is one example of how both writing and speaking create our world. Every morning when I say my document, I say how much I love Amy and how much I appreciate her. I am creating my world through my speaking. Once when I was working with Karan Rai, he said, "Every time I'm here, you have your 'A' game on. How do you do it?"

I said, "It's not just me. You are creating your coaching experience by your speaking and thinking. You could undo the magic any time you wanted. When you woke up this morning in Manhattan and started getting ready for your flight, if you said, 'What in the world am I doing?' or when you got to the airport, if you said, 'Damn, this flight costs a lot of money,' you could undo it all."

That is why I am not casual with my speaking. It is creating my world. If someone calls me and says, "Call me when you want to chat," I will say, "I won't be doing that. I don't chat." Some people think I'm brusque, but creating my world through my speaking is more important to me than social grease. If I take my word casually, it takes away from my ability to create my future through my speaking. I am not willing to do that.

Vignette

Kai Jordan

When I sat down with Steve for my *Be With* session, I didn't know what to expect. I thought it might be like a coaching session. The first thing Steve said was, "So what's present for you today?"

I felt this rush of energy. I said, "I need to improve my leadership. I feel that in the coming years, I'm going to be required to step up as a leader and really be someone who needs to understand how to lead and how to guide large groups of people."

And as soon as that came out of my mouth, he pulled out his phone and he held up his finger and said, "One second." He dialed a number on the phone.

I was sitting there thinking, "What? He's on his phone!? I thought we were doing a coaching session! He just jumped on his phone." He dialed this woman and said, "Hey Anne. It's Steve Hardison. Are you and Werner Erhard still doing the Being a Leader program?"

I could hear her on the phone. "Yes. Is that something that you're wanting to do?"

Steve said, "Do you remember you offered me a ticket?"

She said, "Yes, of course. We'd love to have you in the room. Just let us know if you want to come."

"Well, I'm actually sitting here with a gentleman named Kai Jordan. I think the program is going to be perfect for him. I'm going to have him get in touch with you. I think he should do the program."

"Sure. Have him send me a message. I'll give him anything he needs."

"Great," responded Steve. "Say hi to your husband. Love you. Love you both. We'll see you later."

He hung up the phone, looked at me, and whispered, "I'm going to get you that ticket."

I thought to myself, "What just happened? Where was the coaching? He didn't ask me any questions. He didn't do any processes with me!" I was sitting there in shock. Within three minutes from the moment the words "I need to improve my leadership" left my mouth, there was a solution on the table. And I was committed to it. I was stunned.

Steve messaged me the next day. "Anne's got a ticket for you. You just need to pay for your room and board. Contact her as soon as possible." Before the day was over, I had the ticket. I was enrolled. And I was heading to the Being a Leader course. It's a $5,000 program. I had already recouped the payment for the *Be With* session.

What I got from this is that Steve isn't just a coach. He's not sitting there trying to help you get through your problematic thinking or unlock your full potential. He's there to create. Steve's a creator, and being in his presence is an opportunity to create things you never thought were possible. It's an opportunity to create miracles.

In that moment, I realized you can't call him a coach because he doesn't fit into that spectrum. I've seen a lot of coaches, and I've seen how they work. This is a creator. That's the only way you can describe what happened.

Chapter 31

Sacred Connections

His cell phone rings. "This is Steve."

"Is this the Steve that coaches Ron and Mary Hulnick?" asks the caller.

"One and the same."

"I want to talk to you about coaching—but I'm not sure I can work with you."

"Wait a minute. You just called me about coaching, then you said you aren't sure you could work with me. That's interesting. But let's start with *why* you couldn't work with me."

"You are a Mormon."

"And?"

"You believe in sin, redemption, hell—all that stuff. I'm an atheist. I think all that is a little crazy."

"Let's get some things straight," says Steve. "There are certain things you would need to do if we worked together. First, I don't travel. You come to my office in Arizona. Second, you pay up front. Third, if you don't keep the agreements we make, your coaching agreement is finished. No refunds. Fourth, if you start believing in God or a religion while you are working with me, I will fire your ass. If you are an atheist, I want you to be a kick-ass atheist. I want people to be their best. I don't care what they believe. I care that they live what they believe."

Many of the people Steve works with are very spiritual. Some are also religious. Steve is both spiritual and religious, but when he steps into his office, he does not coach from his religion.

Steve works with people who believe in angels, auras, crystals, energy, shamans, Shakti, Jesus Christ, Moses, Krishna, and Allah, to name a few. He works with some people who access spirituality by attending church and some who do so by going on ayahuasca retreats. Some study the Torah. Some study *A Course in Miracles*. He honors each person for their belief and their spiritual processes. He works with each person inside their belief.

As a teenager, Steve had friends who were conservative Mormons and friends who were pot-smoking hippies—and everything in between. He has space for all kinds of people and all kinds of belief systems. His clients experience Steve's acceptance.

Melanie Waite says, "Steve is very nonjudgmental. Even though I'm a Mormon, if I were to say, 'I believe this part of Mormonism, but not that,' and 'I want to live this, but not that,' he would say, 'Okay, great. Let's make you the best non-Mormon Mormon there is.' He doesn't have a should or shouldn't."

Michael Serwa experiences Steve as Melanie does. He says:

Steve and I are so similar and yet so different. Here I am, a single man who doesn't want a committed relationship. I like to play the field with the ladies, and he got married at twenty-two. He's religious and I'm not religious at all. These are pretty big differences. But he has never had an element of judgment. He has never said, "Michael, when are you going to get serious and commit to one woman?" or "When are you going to find Jesus?" That would have put me off.

Led by God

Abigail Olaya's first words to Steve were, "God told me to work with you." She isn't the only one who felt divinely directed to work with Steve. Roxane Beck says, "When Iyanla Vanzant said Steve's name at the Celebrate Your Life event in Phoenix, energy like Shakti shot through me." A few months before Norma Bachoura contacted Steve, she saw him in a dream and knew she was to work with him. She knew the dream was from God.

Laura Minard also dreamed about Steve—seven years before she knew anything about him. At the time, she thought the person in her dream was an older version of a high school classmate. Fast forward seven years, Laura was praying for a new coach. She had outgrown her previous coach and spiritual teachers. She connected with Steve through Facebook and set up a *Be With* session. When she met Steve in person, she realized the person in her dream was not her classmate. It was Steve.

Below are three first-person accounts of people who were led to work with Steve in extraordinary ways.

Edith Croteau

I'm a spiritual coach who has studied life-coaching, homeopathic medicine, physiology and hormones, I also specialize in trauma, addiction and suicide intervention.

I have always had a great connection with my inner voice, from the moment I was born. It was very present at a young age. This connection kept me alive through many critical situations in my life and death experience.

Some people have an angel or a guide or someone else. For me it is more an energy vibration, a knowing inside that comes as a thought, a voice or an image. Now, I also have the capacity of leaving my physical body to visit other places in other dimensions.

Six years ago, I went through a serious situation with my health. So, I asked my inner voice to give me someone, somewhere, that I could talk with or work with one day.

It took days to arrive. Finally, in the middle of the night, I woke up and I had a name in my head. This time it was written down. I asked why it was written. It was written so I could not misspell the name. So, I got up, ran to my desk, and wrote it down: Steve Hardison. Before that moment, I had never heard of him or come across that name. The next day I did some research and I found his contact details. I connected with him.

Dr. Chris Baek

In a recent dream, I received several messages about Steve. The guidance came sporadically throughout the middle of the night. Words were spoken to me. It's unclear who was speaking to me— everything was dark and I didn't see anything—but I think it may have been an angel or just a more enlightened version of myself. The entity did not reveal herself. I only heard her speak.

I was told that Steve Hardison was sent to me to heal, and that I needed to work with him to transform my life. I was told that he is the "real deal" and to invest in him.

I was told that Steve Hardison . . . came down to earth to help people. He has something to share and has been sent to transform me.

I was told that Steve Hardison has the ability to heal and transform.

I was given confirmation of my mission, which Steve was sent to help me with.

Based on this guidance, I received a resounding 'YES' from the heavens. The gates have been opened, and the procession will begin with support from God and the angels. So excited!

Karen Davis

When I was eleven, I fell from a tree swing and hit my head on a boulder. Suddenly, I could see my body down below me. I was out of my body. I was in spirit. I found myself moving towards a warm light. All fear, anger, and frustration dropped away, and what was left was the pure essence of love. It was incredible.

At that time, there was a lot of turmoil going on in my life at home. My parents were going through a divorce. My mother had paranoid schizophrenia. It is sad to say, but I didn't want to come back. When I was out of my body, there was some convincing going on, trying to get me to see that I needed to go back, but I really didn't want to return.

I entered this space and there was something I refer to as 'the screen.' It was not like a television screen. It was massive. I saw my whole life replayed on the screen. Then I was shown something on the screen, something about what was next if I went back. I don't remember what that was. I remember all of my near-death experience, everything from the time I hit my head all the way through my out-of-body experience and then coming back—except for what was next, the reason I needed to come back.

In 2007 I did a regression trying to remember the part I couldn't recall. The woman I was working with took me back through the whole experience and I remembered everything—except for that one part. She taped our session, but the recording didn't work. She said, 'Karen, I don't think you are supposed to know that part.'

Fast forward to February 2020. I'm sitting in Steve Chandler's ACS (Advanced Client Systems) course. I was watching the people in the room who hadn't experienced Steve Hardison before. I was able to see his intuition at work in the room. He could spot someone in the room and instantly know what was going on. He just knows people. People were crying in the room. He was crying. I can hardly describe his way of being. It was absolutely amazing.

Steve was talking to Alisha Das, who was sitting right in front of me. He tipped his head down and I suddenly saw the screen in my mind's eye directly above me. It just dropped in and it was still blank. That is when I felt really drawn to work with Steve. The communication was instant, and it was clear: 'Work with him.'

Sacred Connections and Coaching

The divine influence does not cease once clients connect with Steve. Aaron Benes sent Steve this note:

Steve,

When you speak with me, I feel like God is talking directly to me. Thank you for being you, all that you did to become that, and all that you are doing with me so that I can fully step into who I am. I continually thank God for bringing you into my life—you are a blessing.

I love you. Be healthy,

Aaron

During the years Martine Cannon coached with Steve, often the night before a coaching session with Steve, she would be awakened in the middle of the night. She writes: "I'd snap bolt upright in my bed at midnight, and for two hours I would meditate. I would sit there and get downloads from Patanjali (an Indian sage who lived thousands of years ago and who wrote the *Yoga Sutras)*. I didn't even know who Patanjali was at that time, but I would be getting downloads. I'd go back to sleep, then I'd go and see Steve, and the teachings would match up."

Some people's spiritual experiences in and around Steve's work is dramatic. Many have more subtle experiences. Many express something like what Electra Ariail wrote: "Steve is a radiant exemplar of a Holy Spirit-filled being. Love directs his steps. The Divine dwells within him and informs his thoughts, his breaths, his words, and his actions . . . I believe God uses Steve to touch people, and to give them a glimpse of our Heavenly Father's love."

Vignette

Shenal Fernando

I grew up in Sri Lanka, in a Catholic family. I came to the UK when I was about eleven years old. I had so many questions about God and how to connect with God at the deepest level possible. I used to meditate and pray and have these visions. There wasn't really anyone I could speak to about them.

When I was about fourteen years old, I became involved with another religion. I studied with them for about ten years. I introduced my mom, my dad, and my brother to it. Eventually, my brother and my dad lost interest. But I had officially joined this church. I was in it, but I felt really constrained. There were so many rules and regulations. It was impossible to do all the things that God wanted me to do. Also, I wanted to connect with God at a deeper level, but they believe that miracles and visions don't happen nowadays. I love these people. They had helped me so much. They're absolutely wonderful and brilliant people, but I felt this massive conflict. So, for ten years, my prayer was always, "Father, what do you want from me?"

I quit a reputable job in central London and started a business. It failed. I then fell into the world of transformational coaching and hired Michael Serwa as my coach. Through his Instagram, I came across the name and face of an unusual man called Steve Hardison.

Subconsciously, I recalled a faint memory of me walking in a sunny, parched land in America and a man giving me his hand and offering me water, help, and to stay in his house. I don't know whether it was a dream, a vision, a memory or where it came from. It was faint and it had previously come to me when I was hiking alone in Colorado Bend State Park in Texas. It had something to do with the desert. I just had a feeling that a kind American man was going to show up in my life out of nowhere and help me to become successful and teach me everything I needed to know about life. Far-fetched? I chose to believe it.

I went to Steve Hardison's website and felt a deep resonance, an ecstatic vibration. I was so excited that I couldn't maintain any real focus. I attempted to read anyway. I wanted to connect with him, but I felt I wasn't in a position to communicate with this famous person who works with important, wealthy people. So, I let it go.

One morning, I was again moved to email him and this time I didn't resist. I wrote, "I would love to meet you one day, even if to just give you a hug." Simple. It was nothing short of a miracle when Steve replied that he would be in London the very next month and invited me to meet him at an informal meet-and-greet. I had a feeling that my life was about to be changed.

Out of sheer excitement, I arrived thirty minutes early to the London Marriott Hotel on Saturday May 11, 2019, at 3:30 p.m. and waited for him at reception with gifts of fine tea from Sri Lanka and a red T-shirt souvenir which read, "Loving you more. SF." Already a beautiful couple from the Netherlands had flown in and were waiting. As Steve walked in, I walked to him. I was the first to greet him. As our eyes connected, I felt electric love. I knew that I had known him for millennia.

Steve spoke for two hours and completely filled the room with light and holy vibrations of pure Love. Several times he told everyone about my offer to chauffeur him and his dear wife Amy around London and how I had invited them to my house for a traditional Sri Lankan dinner and music. His appreciation of me was so honest and loving; it was heartfelt. I felt his Christ-like love in my soul. It was that tangible.

As we were wrapping up and saying our goodbyes, I approached Steve and it exploded out of me. I said, "I'm pulled violently in two different directions. What does God want from me? I'm trying to force myself to live in a way that he wants." I burst out crying.

That's when Steve said, "We're going to speak after everyone leaves." After the event, we found a room. He looked at me. He was intense, even angry, but I knew it was from a place of love. He said, "What are you doing?" It was almost as if God was telling me "Come on Shenal . . . Do you really think that I would want this for you? What are you doing listening to these people? You're more connected than that. Stop being weak."

Steve started saying a few things, a few analogies, but it wasn't the words. The conversation was just a tool. I was downloading information from God. God knows me. Steve is connected to God. So, God used him to speak to me. From my time with Steve, both during the meet-and-greet event and our personal time afterwards, I felt myself expanding, expanding, expanding, unlocking, unlocking, and unlocking.

Suddenly, Steve stood up and said, "When I die, God is not going to say, 'You stole a candy bar when you were five!' He is going to say, 'You learned to love. I like that.'" In that moment, I realized that it was entirely possible that everything I thought I knew about God was wrong. Perhaps God was not the stories I had conjured up about Him. I had to rediscover God for myself experientially, and not just go along with books and traditions.

I expected Steve to come and sit back down again—and he just walked off. But I got up and hugged him. I hugged him harder than I've ever hugged a human. There was so much love there. It was incredible.

Vignette

Byron L. Applegate

I had started a new business hiring lawyers to do debt collection in all fifty states. We had contracts to do the debt collections for three of the top ten credit card issuers in the country. We had a ten-million-dollar valuation from an investment banking firm. We thought we had arrived. We were arranging the lease of a private jet—a Dassault Falcon—just two months before 9/11. In the wake of that tragedy, the value of our company tanked. All of our contracts went on hold, but our office, staff, and overhead did not. I was borrowing money at a reckless pace to try to save the company and keep up the façade of my lifestyle. On multiple occasions I could not sleep, so I just went to the office and worked through the night. I started drinking heavily and eating terribly. I was losing my mind.

One night I had a dream that is hard even for me to believe happened! If you have ever seen or read the Charles Dickens' classic *A Christmas Carol*, you know that after he dies, Ebenezer Scrooge has angels walk him through his life. Well, this night I had an angel in my dream walk me through the aftermath of my suicide. The angel was Steve Hardison. I kid you not. It was the freakiest dream of my life.

We (Steve and I) walked through the future of my family once I was gone. We went to a baseball field in a small town in Utah where my son was playing low-level baseball with no father there to watch him and no mother there either because she had to work. My wife, Cora, had moved home to her family ranch to have her family help take care of her and help raise our three children. My kids were broken. They had lost their confidence and their zeal for life. They looked lost and afraid. My wife was their sole provider, not just financially but emotionally and spiritually. Their lives were sad and empty. They were lost and it was all my fault.

I remember Steve held my hand and told me that it was not the loss of money that had left them desolate. It was the loss of their father. They needed two parents for a balance of love, guidance, and encouragement. They needed someone to believe in them and point them in the right direction. They needed a father! He shared with me how his amazing mother had raised him and his four siblings by herself. He spoke of her with pride and admiration, but also conveyed how hard it had been on her.

When I awoke in the morning my head was spinning. I was in that post-dream fog where you don't know if you are really awake or still in the dream. I felt lost. I walked out to my pool and fell in naked. I floated about looking at the sky and trying to get my head around what had just happened. Was I really that suicidal, or were these thoughts just fleeting? Was there a way out of the mess I had gotten myself into? Was the life insurance enough to take care of my family? *Cora is a beautiful girl*, I thought, *of course she will find someone better than I am.*

Then Cora came out to the pool, carrying my robe. She said,

"You had better put this on. Steve Hardison is here to see you."

At this point in our lives, Steve and I did not even speak annually. We had a screaming match a couple years before this. That had taken him off the pedestal I had placed him on. That story is neither good nor bad and not really important other than to clarify that we were not close at this point in time. Steve had never been to this house. I suppose he got the address from our Christmas card. As I walked into the living room, he grabbed me and bear-hugged me tightly with tears in his eyes.

I looked up into his big, blue eyes with a sense of shock and awe and asked him, "Steve, why are you here?"

He said, "I have been with you all night."

As I told him about the dream, he said he already knew that. He had the same dream, and when he awoke, he knew he needed to come over immediately. He needed me to know that my life was worth living and my family deserved to have a father. We spent the next few hours talking on the couch. We discussed everything from business, to family, to church, to money, to suicide.

When we talked about my business, I told him I was afraid I was going to lose everything. He kicked into coach mode and laid out the harsh reality that I was already bankrupt and was just avoiding the inevitable. He hit me right between the eyes with that type of brutal honesty only Steve Hardison can get away with. You know, where he just cuts you open with a verbal samurai sword, then nurses the wounds with love and compassion and fills you with hope. If you have ever been coached by Steven Forbes Hardison, you know exactly what I mean!

He told me who I was being and how I was responsible for the results I was experiencing. September 11 was just an event, and I was not a victim. He said he would help me rebuild and that it was only money. He helped me see that I have what it takes to do so, but I had to live in order to do it. He helped me see that my family could not replace me.

In true Steve Hardison fashion, he made me give him my word and commit that before I did anything to end my life, I would call him and give him the chance to talk me through it. If you know Steve, then you know that your word is all you have, and commitment is how we know what to do next. He told me I was not safe to be alone and I was not safe to drive. He again had me give him my word I would not drive for a week and I had to check in with him before I could start driving again.

I spent the next week having someone by my side 24/7. I rode with friends wherever they were going, just to avoid driving. I even went golfing with a friend and his buddies just to ride in the cart, since I was not a golfer at the time. I told my wife the truth about how bad things were and spoke with Steve multiple times. I shut down my company and sold my house. I went through Chapter 7 Bankruptcy and started over. The weird thing is, the bankruptcy was a huge relief. It was like somebody took the elephant off my chest. In a rental house, I still slept in the same bed, with my same beautiful wife. I pet the same dog and rediscovered my children. I rebuilt my life. Thank you, Steve, for saving it!

Chapter 32

The Cost of Coaching

"When I first learned about Steve Hardison," says coach Lisa Hale, "the first thing I heard, to be really blunt, was how much he charges his clients. I was kind of gobsmacked by that. My first thought was 'What kind of a coach would you have to be to command those fees?'"

Then she heard Steve has an extensive waiting list. It would take years if he were to coach everyone on the list. Twice gobsmacked, she considered, "What kind of a coach would you have to be to command those fees *and* have a waiting list that long?"

Steve answers that question with an analogy that is timeless, but which is spoken in the context of the early 2000s, when he first said it. He says:

> If you go over to Bank One Ballpark at game time, you will see a man who is almost seven feet tall. His name is Randy Johnson. He has won the Cy Young award five times. In 2004, he pitched a perfect game. That means you don't walk anyone. There are no errors. No one scores. There have been

only twenty-three perfect games ever pitched in the history of Major League Baseball. Randy Johnson pitched a perfect game when he was forty years old, the oldest pitcher in the history of Major League Baseball to do so.

If you drive around the valley, you will see intersections where there are day laborers standing at the corners, hoping they will get hired that day for minimum wage. If you keep driving, you can find plenty of doctors and attorneys who are making six-figure incomes. If you drive to Bank One Ballpark, you can watch Randy Johnson pitch for the Diamondbacks. He is getting paid $52.4 million. Why? Because there are very, very few people who can pitch a perfect game and throw a baseball one hundred miles an hour. But that's not all.

If a pitcher throws the ball at one hundred miles an hour and it's right across the center of the plate, any Major League Baseball player can hit it out of the park. What makes Randy Johnson so valuable is he can throw a ball at one hundred miles an hour and he can put it on the edges of the strike zone so that when the batter connects, the ball will likely be on the ground or popped up.

The fewer people that can do something, the more a person who can do that thing gets paid. No one does what I do when I coach.

Scott Parker is one of many who holds the same opinion. He says, "Believe me, Steve is worth every dollar. When I was sitting with Steve, I never thought about the money. In fact, if anything, I thought he doesn't charge enough. I was thinking, 'This stuff he is doing is magic. This is the most unbelievable thing I've ever seen.'"

But that's not the only reason Steve charges what he does. It is also about commitment. Lisa Haisha says, "Anyone who pays that kind of money is not going to pay it and then go back to who they were. Working with Steve is a really strong investment in your life. I'm going to get back tenfold of what I spent because it's going to shift who I am as a person. And that's what started happening. Just boom. Everyone's like, 'What is going on here?'"

There is yet another reason. "He charges that fee because of what it draws out of his clients," says Rich Litvin. "They have to tap into resources they never knew they had. They have to enroll their wife, husband, or business partner. And they have to show up in a way that never seemed possible before they chose to work with Steve. The value they get *before* they have even begun coaching with Steve is extraordinary."

In the gap between paying Steve and beginning his coaching, Townsend Wardlaw reflected, "This may sound a little strange, but if Steve dropped dead tomorrow and I never got to actually work with him, I already got my value. I got my ROI [return on investment] on my two hundred grand. My whole world has shifted from our one conversation."

Gina Carlson shares her experience:

On February 1, 2014, I showed up at Steve Hardison's office with a check for $150,000 to begin our journey. On a side note, how I even came up with that much money (twice, because I had multiple agreements with him) to pay Steve's fee astonished me, and all without mortgaging my house, borrowing or going into debt. This in and of itself was no small feat for this working, single mom. And full disclosure, I did ask Steve for the single mom discount. He replied, "I would never do that to you; I would never de-value you like that. You are a powerful creator and if you really want to work with me, how you will pay my full fee will occur for you."

I left his office in a quandary. By the time I flew back to Los Angeles, I had come up with seven possibilities for how I could pay his fee. It was almost like the accomplishment of creating the money to pay his fee was so beyond what I ever would have thought possible that I didn't even need the coaching after that.

Martine Cannon was so committed to work with Steve, that she was willing to sell her home. "I knew my life was more important than my property. But as soon as I was committed to selling my house, other options popped up. Someone said to me, 'You have plenty of equity in your house. Let's just release that.' I replied, 'I know that money can be released for renovations. Well, this [pointing to herself] is the house that is being renovated.'"

Jeff Dinsdale was twenty-three when he hired Steve as a coach. "I went through a lot to create the funds to work with Steve. My first day sitting in his office, I said, 'Now I know why you charge what you charge.'"

"Why is that?"

"It is because now I know I don't need you."

"You got it," Steve said. "You got it."

The fees Steve charges commit his clients to be fully engaged in their work. But it is not a unilateral commitment. They also commit Steve. Right? If he is going to charge what he does, he had better deliver. Right? Nope. Steve is crystal clear on this. Ask him, and you will feel his energy start to rise. He guarantees that he will step into his office with one hundred percent of his heart, mind, and energy. The rest is up to his client.

"If you hire me thinking I am going to make it happen, you're nuts!" says Steve. It's a clear message he sends to each of his clients. The words may vary. To Clate Mask, he said, "Clate, you will get your desired outcome if you do what you agree to do during our coaching sessions. But this isn't about me. It's about you. Think of it as going to the gym and I'm your trainer. If I do the sit-ups, it's not going to make your abs tighter. This is on you. You are responsible to take what we create in the office and make it happen." It's a lesson that is sometimes learned the hard way.

Tom McGovern says of his coaching experience, "Frankly, one of my objectives wasn't met. It was a business goal. And clearly, it was on me." Steve will coach, share, direct, and inspire, but his client is responsible to act. McGovern goes on to say, "I recently looked back over my notes. The first note I read was something that I still haven't nailed down. Had I really embraced it, it would have changed the last ten years. Steve absolutely saw it and he had the solution for it. The stuff he shared with me and how he shared it was brilliant."

Do these misses depreciate Tom's coaching experience? Tom relates:

> One of the objectives we created during our time together was about me parenting my then young son. I'll never forget it. He said, "You say you want to be a good parent, but the truth is that you want to parent your daughter. You don't really want to parent your son." And he was right. We worked on that. Together we shifted how I was being with my son, and it changed everything. We have a fabulous relationship. So, was it worth $150,000 plus travel time and cost? Yeah, absolutely. Absolutely.

The stuff that comes up around money can be difficult. Jordan

Dangelo was getting married in a month. A month before that, his fiancée (now wife) lost her job. It was stressful. Jordan had a nest egg. He could use it for a down payment on a house or he could hire Steve for ten hours. It was an easy decision for him. It wasn't so easy for his fiancée. He went with the ten hours. He writes, "Every two hours was an experience unlike any other. Time stopped as we dove into everything in my mind that was limiting me. I learned the true meaning behind forgiving oneself. These ten hours changed my life. My marriage has been absolutely blessed by my ability to forgive myself and just simply love."

Tom McGovern relates this experience from 2010:

We were set up for our session and Steve said, "Hey, have you seen the movie *The King's Speech*?"

"No."

"Well, it is showing in a half an hour. Do you want to go?"

"Okay. I guess so. I thought we were going to have a coaching session."

I'm thinking, "That's a $3,000 movie. It better be a damn good movie."

About halfway through the movie, I don't know why I'm there. I'm getting a little bit pissed because I'm spending $3,000 for a movie. I didn't see the value. But then there was a part in the movie where the king looked over at the speech therapist who was helping him overcome his stammer and he said, "I have a voice."

Steve looked at me and I looked at him. I was like, "Yeah, that's me." I am not quiet, but I can take the backseat to people. That was the $3,000 lesson: I have a voice. It was worth it all. Whether it takes a minute or two hours, the point of coaching is to make the point. And the point was made. It was the most expensive movie ever, but it was great.

Steve recognizes that issues about money can be hard, but his focus is not on the cost. It is on the value. Stephen McGhee says, "The value he provides is exponentially greater than his fee." Cost is quantifiable. Value is less so, but just as real. Aaron Benes says, "Every single session, there's at least one miracle, and usually multiple miracles. He got me to see my self-worth. I don't know how I could ever put a price on that."

Ethan Okura uses an analogy. "Without a doubt, the value I have received from working with Steve far exceeds the value I received from my Columbia Law School education, which I prize dearly."

One afternoon, Steve was coaching with Andrew Lehto. Andrew looked over at him and said, "Can I tell you something? You have earned your annual fee, just in what you taught me right now." That happened six times in that one session.

After the sixth time, Steve said, "You know, that is now $1,200,000 of value just from today. I'm a great value."

Vignette

John Patrick Morgan

"100 Hours with Steve Hardison"

The following is abridged from a video John Patrick made and posted on the internet.

I flew out just for a two-hour meeting. We sat in his living room. He asked me two questions: "Who are you?" and "Why are you here?"

"My whole life," I said, "I've learned to excel by hanging out with the best people in the world. As far as I can see, you're the best in the world at coaching and creating, and I want to be around you. And there's another reason. My experience of you is that the way you live is truly fearless." Later, we created a name for living fearlessly. We called it "nothing," as in having nothing between my intuition and my action. I wanted to work with Steve to create more nothingness in my life.

After my two-hour *Be With* session with Steve, I said, "I'll be back. I want to work with you. I just have to create the money."

At that point, I was making probably just under $250,000 a year. I was going to have to come up with $150,000 to invest in coaching. I wasn't sitting on that much cash for sure. It would take a while, but I was going to do it.

Two years went by. Long story short, it didn't happen. I realized in the summer of 2016, that wanting it wasn't creating it. On August 23, I sent Steve an email. "By Christmas Day this year, I will have the money to work with you."

Short email back. "Great, looking forward to it."

Then I realized, "Oh shit, with taxes and expenses and all the other stuff, I have to make more than $200,000 in the next four months. I had never made that much in a year in my current business."

I was determined not to go to a place of scarcity or acquisition, or to overwork so I was ignoring my family, or any of the ways that might produce the money but would be counter to the whole point of hiring Steve. That would be hypocritical.

A week before Christmas, I was 100 percent short of my $150,000.

I pulled it together by Christmas Eve. I made all the money I needed to make. I was able to email Steve on Christmas Day. "I'm in!"

When I sent him the money in one lump sum, my hands started to sweat.

"Wire transfer is complete."

"Oh, where's the undo button? You can't do that? Oh shit." My heart started to race. Just telling the story right now, my palms are starting to sweat again. I just transferred six figures, way more than I have ever spent to buy anything before. I didn't even put that much down on a house. I thought, "Oh shit, what if he dies?"

I created my answer: Even if he dies, I'm still going to spend one hundred hours in his office. I'm going to read his books. I'm going to read his notes. I'm going to sit there. I'm going to coach myself. And, this is the important part, I committed to creating the return on investment no matter what. At that point, I wanted to create a ten-fold return on my $150,000.

Steve told me on our first day that I was welcome to show up at his office thirty minutes before our sessions. The door would be unlocked and the office ready. For the next fifty trips to Phoenix, I took an early flight out of Los Angeles. I pulled up to his driveway, thirty-one, sometimes thirty-two, minutes early. I walked really slowly so that I would get into his office exactly thirty minutes early. I wanted to be in that space every single minute I had access to it. It was a big deal for me. It was a big deal financially. But it was also a big deal because of who Steve is.

There's an aura that surrounds this man. There are stories of him being loving and powerful in a way that you don't really experience on Mother Earth. Steve and I have gone on field trips as part of my coaching. I experienced his love and his power firsthand, not just through stories. He is present and loving with every living being he comes across, whether it's the homeless person, the billionaire that shows up at his house for coaching, or the tortoise that lives in his backyard. Same love, same presence.

To be with somebody who is that way is a gift. Why? Because we learn through emulation. Steve's way of loving everything and everyone in the world rubs off on you. When I look back at the hundred hours I spent with Steve, the most valuable thing I learned was how to love: how to love others (despite what you might see in them or not see in them), how to love everything (despite what it might look like or not look like to you), and how to love myself. I have grown so much in my capacity to love myself. If this were the only thing I got from working with Steve, it was worth what I paid, ten times over.

The reason I wanted to work with Steve is I wanted the power that he has, the power to create in the world, the power to create the kind of business he has, and the power to create miracles. And I wanted to create through love. Steve is a powerful man with a loving way of being. That is what I wanted to be.

Over the hundred hours we worked together, Steve and I looked at all of the ideas that I had about myself that were an obstacle to me being who I really am. What does that mean? I have thoughts about myself and the world when I feel fear and I have thoughts about myself and the world when I'm feeling loved. I call the loving thoughts "who I really am," and the fearful thoughts "who I'm not."

We spent two years looking at all of the ways I was seeing myself from fear and changing them, one idea at a time. I was able to access new ways of seeing that were more loving. I would take those home and practice believing them.

I wish I could take you into every single session and every single conversation we had and show you the gifts I received through being with Steve. I wish you could see how I left his office walking on a cloud, feeling so confident in myself, so happy, so peaceful, so certain.

I hope you are having some thoughts of skepticism. "How is this possible? How can one man be so wonderful? Is John Patrick Morgan just some guy who linked into the Steve Hardison myth and fell for it all?"

Maybe, but I don't think so. You see, I'm not your average

follower. I don't like following people. I'm very much a maverick. I'm not really a part of many communities. I'm kind of an outsider. I really despise the idea of following somebody in such a way that you abdicate your own personal uniqueness and power and responsibility. So, I brought very heavy skepticism to my work with Steve Hardison. It was perfect because we had some really great conversations about some ideas I had about Steve that were an obstacle to our work.

Regarding the fear that people get drawn into Steve's orbit and then lose their sense of self and their center, or the idea that they are just following some great salesperson, it's so not that. Unlike some kind of manipulative leader who just wants people following him, the closer people get to Steve, the more he helps them find themselves. Steve has an incredible power to help people find their own truth and their own uniqueness. It creates this incredible magnetism that moves people towards him. The closer they get, the less they need him. The more they love themselves and the less they judge themselves, the less they need him. And that's why at the end of our one hundred hours, I'm even more comfortable not having Steve in my life than I was before.

Our work has changed the destiny of my entire family, my wife, my son, my mother, my clients, and people I've worked with over the past couple of years when we've been working together. The best decision I have ever made is to work with Steve Hardison . . . Okay. The best decision I ever made was to marry my wife and to have my kids. But the other best decision I ever made is working with Steve.

Love is, you are that, so much.

Vignette

Clate Mask

In December 2009, Clate Mask committed to start coaching with Steve in March 2010. This vignette picks up the story on March 9, 2010.

Steve was expecting me to show up with a check at 3:00 p.m. and start our coaching. I called him at lunchtime and left him a message: "Hi, Steve. This is Clate Mask. We're supposed to start coaching today. I just want you to know that I am committed to coaching with you, but I can't start today. Confidentially, we're doing a layoff in the company and I'm working on all the details of that."

In my mind, it was crystal clear that if I was going to lay off ten percent of my employees, I was not going to take money—some of which would be personal, some of which would be company—and put it into coaching. That just wouldn't look right, and it wouldn't be right for our employees. So, I left a perfectly reasonable message, and thought that I was off the hook.

He called me back. "Clate, I just want you to know that if you're committed, we'll be meeting today at 3:00. And if you are getting ready to do a layoff, there's nothing more important that you could do than to meet with me to figure out how you're going to navigate these challenges."

It really struck me how he didn't just beat me over the head with my commitment, which he could have done. Rather, he reminded me of my commitment. It was also striking to me how confident he was in the value of the coaching that he would deliver.

"If you want to keep your commitment," Steve said, "I'll see you at 3:00." Now, at the time, we didn't have a ton of money in our bank account. I'll put it this way. It would reduce our balance by more than half. It was a big deal to do that. I went to the bank, got the money out, put it in this little box, and went to his office and sat down.

That was the beginning of our coaching. My head was full of all kinds of concerns about having to lay off people. There was board unrest, even mutiny going on. There were so many issues at the time. Those first few months were super tumultuous in the business.

Shortly after I started working with Steve, we had a really rough board meeting because the company had performed so poorly during the first quarter of the year. One board member in particular was telling the other board members that they should replace me. Then at the July board meeting, things erupted. One board member was calling me out. I got upset, and he got upset, and there were fireworks. It came down to this: either he was going to go, or I was going to go.

There was a lot of evidence to suggest that they were going to replace me. So, I had what I considered to be a well-reasoned fear. Steve helped me face the fear, understand that fear, and see how that fear was holding me back from being the leader I needed to be.

When my lead board member came out to meet with me, I knew the meeting was to either fire me or back me. She sat down; I sat down. I explained to her: "I see the issue. This is what I've done. I've taken care of this. I've resolved that. I'm working on this. This is what's going to happen when I do. We're going to get the company back into a safe place. We'll be cashflow positive by the end of the year. You can take that to the bank."

She sat back in her chair and said, "Okay, I was hoping I would hear something like that. Let's do this."

Later, our corporate attorney told me, "I've seen this type of dynamic many times in my career where the board presses on the CEO. And I've never seen it work out the way this worked out. I'm honestly scratching my head about how you did this. In my career, this isn't how it goes. How did you do it? I genuinely want to know."

I said, "I work with a coach and he's really amazing. He helped me see what I needed to see in order to work my way out of this."

"I figured you must have been talking to somebody, because there's no way a venture-backed entrepreneur could do what you did." He went on, "I'm intrigued. What did your coach tell you?"

It was nothing he told me. Steve didn't tell me to do anything. He helped me see how my fear was preventing me from being the leader that I needed to be. And he helped me see that if I had that fear, then the board should fire me because I wasn't leading the way I needed to lead. He woke me up to lead and helped me get rid of my fear.

What price do I put on my coaching with Steve?

The most recent valuation of the company put it at $500 million. If I hadn't coached with Steve, I would have lost the company.

Chapter 33

The Millennials

S teve doesn't coach for money. He charges what he does so people are committed. Steve is clear there are things far more important than money.

Mark Silverman was ready to hire Steve, until he learned he would need to fly from his home in Virginia to Phoenix every two weeks. With two young kids, he knew "that ain't happening." But he stayed in contact with Steve over the next five or six years.

Mark was excited when he heard that Steve was speaking at Steve Chandler's and Rich Litvin's event in London. Here was a way to see Hardison face-to-face. Then Mark learned that his son had the opportunity to play baseball in Spain. Ten days of baseball and sightseeing in Spain—and Mark could go with him. It was at the same time as the London event. Mark called Steve and said he could fly from Spain to attend the event in London and then rejoin his son a day or two later. Steve said, "If you leave your son to come see me, I will refuse to see you. You spend every moment of those ten days with your son."

Other evidence that Steve's fees are a means to an end and not the end in itself are the people Steve has coached *pro bono*, particularly, those of the rising generation. Below, four millennials share their experiences with Steve in their own words.

Robert Harding

I was about seventeen years old. I was in high school. I was playing on the football team and enjoying life. We had what was historically a really, really horrible football team. Surprisingly, this year we put together a squad that was doing amazing and was making news, at least locally.

Steve came to one of our games. We were supposed to steamroll this team, and we were getting beat up in the first half. Steve came down to our sidelines. I didn't know who Steve was. To me, he was just some random guy running down our sidelines screaming at our players. At half time, he was in our locker room. [Note: Steve's friend and Mesa High's football coach, Kelley Moore, had invited Steve both to stand on the sidelines and to come to the locker room.]

I don't remember the full details of what he said. I just remember it really moved me. Steve was banging on lockers and telling us about our potential, how great we were, and how fantastic it would be for the city if we played well. He closed with, "You guys have the potential to be the greatest. Why don't you go do that?" We went out and played the best half of football our team had ever played.

A few months later, he was at our football banquet at the end of the year. Once again, Steve saw the potential in this group of high school guys. The school wasn't the most affluent. There were a lot of kids that needed help, kids who probably weren't going to go to college. He saw that.

At the banquet, he gave another awesome speech. Once again, I don't remember what he said word for word or even any of the highlights of it, but I knew in my heart that this guy knew what he was talking about. This was someone I needed to pay attention to. At the end of his speech, he made an invitation. "I have a dozen books here. Anybody is welcome to take one. Read it. I have my card in there too. If you had a good experience, give me a call."

I was eighteen. I had just gotten out of high school. I didn't want something to read. I wanted to have fun and do my thing before I went to college. But he had had such an impact on me, I picked up a book. Out of eighty kids, I was the only person who took a book. I read it in the next two days. I sent him an email and said, "Hey, this is awesome. The book was great. You've had such a great impact on me. I don't know what it means. I just feel inspired by you. I just wanted to let you know that."

I was the only person who reached out to him. I'm glad that I did because from there, he took me under his wing. I was a kid graduating from high school. I didn't have any money, but I met with him once a month, emailed with him, and called him. I took a lot of his time. Looking back, knowing how much people pay to be coached by him, it's amazing that he took so much time out of his busy schedule to coach an eighteen-year-old kid that had no prospects. I didn't know what I was doing with my life. He took time to share with me what was good in his life and what could be good in my life. A lot of things came from that one decision to reach out to him.

Every single second I was with him, his focus was one hundred percent on me. I felt like I was the only one in the world, even though his wife was in the room next door, even though he had a million other things going on, even though I wasn't paying him a dime. I was his focus. That completely changed me. It helped me realize that his way of being was something I wanted to implement in my life.

I ended up converting to The Church of Jesus Christ of Latter-day Saints and going on a mission. Before I left on my mission, Steve committed me to make it the best experience I had ever had. He wrote me consistently. He helped me out financially. He was always, always there for me. He taught me to go out and create each day. Every day is a masterpiece. Go out and give it one hundred percent and create. That was always in the back of my head. As a result, I had a very successful mission.

When I came back home and started my own life, he was in the background of everything that I was doing. I didn't know he was talking me up to so many different people. I had no clue. I probably had a dozen job interviews because of him. I met his sons, Blake and Clint. I am partners with them in commercial real estate. I now have a career I can succeed with. Steve has set me up financially for the rest of my life. I wouldn't have this if it weren't for Steve. My best friends are his two sons. We have spent pretty much every day together for the past six years.

If I went back and stacked up all the hours that he spent on me, coaching me or putting me in a position to succeed, it would be hundreds of hours, simply because he wanted to help one kid out. Steve has altered the course of my life. And not just me, but now my son, and eventually my son's son. Generations to come have been completely changed.

Todd Runyan

I was a young teenager when I first met Steve. My family had moved in just down the street from him. We were in the same church congregation. A lot of people thought Steve was a little eccentric.

Steve essentially doesn't care what anyone thinks about him.

I had my most profound experience with him when I was a junior in high school. I don't know how it happened, but I think Steve extended an invitation to meet with me to my parents. My parents and I met with him. It was an interesting meeting. Steve took Post-it notes and started sticking them on his head and going through some distinctions about thoughts and language. I remember I didn't really want to open up with my parents there. Steve picked up on that and asked me if I wanted to meet with him one-on-one. I took him up on that.

The biggest thing in my life at the time was sports. I was naturally really good at the 300-meter hurdles. Because the hurdles were spaced out, my hurdle form didn't need to be that good. I could catch up sprinting between the hurdles. So, I was pretty good at that event.

But the 110 high hurdles were a different story. That was a nightmare. I couldn't even run the race correctly in my head. Even in my visualization I was crashing.

Steve helped change all of that. I met with Steve for about a month, for four sessions. One of the things that came out of that was the creation of what Steve termed the "velvet bullet." He said, "I want you to feel like you're smooth and super fast over the hurdles."

That was cool, and it helped with my hurdles, but that wasn't the distinction that shifted things for me. It was when Steve said, "You are extraordinary, brilliant, and free." That one took hold of me and is still a part of me today. EBF. That enabled me to get out of my head.

I went from being a Junior Varsity athlete in that event in my sophomore year to fifth in the state in my junior year. And then in my senior year, I was the state champion. I attribute almost all of that to the work I did with Steve.

I have tried to do with other people what Steve did with me. I couldn't. It's not formulaic. You can't reproduce it by going through the steps. The best way I could describe it was that Steve was a conduit allowing me to see my potential. It's hard for me to overstate what he has done for me in my life.

Sebastian Hidalgo

I have known Steve since I was three years old. When my family moved into the neighborhood, Steve and Amy immediately came to our front porch with a warm welcome, a set of plastic drinking cups, and a trampoline for my siblings and me, who were all under the age of seven. My family's relationship with Steve quickly became intimate.

In 2012, when I was fourteen years old, Steve approached me, with his gleaming eyes, large smile and towering stature, and asked me if I would consider being his personal landscaper at his home. He told me that he would give me time to think about it and that we could arrange a date and a time for us to meet at his home and go over the responsibilities that I would be accepting. I accepted the opportunity. We met on the given day and he explained with great detail what he expected of me. At the time, my high school did not hold classes on Fridays, so I agreed to go to Steve's house each Friday morning to do my job. There were days when I needed to arrive as early as 3:00 and 4:00 a.m. in order to complete my work at Steve's and also fulfill other responsibilities for that particular day.

After each workday, I would let Steve know that I was finished for the day. We would then do a thorough walk-around of the exterior of his home to ensure that I did an acceptable job. He would praise me for my work, and then he would share invaluable life principles. Five of the principles Steve shared with me are:

1. **Limitation creates value.** If there were a million people who could play basketball like Lebron James, nobody would know who Lebron James is. The more limited you are, the more valuable you become.
2. **Whatever it is that you are doing in the moment, be the best in the world at it**.
3. **Create a lens through which you see the world.** You control what affects YOUR world. What you allow to enter your world shapes who you become.
4. **Be My Word (BMW). If you make commitments, keep them**. If Steve tells you that he will be at a certain place at a certain time, he will be there at that time. If he says he will spend X minutes with you, expect for him to spend exactly X minutes—no more, no less.
5. **Fear does not exist in the world.** I could never bring Steve a cup of fear. You cannot find fear. You can only create it in yourself.

Fast forward eight years. I had graduated from high school, served a mission, enrolled in college, and gotten married. Steve came up to me at church and said, "I'd like to give you this watch." It was a $3,000 watch. He had bought it in Switzerland. I loved it because Steve gave it to me.

A few months later, Steve asked me how my wife and I were doing. I said, "We're young and we're poor, just like any young married couple, but we are loving it." Steve offered to buy the watch back from me for what he originally paid for it. I refused. The gift has a lot more value to me than the $3,000 because it came from

Steve. I was moved that he was essentially going to buy his watch twice so he could help us out. You're always going to win when you work with Steve.

David Bennett

I was a bad student in high school. We had an academically strong school, so bad around here is being a "B" student. That's about what I was. I was not really interested in college or med school. I was into building guitars. I'm good with my hands. I was going to do that for my profession. Then I realized that building guitars probably wasn't the best career choice. "Well," I thought, "I guess I'll be an orthopedic surgeon."

That isn't as random as it sounds. My little brother had arthrogryposis, which is a really severe bone defect disease. He had a bunch of surgeries at the Shriners Hospital in Utah. They actually lengthened his bones. So, orthopedics had caught my interest.

Steve was very encouraging. He thought it would be a great career and a great direction for my life. I said, "Yeah, but I'm not smart. How am I going to do that?"

Steve taught me that if I wanted something, I should write it ten times every day. He also taught me how to visualize my goal.

"All right. That's a simple thing." So, I started doing that.

I didn't realize you had to go to med school to be a surgeon. I thought it was a separate thing. It seems dumb now, but I thought it was a separate journey. I knew you had to get good grades to get into med school. I had no clue how to do that. But I used that same technique. Every single day I wrote it down: "I, David, get perfect grades." I got great grades in undergrad and went to med school at Howard University in Washington, D.C. Steve and Amy flew out to my graduation. It was just my family and Steve and Amy. I did well in med school and matched into my first choice in orthopedics at the University of Arizona.

In all the time I spent with Steve, he never told me what I should do. I chose what I wanted to do, and he showed me how to reach it.

Visualizing has made me a better surgeon. Before every surgery, I go through every step in my mind. I usually write it out so my team also knows each step. I have found that the outcomes are far superior when I do that. It's staggering how much better the outcomes are. The surgery goes twice as fast, with about an eighth of the negative outcome. I learned that from Steve.

Of all the principles Steve taught me, visualization was the biggest one. I would say that is something everyone should know how to do. Honestly, I can't even imagine what my life would be like without it. Steve really helped me shape the direction of my life.

Chapter 34

TBOLITNFL

TBOLITNFL is a mouthful, until you realize it is simply the acronym for "The Best Offensive Lineman in the NFL."

But it is more than an acronym. It is a story, an event, a video, a website, and an experience. It appears to be about a football player. It's not. Lorraine Warren got that. Ten years after watching the video, she emailed Steve: "I remember you asking me to watch the video TBOLITNFL. What you don't know is that I cried for several days after watching that film. The possibility that I saw for my life really scared me and brought me to my knees."

TBOLITNFL provokes knee-buckling possibility. It is a wake-up call, but not like xylophone tones, birds chirping, or even annoying techno beeps. It's like the errant fire alarm in the middle of the night that jolts you out of sleep and shoots adrenaline through your system. It says, "Wake up. It's time to live big."

It was Sunday morning, September 5, 2010. Printed newspapers were still a thing. Steve was perusing the Arizona Republic and saw that Matt Leinart—a former starting quarterback for USC, a Heisman Trophy winner, and a first-round draft pick—had been released from the Arizona Cardinals. This man had talent, yet ESPN was saying nobody wanted to pick him up. The Arizona paper was saying, "He's a washout." Steve knew he could help Matt Leinart with the critical missing piece—his thinking—if he could speak to him in person.

Steve contacted his friend and former Cardinal, Vai Sikahema, who gave Steve the phone number for Deuce Lutui, a teammate of Leinart's. When Steve and Deuce connected on Monday morning, Steve explained that he could help Matt. "Deuce, it's what I do for a living. I work with people's thoughts. But I can't do it on the phone."

"So," said Deuce, "you only do this face-to-face?"

"Yes."

"You won't be able to help Matt then. He's gone to Texas. He's with the Houston Texans." That information had not yet been released.

Steve thanked Deuce and was ready to hang up when Deuce blurted, "Would you do with me what you were going to do with Matt?"

Steve heard the hunger. He liked that. "Deuce, I can't do with you what I was going to do with Matt Leinart. You're not Matt. But I can do with you what I can do with you."

Deuce had one day off a week, Tuesdays. Steve invited Deuce to look at his schedule and find a Tuesday in the future where he could meet with Steve for two or three hours. Steve would make it work with his schedule.

"Tomorrow is Tuesday," said Deuce.

"I have clients tomorrow."

"Can I come tonight?" asked Deuce.

Steve could work with that kind of desire. Steve had a family dinner that night, but he agreed to meet with Deuce between his clients the next day. "And Deuce," said Steve, "come on time—American time, not Tongan time. If you're late, we don't meet."

Deuce showed up early. When Steve opened the door, a massive Tongan loomed in the doorway. Deuce was 6'4", 386 pounds. He filled up his 5X jersey. He had tattoo sleeves on his arms and legs. He looked formidable—except for his smile.

Steve invited him into his family room. "Deuce, tell me about yourself," prompted Steve. Deuce spoke about living in Tonga, coming to America, and the car accident that killed his sister and put his father and brother in a coma. He talked about his wife, his children, and his God. After forty-five minutes, Steve invited Deuce into his office.

Deuce took one step into his office and backed out. He had sensed the sacred. "What do you do in here?"

"We create miracles," said Steve.

Deuce took his shoes off and stepped in with reverence.

"Deuce, do you have anything else you want to say before we begin?"

Deuce spoke for forty-five more minutes. When he had nothing left to say, Steve said, "Deuce, I have just one question for you." Steve leaned forward in his chair. "Who is the best offensive lineman in the NFL?"

Deuce looked up in thought. He was checking his NFL Rolodex.

"Thanks for answering my question, Deuce."

"But . . . I didn't answer your question."

"Oh, you did. It was loud and clear."

"I'm confused. What are you talking about?"

"Ok. Let's change places. Just pretend I am Deuce Lutui. Ask me, 'Who is the best offensive lineman in the NFL?'"

"Okay . . . Who is the best offensive lineman in the NFL?"

Steve vaulted from his chair, grabbed Deuce by the shirt with both hands and roared, "IF YOU HAD ANY IDEA WHO I WAS, YOU WOULDN'T ASK ME SUCH A STUPID QUESTION!" Steve kicked his chair with his exploding energy. Then Steve brought the volume down and the intensity up. It was far more unnerving. "Listen. I am Deuce Lutui and *I am* the best offensive lineman in the NFL. That's who I am."

Steve stood up, smiled, and said in a conversational tone, "Deuce, we're out of time. I have a client coming shortly."

Deuce looked dazed. He stepped outside the office and slid into his sandals.

"Deuce," said Steve, "if you got that inside of you, your whole world would change."

Steve walked Deuce out to his truck. With each step, possibility dawned. By the time Deuce reached his truck, he said, "Steve, I want you to fly to St. Louis on Sunday. I want you to watch me play football. I want you to go to all my away games. I want you to come to all the home games. We can put you up with the team."

"Deuce, you can count on me *not* doing that. But I will make you one deal. Drive somewhere, sit quietly, and think about what happened in the past three hours. Then go to my website and read it carefully. Sauté in it. Read everything my clients say about working with me, but read it as if it were about you. If you do that, I will come to your first home game. If you don't want to do that, it was nice meeting you."

Clate Mask, Steve's next client, arrived as Deuce was climbing into his truck.

"Who was that?" Clate asked, as Deuce drove away.

Steve gave him the short version.

Clate said, "Let me know if you hear back from him."

That night at 9:50, Deuce sent Steve this email:

> A few things I wrote down after our session and going onto your website:
>
> This has locked my future and has secured my goals
> The best in the game!!!
> The best OL in the NFL!!! best pro bowler there is!!!!
> Best at my craft!!!! Best on the team!!!!
> Captain!!!!! PAID!!!!!!!!! I AM!!!!!!!!!!
> The scary thing is this isn't enough for me nor good enough.
>
> Love you brother.
>
> I want you to witness this at every game, at every play. Please let me have you at every game you are able to make. It will bless my life to know you're behind me, literally watching my every move!
>
> Again, The best in the game!!! The best OL in the NFL!!! best pro bowler there is!!!! Best at my craft!!!! Best on the team!!!!
> Captain!!!!! PAID!!!!!!!!! I AM!!!!!!!!!!
> Ofa atu
> TBOLITNFL
>
> Deuce Lutui

At 9:50 p.m., September 7, 2010, TBOLITNFL was born.

The first thing Steve did was respond to Deuce: "Deuce, powerful, like you. So let it be written. So let it be done!!!"

The second thing Steve did was give Clate an update. Clate wrote back: "I am a God-serving man, a great father, and the CEO of a billion-dollar software company called Infusionsoft." TBOLITNFL was only minutes old and it was already creating possibility.

Launching the Vision

True to form, Steve shared the Deuce Lutui story with his family, friends, clients, and the people he saw at the car wash, the mall, and the grocery store—pretty much everyone. Steve's son, Blake, told the owner of his company, who called Steve and asked him to come and share the experience with his company. Steve said, "That's not what I do." But the owner persisted. He touched Steve at a tender spot. "Your son works here. Come help our company."

Steve agreed. "I'll give you one hour."

They met at King's Fish House restaurant in Tempe. They expected twelve people. There were sixty. They were packed into a room that accommodated forty-eight. Steve shared the story with his signature passion. People were inspired, but not because one football player was electrified by his possibility. Deuce was everyman. People walked out of King's Fish House inspired by who they could be and what they could do.

The King's Fish House audience didn't just think about what Steve said. They gave the story electronic wings. They gave heft to it as a movement. One person created a website where the written story was posted. One man rented a billboard so that for eight seconds out of every minute, twenty-four hours a day, for thirty days, "TBOLITNFL" flashed at the cars driving on the freeway.

Steve shared the story over and over, so often the tellings strained his voice. After Steve rasped the story to Dr. Gibson in

California, the doctor enrolled his friend, Julie Blake, a vocal coach, to help. Soon, she was on the phone telling Steve what he needed to do to restore his voice. When he could speak, Steve shared the Deuce Lutui story with her.

"Would you come to Utah and do what you did at the restaurant?"

"That's not what I do. And I don't love traveling."

However, it just so happened that Amy was presenting a paper at the Sperry Symposium at Brigham Young University on October 29, 2010. They were already going to be in Utah. If Julie wanted to make something happen on October 30, Steve would do it. Julie took on producing the event. She even got Steve to agree to do something he never does. He let her tape the event.

Fifty-four days after TBOLITNFL was born, Steve was standing in a room at the University of Utah, speaking to an audience of six hundred people. He spoke from his heart as he related the series of events that brought Deuce to his home. He re-enacted the pivotal moment in his office, with Chris Dorris acting as proxy for Deuce. Even though Chris had been at King's Fish House, even though Chris knew it was a re-creation, when Steve grabbed his shirt and got in his face, Chris was rattled. "I was so proud that he chose me for that moment. That was pretty great, but at the same time I was scared shitless. I was afraid this could actually get out of hand." It didn't. But Chris's shirt, his favorite Greg Norman shirt, was a casualty to Steve's exuberance.

Steve finished telling the story of Deuce, then he drove home his message. "Listen. Commitment rocks the world. You want something to shift in your marriage? You want something to shift at work? You want something to shift at school? Get committed. When you are committed, the world lines up to support your commitment.

It's like a black hole. Commitment has gravitational power. Everything you need moves to the commitment."

Steve read a statement by W. H. Murray from *The Scottish Himalayan Expedition:* "Until one is committed, there is hesitancy, the chance to draw back, always ineffectiveness . . . The moment one definitely commits oneself, then providence moves too. A whole stream of events issues from the decision, raising in one's favor all manner of unforeseen incidents, meetings and material assistance, which no man could have dreamt would have come his way."

Steve finished, "I give you the same challenge I gave Deuce. Go find a quiet place. Ask yourself 'What is it I want? What is it I could commit to?' And look inside. Be quiet long enough to see something."

The Response

The emails came from every state in the United States. They came from Paris, Luxembourg, and Germany. They came from Russia, Australia, and the Czech Republic. They all had the flavor of this one: "I don't know who Steve Hardison is. I don't know who Deuce Lutui is, but what I do know is that I'm going to be the best confectioner in all of Scotland" (Isla Morrison). This email came with two pictures: TBOLITNFL spelled out with cupcakes and TBOLITNFL spelled out with seashells on a beach.

A CEO in London wrote, "Hi, Steve. You, sir, are magic in motion. That document belongs deep in the fleshy tables of every heart. I have gone through it three times, made notes, and carry a small black notebook that has my own version of TBOLITNFL in it. It would be surprising if everyone reading this document doesn't create their own personal internal commitment." (Steve later called "personal internal commitment" *declarations*, or, cumulatively, *the document*.)

Fred Beljaars from the Netherlands wrote, "My coach sent me a video of Steve doing TBOLITNFL. I watched the long version three times in a row. Awesome! I was in love." David Gerber wrote, "I've watched TBOLITNFL five times and it impacts me in new ways each time I watch it." Eric Lofholm wrote: "Hi Steve, Gary Henson sent me the info on TBOLITNFL. I was so inspired by it I shared it at CEO Space today where I spoke to 300 people. I will share the story with several thousand people in the next year during my speeches and webinars. Warmly, Eric Lofholm, The World's Greatest Sales Trainer."

Jenn Walter wrote:

I had never heard of Steve Hardison. To be honest, I thought coaches were for weight loss and athletes. Parker Winder shared with me Deuce and TBOLITNFL. I am a Packers fan, so my first thought was, "Who is this other football team and why would I care?" But I trusted Parker.

Holy Buckets, Batman! I believe I may have watched that video twice. Who is this man? Who talks like this? Who does this for another person? I was hooked.

Steve has no idea of my journey, but he helped put a spark in my mind that started a fire in my heart that fueled my passion for transformation. I am the creator and master of my life!

Four years after viewing the video, Emma Holmes in England wrote to Steve:

Hi Steve,

I hope you and dear Amy are well! I am not sure if I have shared this with you—around 2016, I created my commitment as TBOSDJTITW = The Best Online Scratch DJ Tutor in the World. Shortly after, a leading DJ software company contacted me to create some video tutorials for them and referred to me as exactly that. I love sharing the TBOLITNFL video with my clients, and all who take the time to absorb it are transformed. Grateful for you.

Shortly after Rosie Bernardo moved from Los Angeles to Miami, she watched the TBOLITNFL video on one of her breaks at the school where she worked. She says, "I can't even explain what went through me, but basically, I said, 'Holy shit. Somebody is as loving as I am.' I had felt embarrassed about the acts of kindness I did. I felt like maybe they were over the top. This video gave me permission to keep doing them." It also inspired her to "stick with this coaching thing," which she was doing on the side. Rosie relates:

I started giving the Steve Hardison video to people. One of the people I gave it to was my cousin, before he was the mayor of Miami. After watching the video, he literally drove to my apartment and he gave me a $100 bill. He said, "Thanks, coach." He had written his personal internal commitment on a napkin. This was before he was mayor, but he was already on that trajectory.

I started a coaching group called The Power 10. It was an after-school coaching program at the adult school. I had enrolled ten young adults in it. There was a young guy from Miami in this group. I believe his name was Adid and that he was originally from somewhere in Africa. Sometimes I substituted for the teachers at the school, teaching their English classes. Adid had been in one of the classes I had substituted and he wouldn't do anything. When he came to The Power 10 program, I said, "Adid, can you just watch this video?" He agreed and started watching it. Shortly after, he said, "Miss Bernardo, this is boring."

"Just take it home, and watch it at home," I pled.

So, he went home and watched it. Two days later, he was frantically searching for me at the school. When he found me, he said, "Oh my goodness. I watched the video and I started crying. I don't even know why, but I was sobbing. So, I watched it again. I think I watched it five times. And then I started writing my commitments. I don't know what was going on, but all these words started coming out of me."

"Wow. You know what?" I said. "I'm going to tell Steve about you." So, I sent Steve an email and I asked if he would sponsor Adid. It cost $100 for each kid to take this training with me. Steve agreed and even wrote an email back to Adid.

I continue to send that video to every person I know when I think they'll be open to watching it. I send it to every client before I work with them. It doesn't matter who it is, every single person experiences a transformation watching that video.

Postscript

Deuce Lutui caught the vision of what he could do. He was on fire. He had a killer season. But ultimately, his football career floundered because of his weight. Deuce decided to move from the Cardinals to the Bengals. Will Keiper writes:

His lucrative new contract was conditioned upon him passing the Bengals' physical exam. Among other things, the exam included stepping on a scale to check his weight. In another single, powerful moment, Deuce's world changed again. The scale declared he was carrying 381 pounds; he should have been thirty or forty pounds lighter.

The Bengals said, "No, thank you Deuce," and less than twenty-four hours after he left for the promised land of his new contract and team, Deuce was on a plane back to Phoenix . . .

Some estimated that he left more than six million dollars over two years on the Bengals' table. If this was the case, it represented about $200,000 per excess pound he carried onto that scale in the Bengals locker room.

The next day he signed a modest, one-year contract with the Cardinals.

Deuce's final year as a Cardinal was bleak. Things went downhill from there. Does this disappointing conclusion invalidate TBOLITNFL? Only if TBOLITNFL was about a football player. It's not. Every time Steve shared Deuce's story, it was always about waking someone up to their own possibility and inspiring him or her to commit to making it happen. Deuce woke up. He was inspired. But he failed to do what he needed to do to make it happen. As such, the doleful finish of his football career is not a footnote to TBOLITNFL. It is not something to be swept under the rug. It is truth told in relief. A personal internal commitment is not a magic wand. It is a powerful commitment that brings dreams into reality by consistent, daily actions. Miracles happened. Dreams were actualized. Chris Dorris, who stood in for Deuce at the University of Utah, concludes, "I cannot believe—I definitely will *not* believe—that the value of these powerful stories is in any way lost by virtue of someone either choosing a different path or forgetting their power."

Conclusion

TBOLITNFL continues to be read and watched. It has been more than ten years since Steve spoke at King's Fish House and the University of Utah. Steve still gets emails like this:

> Thank you for sending TBOLITNLF to me. I'm inspired by Deuce's commitment. It does the same thing for me that it appears to have done to the others who have read it. It makes me want to be my best. It makes me want to play bigger in every area of my life, to man up and take the challenge of me. I will watch in great expectation, and cheer on number 76 this year, with a love I have for the greatness in human beings when they're being all they can be. Thank you for all you've done in my life to bring out the greatness of me.

Man up. Woman up. Play bigger. Love the greatness in humanity. Tap into your own greatness. That is what TBOLITNFL is all about.

Link to TBOLITNFL video:

https://www.youtube.com/watch?v=3n7Kvu-KrEg

Vignette

Chris Dorris

In October 2010, Steve called me and said, "Chris, you know Julie Blake, right?"

"Of course," I said. "I just spoke with her yesterday. She invited me to go to Utah for her event. I told her I was at the Fish House in Tempe when you did the original TBOLITNFL."

What I thought but didn't say was: "No way am I going to Salt Lake City. I am not going to miss an Eagles game."

Steve interrupted me. "She's having a hard time pulling this event together. This is what I want you to do. First thing tomorrow morning, at 7:00 a.m., call her. Do NOT tell her that I told you to do this. That is imperative. Call her and ask her what she needs. And whatever she asks for, say yes. If she asks for fifteen Harley Davidsons, you figure it out. If you do this, I promise you will experience miracles in your life both personally and professionally. Are you willing to do this, Boatness?" (Steve calls me "Boatness." I call him "Admiral.")

"Yeah. Because I love you."

"Pray to God she asks for something huge." Click.

I jumped in because I love, love, love this stuff. I really do feed off of it. Now, we got game. Still, I was scared shitless and uber-energized. I was scared and pumped.

So, the next day, I called Julie. "Hey Julie, it's CD. Is there anything you need to pull this together? Because I know it's a big deal and you are really working your ass off."

Julie said, "Chris, you're a godsend!"

"What can I do to help you?"

"Can you please be here? It would be so great to have you here," Julie said.

I host a big party at my house every Sunday during football season. My house is the place to be. I hate missing games. But I made a commitment to say yes to everything. I told her I would be there.

"Oh, that's great," Julie said. "And can you pay for the venue?"

"What?!"

I thought, "I just hired Steve Hardison. How much disposable cash do you think I have sitting around? I'm freakin' broke. I'm pumped about it, but I'm broke."

But I committed to say yes to everything. I told Julie I would pay for the venue.

She said, "You probably want to know how much it is."

I guess I should have, but it didn't matter. If it were five bucks, I didn't have it. And it was thousands.

I said, "Game on."

She said, "Thank you, CD. Can you wire that to me tonight?"

I'm the "yes" man.

She gave me the wire information. I'm thinking, "I have to get the money."

I plopped down on the top of my stairs and sat there and thought. It took me forty-five minutes to come up with a solution. I was excited about my idea, but in retrospect I realize I should have sat with it for another fifteen minutes. I would have come up with a much better solution. But who cares? I came up with one. And all that matters is that there was one, one I would never have even considered if I had not taken that leap.

I had just made an agreement with a new corporate client to pay me in advance for some work I was going to do for them. I called and told them about TBOLITNFL and what I was doing and asked if I could come pick up a check that day. They said, "Oh, we'd love to be a part of that." The takeaway for me is that if I ever need to create anything, I can do it like *that*. That's what TBOLITNFL is all about in the first place.

I was on my way back from picking up the money from my client. I was all amped up because I felt like a freakin' powerhouse. I couldn't wait to get home and wire the money to Julie. I was also thinking about getting my plane ticket, since I was now going to Utah for the event. At this time, I was also in the middle of creating my first ever audio program, a five-hour course called "Creating Your Dream." I called the production company and said, "Can I get 500 copies of disc one? Can I get them tomorrow? Because I'm leaving tomorrow." I gave the discs out at the event and that led to clients. Miracles were already starting to occur. And they are still occurring.

So, I was driving and thinking about all this stuff, and my girlfriend called. I started telling her how excited I was. She said, "Hold on. You just hired this guy. And you're paying for his venue?" She's going off. I'm like, "Sister, you are so getting in your way here. You are not bringing this vibe down." And that vibe has never come down.

I went to the event in Salt Lake. Steve brought me up on stage. People are still talking about that. People hired me from that. I'm still using it. I created an "All In" audio program, which has now become an online course, and is now a fundamental element of my corporate training. I teach that goals are for those who don't have the guts to make a decision. A goal is, "Oh, I hope I can pull this off." A decision is, "This has to get done, like now."

Steve was right when he said, "I promise you, I promise you, you will experience miracles in your life both personally and professionally."

This story has changed my life.

Vignette

Luisa Molano

(From a Facebook post on January 19, 2021)

Today I received an invitation to celebrate myself. It came in a vase with beautiful flowers from my coach [Varian Brandon].

The card said: Because today marks six months of you choosing you! Congratulations, Luisa, on your courage to become . . . so much love!!!

My eyes immediately welled up with tears, and then I realized I didn't know what the six-month milestone even was!

I pulled up my calendar, went to the month view, and quickly swiped back to see what happened six months ago today.

I saw it and my eyes immediately welled up with tears again.

Six months ago was July 19th, the last day I had alcohol.

I've never had an issue with alcohol or drinking. Actually, I was always that girl who, after a few cocktails, ended up exchanging numbers with random souls in the bathroom, swearing we'd grab lunch or cure cancer together the following week.

But I also used alcohol to numb, and I knew it. After a long or "hard" day, it always "did the job." But it worked, so I kept doing it. My life, my rules.

But on July 3rd, something happened. I took my commitment to myself and my purpose here on earth to a new level after watching Steve Hardison's TBOLITNFL video (if you haven't seen it, you're missing out on the chance to see a miracle unfold in the span of two hours).

I cemented it with a tattoo because, well, I have a flair for the dramatic . . . what can I say?

Steve says that when one is committed, everything moves to the commitment, like a black hole.

That day I committed to seeing with new eyes how each action, thought, belief and habit would either move me closer to my purpose—or away from it.

Two weeks later, on July 19th, I woke up and clearly saw that alcohol wasn't doing me any favors.

It wasn't bad; it simply wasn't useful in helping me to accomplish what I am here to do.

I celebrate this with you Varian because you've been my champion since October 25, 2019 . . . Coaches are people, just like everyone else. But coaches are also guides who have chosen a personal legacy in service of the soul of the planet. And, some coaches are angels, as Varian has been for me.

Vignette

Stephen Sainato

I'm currently in Jersey City, New Jersey. In 2011, I hit rock bottom. I was in enough pain that I was ready to request and receive support. My brother, Nick, said, "Steve, man, you just got the smack of God. You have got to make this the best thing that has ever happened to you."

I said, "Okay man, I'm going to do it. I'm going to get sober." I thankfully recovered and got sober. I was in and out of court. Here I was, a defendant, and I go and sign up for the law school admission test. I had tons of fear and limiting beliefs: I can't read fast enough. Everyone else is smarter than me. I don't have enough time. I have to work. I have to attend 12-step meetings. And on and on. I had to rise above ALL of these diminishing and disempowering thoughts.

I had made friends with a judge while bartending. He invited me to his chambers to connect and discuss the law. He was talking about how he is able to be of service to the community and all of these wonderful things. And I said, "Judge, I don't know if you're a believer, but I swear, God's talking right through you."

He confirmed, "I am a believer." He pulled out a Bible and said, "I read this every morning before I sit on the bench. I want you to come to my church." So, I went to his church, and I heard him share his story. It rocked me. I was deeply moved and inspired and felt something shift inside of me.

I thought, "I'm going all-in. I'm doing this. For the first time in my life I'm giving something everything I've got." I started listening to inspiring videos every morning. That transformed my entire psyche. I began to believe in myself. I began to show up like the freakin' Terminator. I maintained that level of commitment for three years and I graduated first in my class. It was a true miracle.

I went through the journey to become a lawyer. I practiced at one of the best firms in the world, based in New York City. Shortly into practicing, I felt deeply unfulfilled and chose to make a bold move: I left the law and transitioned into coaching.

I was struggling emotionally. I was excited and inspired yet often paralyzed by fear and anxiety. Then my friend, Mike, sent me an audio of TBOLITNFL. I had never really heard of Steve Hardison. I heard his name, but never heard his voice or anything. I was curious.

I was listening to this audio and it was like my soul recognized it. It hit me so hard. I was walking down Lexington Avenue in Manhattan, listening and in tears. I was so moved by his being, by his authenticity, by his power, by his love, by his service-oriented spirit. The shift that had occurred for me with Judge Wright happened again. I made an internal commitment to go all-in and become the best coach I could be. That was a profoundly pivotal moment for my life.

I went on Facebook and sent Steve a friend request. He wrote me back a really beautiful message and sent me one of Steve

Chandler's books. We exchanged messages a few more times. He sent me another book by Nadine Larder called *Conquering Fears to Create Masterpieces*. As I was flipping through the book, I saw the declarations infused on the masterpiece wall. Again, I was rocked spiritually and emotionally. It was like Spirit wrote right through me as I began to declare who I BE. I declared, "I have a full coaching practice with a waiting list of clients." This is at a time when I had maybe one or two clients.

Within a few months, I had a full clientele and a waiting list for both my one-on-one practice and my next workshop. Before I even talked to Steve, he transformed my life. He helped me to fulfil what I believe I am put on Earth to do: to coach and serve.

I have cultivated having conversations with the God of my understanding. My declarations come to me through my conversations with God. He affirms, "You are the possibility of unconditional love, profound service, and Divine power. You are loved, loving, and lovable. You are perfect peace. You are a sunbeam, a spark of divinity, a lighthouse. You are one of the most loving, committed, and powerful coaches on the planet." This is how I begin each day.

Part Three

Steve Hardison—the Man

Chapter 35

Love

"Have I told you I love you today?" Steve asks Amy. He will ask again in a few hours, and once or twice more throughout the day. Amy opens the refrigerator. A sticky note clings to the milk. It reads, "Amy, I love you. Thank you for being my wife. Steve." The date stamp in the upper right corner reads, "Now and forever." The toothpaste bears another note. This one says, "I love you today. SFH." And there are the frequent refrains: "What can I do for you today?" and "Let me tell you how amazing you are . . ." Amy gets it. She knows Steve loves her. It is the bedrock of her world.

It is also signature Steve. Steve does everything with intensity, including how he loves. People notice. They can't help it. He speaks of his love for Amy openly, boldly, effusively. He creates Amy as only a master creator can. It's memorable because, frankly, it is exceptional, in both senses of the word. And it smacks of possibility.

Gary Mahler attended one of Steve Chandler's coaching schools. He says:

Steve was there with his wife Amy. I have never seen any man treat his wife so beautifully and lovingly. When he spoke, he spoke with a power, love and conviction I had never heard before. He spoke of his commitment to his family, his devotion to his wife, and how he lived his life in service. As I listened to him speak, I saw a new possibility for myself. I saw where I wanted—no, needed—to step up to be a better man, a better husband, a better father, and a better coach.

Amy and Steve

Yayati Desai says, "I adore the way he treats his wife, Amy, and the love he has for her. It's inspiring. If all husbands around the world were like that, the world would be a different place. I aspire to be like him. Being a coach like him is my second priority; being a husband like him is my first."

Dr. Lorraine Warren writes, "I love the way he speaks of his wife, Amy. I love the way he loves her. I love how much he loves her. I love her because of how much he loves her. It's infectious. And, I have never met her in person! I have even had the thought, 'I would love to marry someone who loves me the way Steve loves and cherishes Amy Hardison.'"

Who wouldn't? It's the stuff of fairy tales.

So, what is the secret?

When people observe Steve and Amy, some say, "I bet you guys never fight." Is that the secret? Definitely not. During her interview for this book, Iyanla Vanzant said:

I'll tell you a funny story. I have never even told Steve this. Steve introduced me to Byron Katie. I knew her work, but when Steve calls me and says I need to do something, I do it. So, when Steve told me to go to Katie's School for The Work, I went and took my entire staff. Steve was there with Amy. I don't know what happened, but one evening, he and Amy were over in the corner in the hallway and they were having some kind of a disagreement or an upset. I just happened to be passing by. They were not screaming or yelling. But I see energy—and the energy was intense. They were standing eye to eye, toe to toe, like they were going to duke it out. And Amy, who probably weighs 120 pounds with all her clothes wet, was not backing down from Steve. He was looking down on her; she was looking up at him.

They were going at it, but you couldn't hear a word. It was almost like a whisper. And I said, "Let me get a little closer." I just kind of lounged around over in the corner.

I couldn't hear what they were saying, but I said, "I like that. I'm going to learn how to do that." My partner of fourteen years and I never had an argument, never raised our voices at each other, ever. I wanted to learn how to do that. And I did.

So, the secret is not that Steve and Amy never fight. It's not that they are naturally compatible. It's not that they are natural soulmates. Their children have often asked in disbelief, "How did you two ever get together?" Their magic formula is simple. They constantly create their love and their relationship.

"You create love by what you say and what you think," says Steve. "When people fall in love, they say, 'She is the most amazing person I've ever met' and 'He is wonderful. I can't wait to see him.' They get married and a few years later they say, 'All she does is complain' and 'He's so selfish.' You create falling in love. You create falling out of love."

Steve uses an object lesson to teach this to his clients. When a client says he wants more love in his relationship, Steve writes a check for a million dollars and hands it to him. "Just bring me one cup of love and that check is yours." Steve has never paid out, "because the only place love exists is in language." This is "the cup of love distinction." It is true for all the intangibles: trust, happiness, faith, love, etc. Steve elaborates, "You don't have to create physical objects by your speaking. I don't have to say, 'chair, chair, chair' to have the chair exist. It's here. I can touch it. I can sit on it. But love is different. States of being don't exist in physical reality. If you want love, you must speak it into reality, every day. If you stop speaking it, it will disappear."

So many couples are like one particular client of Steve's who walked into his office disgruntled with his wife and dissatisfied in his marriage. Steve had him write down his thoughts about his wife. "She nags. She is too heavy. I don't like the way she breathes . . ." He had a long list. They created new thoughts. The client began to speak them into existence. In time, he transformed his relationship with his wife. The joy returned.

The first place to go to change your thoughts and your speaking is your document. Van Dunham writes:

Steve shared with me how he keeps his marriage first in his life. Every morning he speaks who Amy is for him, recreating her daily. He challenged me to write down who Cynthia was for me. He invited me to read it every morning, but in addition to just reading it, he asked me to also think of one thing I could do each day to show her that she was the most important person to me. I have to admit, it took me close to three months before I started to automatically think of her needs before mine. I did not realize how selfish I was or how much I took her for granted. I knew that she completed me and was strong in areas that I was weak. However, it was a selfish love. This one exercise has helped me realize that love and relationships need to be created daily. Our love has grown and deepened because I still do this every day. This one experience saved my marriage and family.

When you sear your love into your soul through consistent creation, other things—like ego, frustration, and being right—tend to recede. Lisa Haisha met Steve at the University of Santa Monica. She observed, "He shared personal things about his marriage, his negative sides, and how he wanted to shift. I thought, 'Who is this guy that just says it like it is? He doesn't care if he looks bad if it was the truth of his week.' I got that Steve took life and love seriously."

How seriously does Steve take love? Seriously enough that he revamped his document to supercharge his daily creation of Amy. "I am the Universe" became, "I am the Universe and Amy is the center of my universe. I am expansive and spacious, especially for and towards her." Some of his statements received only slight modifications as Steve added "especially for/with/to Amy." For instance, "I am happy and peaceful" became "I am happy and peaceful, especially with Amy." Several statements became far more Amy-centric. A few of these are:

I am lovingkindness. I am that no one is worthy of my judgment and that everyone is worthy of my love. I do not judge Amy. I only love her. I love everything about her. I am the distinction "lovingkindness" to her, for her, and with her. She senses my love and is drawn to me because I love her for who she is and who she isn't and for what she is and what she isn't. I am her lovingkindness, but only always.

I am strong, healthy, and attractive and I am all of those for the center of my universe. I do what I do in these areas to support and honor my queen, Queen Amy.

I am madly in love with my brilliant, gorgeous, intelligent wife, Amy Blake Hardison. I create ways every day to learn more about her and fall further in love with her. My heart skips a beat when I see or think of her.

In 2017, Steve began signing all his texts, emails, letters, and notes with "SFH/kab." It is another example of the radical recreation

Steve has undertaken for the sake of love. Steve explains:

> My father-in-law, Kent Anderson Blake, was the happiest, kindest, most generous man I have ever met. I was with him on July 16, 2017, when he drew his last breath. Just minutes prior to that, Amy and I were alone with her father. At that time, I prayed to God aloud, so my father-in-law could hear. I said that I did not know the laws of the hereafter, but I had an extraordinary request. I asked God and Kent to leave me some of his being, some of his spirit, some of his nature, some of his attitude, and some of his aptitude for happiness, kindness, and generosity. Having a little more "Kent Blake-ness" in me would be a gift to Amy and a blessing in our marriage.
>
> Shortly after this, Amy, my daughter Steffany, and I watched on as Kent Anderson Blake returned to his Father in Heaven. When I got home and wrote the experience in my journal, the Spirit spoke to me, clearly and concisely saying, "From now until you pass, include the uncapitalized initials of Kent Anderson Blake after your own initials." I have done that. Each time I sign "SFH/kab," I remember my wonderful father-in-law and create myself to be a little more like him.

The result of all this creation is palpable. Lisa Hale, who observed Amy and Steve at one of Steve Chandler's ACS events, says, "I loved the adoring look Amy had on her face toward Steve. That is not something you can fake. They have created this adoration, this renewing of love between them."

Is that all it takes?

While the daily, disciplined creation is foundational, there are a few other things that have contributed to their bliss. Extreme differences can challenge a couple, but they can also bond them.

Louise Phipps Senft says, "Steve lives really large. He is a real life force. And he's really lucky to have Amy who is his cool water." Patrick Provost uses a different analogy. "I think Steve is like a kite that flies high into the air. Amy keeps him grounded. I've seen that over the years. Amy has been brilliant for Steve."

Paul Waite, a mission companion and close friend of Steve's for nearly fifty years, says, "Steve is a hard-charging, hard-working, high-energy guy. He could be demanding and tough to live with. Amy has been his anchor. He would be out there killing dragons and she's back there with a very steadying personality, which is good for him. He came from a place where he didn't have that stability." Marena Hales says, "To put it simply, there can be no Steve without Amy. Her unconditional love, her ability to let Steve be Steve, and the hours she spends listening and supporting him make Steve possible."

In spite of their differences, they are aligned in their basic values, such as finances and family. They prefer a simple life with down time, which they spend together. They aren't big foodies. They prefer Amy's home-cooked, healthy meals to going to restaurants. They love to exercise, read, travel, and go to movies. They love to spend time with their kids and grandkids. They *enjoy* being together. And mostly, they talk. Well, Steve talks twice as much as Amy, but he has always talked the birds out of the trees. They share their hopes, dreams, frustrations, and joys. They share what they are learning and the details of their days. They express appreciation and say, "I love you" a lot. Since Steve's office is at their house, they connect throughout the day with hugs and words. They pray together morning and night. It's a lot of small things—but the aggregate is substantial.

And what is Amy's perspective? She relates:

Several years ago, Steve was getting ready to run some errands. He always makes sure to say goodbye and give me a kiss before he leaves. On this occasion, we engaged in some light-hearted banter. He said, "You know, it is going to be pretty rough on the women out there when I'm walking around looking this good."

"Well, you just remember you belong to me," I said.

At that moment, Steve got serious, looked me in the eyes and said, "I would never forget that. You healed me. You are everything to me."

I love that, because it reflects not only Steve's love and devotion, it reflects all we have gone through to get to this place of unity and peace.

I am everything to Steve and he is everything to me because we have a commitment to love each other forever, which is distinct from staying married. We are committed to being madly in love. That kind of love isn't cheap. It takes a lot of soul-stretching, forgiveness, and patience. In our case (and maybe everyone's), it also took a lot of healing. I was raised in a home with loving, nurturing parents. I experienced unconditional love and an emotionally safe environment without criticism and drama. It was only natural for me to bring that into our marriage. Over the years, that filled Steve's holes.

I have been so blessed to experience being cherished by someone who has so much love to give. He sees the best in me, beyond what I actually am. I have learned so much from him. Steve is charismatic, dynamic, and connects with people better than anyone I have ever met. Over the years, some of that has rubbed off on me. He has been my biggest cheerleader and my biggest fan. Our marriage has been a wonderful adventure and an extraordinary privilege. Each day is sweeter and our love greater.

Steve has a healthy respect for the challenges of love. He frequently says that relationships are the hardest work we will ever do in life. But when we do the work, the joy is exquisite.

Love Beyond the Center

Amy is the center of Steve's universe, but surrounding that center are concentric circles of love that include Steve's clients, friends, and people he has just met. "Love is, I am that" is part of Steve's document. He says it. He lives it. It shows up wherever he goes.

In 2002, Steve spoke at the University of Santa Monica's graduation ceremony. When it was his turn to speak, Steve walked to the podium and looked out at the graduates. He stood in the presence of his love. He was unhurried. He held the room in his eyes.

After five minutes in clock-time and an eternity in speaker-time, he boomed into the microphone, "I LOVE YOU." Then he sat down.

"Chills went up and down my spine," recalls graduate Stephen McGhee, the 2002 student of the year. "He didn't *talk* about love, he demonstrated it. It was the most powerful non-speech speech I have ever heard."

It was an unorthodox graduation talk. Steve could pull it off because he is well-practiced at standing in the presence of love, taking it in, and sending it back out. He does it one-on-one and he does it with large groups. He did it at the coaching intensive co-hosted by Rich Litvin and Steve Chandler in London in 2014.

Michael Serwa attended this event. It was the first time he saw Steve Hardison. He relates:

As soon as Steve stepped on the stage, from that point on, nobody moved a finger. And it's not like he got up there with some presentation, to deliver a sales pitch or anything like that. He just stood there and started talking.

My attention span is not great, so as the previous speakers were presenting, I was listening while simultaneously messaging my date for the night. Some people were going to the bathroom; others were coughing. As soon as Steve got on that stage, silence. It was like we were in a library.

He spoke for about three hours, spending the first forty-five minutes expressing his gratitude to other people. There was nothing about himself. Steve started by acknowledging Steve Chandler and Rich Litvin for what they were doing. He talked about their friendship and the love he has for them.

Then he went from acknowledging Steve and Rich, to talking about Amy and the love he has for her. Everyone started crying. I'm crying! It takes a lot for me to cry, especially in public. I felt the unconditional love he has for her. I have never in my life seen such a profound display of love from one human being to another. I've never seen anything even close to that. No one was moving, and we were all in tears.

He had invited the guy who served him breakfast in a coffee shop that morning. There were other guests as well, people Steve invited. He started speaking to them, acknowledging them in a way that they probably had never been acknowledged in their life.

Lisa Berkovitz shares her experience of that day:

I knew about Steve, but I had not met him. We knew Steve

was coming. His reputation preceded him, and we were all excited. When he arrived with Amy, they came and sat at the front of the room. Steve made it very clear that he did not come as a speaker. He had not come with a prepared talk.

I'm super-energetically sensitive, so that tends to be how I take in information. My experience was that the entire room was literally filled with light and with love. It was pulsing, just radiating through the room in an indescribable manner. I was not the only one who had that experience.

John Patrick Morgan says of the London event: "My applause was NOT for the love that came from Steve. This love was not his. He never created it. He never owned it. He just allowed it to come through him. My applause is for the work Steve has done to clear away that which gets in the way of love."

Steve is definitely present to love. He is present to the magnificence of people. He is present to the privilege of friendship and emotional connection. He is present to people's courage, grace, and grit. And sometimes that love wells up and nearly swallows Steve whole. At such moments, it may render him temporarily speechless. It may summon his tears. It may find release in a profusion of acknowledgement, gratitude, and love. Or it may do all three. Like it did in London.

Love in Action

"Steve sees opportunity and acts on that opportunity," says Ward Andrews. "I think that is the difference. We all see the opportunity and maybe we step back. Steve steps forward. And he'll do it day and night. I received a text from him last week at 3:00 in the morning. It said, 'loving you.' At 3:00 in the morning!"

When Steve is present to love, he doesn't just bask in the warmth. He texts. He calls. He visits. He acts. Deanna Chesley writes, "I love that he will stop by my house just for a hug and then race off in his Porsche." Steve worked with Bill Jensen back in his Rodel days. Bill says, "Steve has called me on a regular basis and chatted. In other words, he was the initiator of keeping our friendship going. When a person reaches out and says, 'I like you and I want to keep talking with you,' that constitutes a great person."

Steve is masterful at microbursts of love, but often he invests more time and effort. When he goes to Utah, he drops by and visits teachers who taught him in elementary school, junior high, and high school. He thanks them for taking an interest in him and for teaching him life lessons. By his actions, he tells them their life and their career matter. He has done this for a long time.

Sylvia Carter was Steve's English teacher in junior high. It was her very first year of teaching. She says, "Any time Steve was in the room, there was energy, enthusiasm, and smiles." After junior high, Steve stayed in contact with Sylvia. She says:

> When Steve got home from his mission, he told me he wouldn't get married until he had my approval of his bride. I told him I would hold him to it, though I figured when he was smitten by some young lady, he wouldn't remember. But one day, I received a phone call from Steve. He told me he was in love and that he needed me to give my approval. Was I honored! He brought that sweet girl to my house and we visited for a long time. I gave him my solid approval.

When Steve learned that his good friend, Rick Glauser, was dying of cancer, he called Rick and told him he was going to take off work and they could do whatever Rick wanted. "Rick wanted to take a farewell tour," says Nan Glauser, Rick's wife. "Rick wanted to see friends they went to high school with, people he had worked with, and some family. So, Steve drove up to St. George, picked up Rick and they drove around Utah for two weeks so Rick could say goodbye. It meant so much to Rick that Steve did this. If there is a word to describe Steve, it is love—kind, real, authentic, meaningful love."

Steve has coached Clate Mask, the CEO of Infusionsoft (now Keap), for over a decade. On occasion, Steve stops by their headquarters. He doesn't just focus on Clate or the executive team. He visits with everybody. Tara LaRue Stradling says:

> When I met Steve, I was Clate's executive assistant. I got to visit with Steve here and there. We became friends on Facebook. I posted two things on Facebook that he reacted to. Once, I posted about loving flip flops and he brought me a really nice pair of brand-new flip flops. Another time, I posted a meme about chocolate being bigger than my head. He brought me five or six Hershey candy bars taped together so I could put them beside my head and show that I found a piece of chocolate that was literally bigger than my head. That was so unexpected and so funny.

Steve notices and acts, not occasionally or when it is on his to-do list. It is his way of being. Stephen McGee says:

> I said something about Jesus Christ in a session once. I mentioned that, in my opinion, Jesus wasn't floating around in white robes. I think he was in people's faces. A week later, this big, heavy statue of Jesus Christ showed up at my house.
>
> He does stuff like that all the time. A lot of people have the thought. The difference is Steve takes the thought and

goes to Amazon, finds the statue, has it shipped to his house first so he can sign it, write about it, write on it, and then repackage it and ship it to me. I see all that stuff. Damn. . . Damn.

Clients

Steve loves his clients. He gets weepy just thinking about them. They feel it. Michael Schantz says of his coaching sessions: "I experienced his absolute dedication to me and my path while I was with him. For those two hours, I was given his undivided attention, heartfelt listening, and unconditional support. In short, I was engulfed with love. That was my experience with every coaching session with Steve for about a year and a half."

Sometimes Steve loves his clients with soft kid gloves, sometimes with coarse grit sandpaper, like when he gets in someone's face to wake them up or when he calls a spade a spade—or a client a liar or a "pretentious son of a bitch." Sometimes, he is thrusting his clients into their possibility. Allison Watts writes:

> About half-way through our year together, Steve vigorously loved me into using my voice. Steve always loves me, but he really loved me this day and I felt his commitment to me this day maybe more than any other.
>
> As my homework, Steve invited me to call at least ten people and share my document of who I am with them. I always get to say yes or no to his invitations. Because of childhood traumas, I believed it was dangerous for me to speak my truth. I reluctantly said yes. I knew I could figure out how to do this with the least amount of risk.
>
> Steve saw what was happening, and he said something I will never forget: "If you don't do this, we're done. I'll

consider you resigned from our agreement and our work together will end." Wow!!! Big tears came up and I got scared. I knew I really had to do this! I was terrified, and at the same time I have never felt so much love. He knew this was exactly what I needed, and he was taking a strong stand for me. I knew in that moment that Steve was more committed to my evolution than to my comfort. Suddenly, I felt profound gratitude for such deep love and commitment from him.

I did my homework and practiced using my voice to create myself and my world, and after the first four or five times, it became fun and much easier and more natural. I ended up making about thirty calls! Now I practice using my voice every day.

Steve has no problem using sandpaper love when the occasion demands it, but he is no stranger to the softer side of love. Stephen McGhee puts it succinctly, "The guy tears up a lot." Karan Rai says:

I tend to hold myself to pretty high standards, and I hold others to high standards also. So, it takes a lot to impress me. But Steve has impressed me time and time again. Of all the amazing things he does, it is his level of compassion that has impressed me more than anything else. Two specific occasions stand out. They were probably two of the more powerful sessions I had with him.

The first occurred at one of those times when I was feeling stressed out about something or other. We were having this conversation about what's important in life, and he looked at me and said, "What are you stressed about? You're going to die. And none of your problems are going to go with you when you die." Then he said that we were going to visit one of his former clients. He was a high-powered attorney. He had made a lot of money. He was in his seventies and was struggling with dementia. He was living in this home that was a care center.

We drove to the care center. Even though this was the first time I met this gentleman, I could see he was just a shell of his former self. I don't even know if he recognized Steve. The thing that will always stick with me is how Steve held his hand and caressed his hair. He was so present with him. It was so beautiful to watch a man be that present with another man. We spent about an hour with him.

The second experience was when Steve asked me if I would be open to visiting someone who was about to die. I was, and so we went to see this elderly woman who had terminal cancer. He visited her regularly. She was living by herself in a small, cluttered house. When Steve walked in, she lit up. Steve lit up. I was moved by the depth of humanity that he brings into these situations. Compassion and humanity naturally flow out of him. It requires nothing but for him to be him.

There are so many things that Steve does that are absolutely incredible: his ability to get you to see the big picture, his ability to get you to believe in yourself, his ability to take really complex issues and make them so simple, his ability to get you to take action. But the thing that inspires me the most is the depth of his humanity and his compassion.

Stephen McGhee says, "Steve has taught me so much about openness and loving and really being a man—a strong, grounded man with heart, with ferocity and velocity, but also with true loving."

Strangers, a.k.a. Friends

"Steve loves people on sight," says Tara LaRue Stradling. "He is unlike anyone I have ever met." Indeed, Steve loves big, and he falls in love quickly. Stephen McGhee says, "I've seen it a number of times. A cab driver would come pick me up after a coaching session and before the cab driver would drive off, Steve would be hugging the cab driver. This is in five minutes."

Steve could fall in love with a person in the time it takes to check out at a grocery store or to get through an airport security line. In 2014 Steve and Amy were at the Istanbul airport. Steve was standing behind a man who was stylishly dressed and appeared to be in his late thirties. They attempted to communicate, but they spoke different languages. They tried sign language and pantomime, without much luck. They shrugged and were on the verge of giving up when Steve pointed to the younger man's shoes, bent over and touched them, and gave him the thumbs up. The younger man grinned. A mutual love for trendy, unique shoes toppled the language barrier. Steve raised his voice and asked if anyone knew Turkish and English and would be willing to translate for them. A twenty-ish man volunteered. Their conversation got traction. By the time they got to the checkpoint station, this Turkish man had taken off his necklace and was putting it over Steve's head. Steve was emotional. They had connected. It was brief but deep.

Steve's son, Clint, makes this observation:

> He's always meeting people. He's constantly having interactions with people, the frequency of which would be exhausting. He has this impactful interaction with the cashier at the grocery store and then with the guy at the gas station and then with the woman who owns the dry-cleaning

business. That takes so much sheer energy, enthusiasm, and interest in other people. It also takes confidence. He is bold in ways that I would never be. And because he does that, he then finds himself up to his elbows in somebody else's problems, but he is willing to jump in and help them solve them.

One time he was at the Arizona Center in Phoenix and there was a woman selling popcorn from her popcorn machine. He watched her for a few minutes and then the next thing I know, he is coaching her on how to create more business. For him, the stakes are extraordinarily low. But he sees that for her, the stakes are extraordinarily high. He sees how she could be a more effective version of herself. As they speak, she says that she doesn't want to always be selling popcorn. One day she wants to be like Iyanla Vanzant. So, dad pulls out his phone, calls Iyanla and then hands his phone to the popcorn woman.

Steve loves this sort of thing. When he retires—if he retires—he envisions plenty of days where he meanders around, meeting people, and helping them. But he is not waiting until retirement.

Following the London event, Michael Serwa had a trip to Los Angeles planned. He was to be a part of a coaching movie called *Leap*. If you live in England, Phoenix is practically next door to Los Angeles, a mere 373 miles. So, Michael booked a session with Steve and a flight from Los Angeles to Phoenix. He relates:

I went to Steve's house and he asked me what I would like to talk about. I told him that after ten years of personal development, I was in a good place. I didn't really need help with anything in particular. I basically wanted to spend time with him. So, we did. He happened to be free that whole afternoon. We spent at least five hours together.

We went to meet some of his clients in his Porsche. I love that. He's this religious man. He is love. Yet he drives a Porsche. On my website, I say that I am as materialistic as I am spiritual and as egocentric as I am compassionate. I clearly see how you don't have to choose a side.

So, we went to Infusionsoft. He coached the CEO at the time. Steve talked to everyone the same way, from the receptionist all the way to the CFO. Then we went to the bank. There were some teenagers, thirteen- or fourteen-year olds, skateboarding outside of the bank. He started talking to them. Again, he was talking to them like they were his own kids, except he had never met them before.

I consider myself a compassionate person. You better be as a coach, right? But my compassion is selective. If I know you and like you, I can be very compassionate. But Steve's compassion is unconditional. He doesn't care if he is talking to a homeless person, some kid on a skateboard, his client, or his wife. He's the same with everyone. I'm not rude to strangers, but I don't engage with them on the same level Steve does. The way he talks to people is an art form. I've never seen anything like it before. He's not doing it to impress me. I'm already impressed, and he doesn't care if I'm impressed or not. He's doing it because that's what Steve does.

LaTrina Williams is the manager of the CVS drug store close to where Steve lives. On the day after Thanksgiving in 2015, Steve walked into her store with a tangle of non-working Christmas tree lights in his hand. He said, "I need to replace these." LaTrina relates:

During that short interaction, a sense of peace came over me.

I didn't want to seem weird, so I continued to focus on showing him the lights. Once we were at the register, Steve asked if we had been open on Thanksgiving and if I had been able to enjoy Thanksgiving dinner with my family. I explained that we were open on Thanksgiving and my family lives in Louisiana. After I said that, it was like "Stop the presses!" Steve said, "So, you had to work on Thanksgiving, and you didn't have dinner with your family? Did you at least have a Thanksgiving dinner?" When I said no, Steve said, "I'm calling my wife Amy. You're going to come and have dinner with us." I was floored, overjoyed, and nervous. When the day came, I was at peace all over again.

I was welcomed by the Hardisons as if I were a family member coming home for a visit. Since the first day Steve and his family came into my life, it hasn't been the same. Steve has given me books, encouraged me with kind words, and stopped by the store to give me hugs. He has been a father figure, a role model, a big brother, the favorite uncle, a man that I'm honored to say I know and love. The gift of love and compassion that Steve Hardison expresses to all is one of the most genuine gifts one could give. The love that Steve has for his wife, his family and friends is a delight. One would think, "How can one person have this much love and express it to everyone?" I am grateful to be a recipient of the love that Steve Hardison possesses.

Steven Pothier, the ecclesiastical leader of the Mormon congregation where Steve worships, recalls the Sunday when Steve was teaching a class for the men. "I remember Steve bringing in a man who was blind and who sold brooms on a corner near our homes to share his story. I had passed by him at least weekly. Steve Hardison gave me the chance to actually get to know this man. This is clearly something the Savior would have done. It is far more appropriate than just speaking about Jesus's teachings."

How did Steve get to know this man and his story? Steve was driving home when he saw a man standing on the corner in the 115° heat, selling brooms and mops. Steve pulled into the parking lot and started visiting with him. He learned his name was Sebastian Ibañez and he was from Mexico. He was here earning money to send to his family. Steve drove to Rosa's, the local Mexican food restaurant, and bought him a bottle of Mexican Coca-Cola. Whenever Steve drove by, if Sebastian was on the corner, Steve would take a few minutes to stop, visit, and buy a broom. Over time, Sebastian told Steve about the adversity he had encountered in his life, including his blindness. He also attested that God had watched over him. Steve asked him if he would be willing to come and share his experiences with Steve's church class. He agreed. By the time Sebastian was finished, more than a few men had tears in their eyes, and by the end of the week, many had new brooms.

Conclusion

Michael Serwa says of the time he spent with Steve in Arizona:

My coaching experience with Steve was phenomenal. Even just walking into his house was amazing. Here is this compassionate, giving, Jesus-loving guy, with all these kids and all these grandkids, and what is the first thing I see? A big picture of himself on the wall. I love that. Who says that you have to choose other people over yourself? Or that if you love yourself, it's somehow selfish? Steve is definitely not selfish, but he sure as hell loves himself, and I think that's apparent to anyone who interacts with him. It really goes well with a theory that I have: for us to be able to truly love other people, we have to truly love ourselves first.

Perhaps Michael is on to something. Yes, Steve truly loves himself. But perhaps he has also tapped into eternal love, the kind that is limitless. Perhaps that is why after Steve has loved himself, there is plenty of love left over, so Amy feels like the most-loved woman in the world. And enough left over so his clients experience "a tsunami of love" (A. J. Richards). And enough left over to care about the blind man on the corner and to befriend LaTrina at CVS. And enough left over to love the person he will meet tomorrow, and the next day, and the day after that.

Vignette

Gary Mahler

Around the time my son Koan was about to start kindergarten, I wanted to bring him along with me for a session with Steve to prepare him for his journey into elementary school. He had always been a rambunctious little boy, and I was thinking we could calm him down. I asked Steve if he had ever done something like this. He said no, but he would do it for me. I was ecstatic. Steve suggested we set the date close to when he would begin kindergarten. And just like that, we had a boy's trip to Phoenix to be coached together by The Ultimate Coach.

My son had heard a lot about Steve. He was excited. When we arrived in Steve's office, there was a gift and homemade cookies waiting for us. The note said "Please open me when you arrive." Steve had bought my son a Lego set, and his wife Amy had baked him chocolate chip cookies.

As soon as Steve walked into his office at 2:00 p.m. sharp, he was down on the floor with Koan. He welcomed him and made mention of my son's best friend, his stuffed bear named Gaga. This endeared Steve to Koan immediately. They talked and played. They spent fifteen minutes on the floor together. Steve then asked Amy to take Koan while we did our work.

Steve said to me, "Koan is perfect. It's you we need to work on." Like magic, Steve slowly showed me where I could change so that Koan could flourish. He also asked me about my daughter. In that two-hour session, we changed ME to help my son become calmer and more at ease. We also began the journey to love the shyness out of my daughter. This was my most prolific session with Steve to date. Two years after this session, my daughter is alive and open. My son is calm and clear. I am love.

The real beautiful part of this story comes that evening when we went to bed at 8:00 p.m. My son said, "Where's Gaga?" We looked high and low. It then occurred to me that Gaga may have fallen out of Koan's backpack at Steve's house. I texted Steve. Within fifteen minutes, Steve called me. I told him the story. He then hunted for Gaga. About ten minutes later, he called. He had found Gaga under his coaching chair in his office. In an instant, he offered to drive Gaga, special delivery, at 9:30 p.m. to us in Scottsdale. I was going to gratefully decline. But then I saw my son, and my pride washed away in softness. Steve drove with Amy, in his Porsche, in the middle of the night, to hand deliver Gaga to my son.

This is true love. This changed me forever.

Vignette

Rephoel Wolf

I read about Steve Hardison quite a few times in Steve Chandler's books. A fellow coach, Gary Mahler (now coaching with Hardison), told me I must watch the TBOLITNFL video. I was enthralled. I sent Hardison a friend request on Facebook. To my surprise, he accepted and sent me a book (*Straight-Line Leadership*). I told him I had already read it, and he sent me two other books.

"Why is he engaging with me?" I thought. I was bewildered. I even asked him if he was really responding or if someone was responding on his behalf? He sent me a slew of messages, leading me to articles, posts, and responses of people asking the same questions.

It sounded weird and automated, so I said, "Now I'm confused. I'm not sure what's going on."

Steve responded, "You can choose to be confused or you can look at it as a gift."

I left it at that. I was still confused, but also convinced that Steve was speaking in ways too cryptic and lofty for regular mortals like me.

But Steve wasn't done with me.

Every once in a while, Steve would send me a link, or tag me in a post he wrote. He even liked and commented on some of my posts! I was touched. And shocked. Why am I on this guy's radar at all? From what I understand, this guy really is the ultimate coach. He is super-expensive, and really, really good at what he does. Why is he talking to me? What is going on here?

I had some brief exchanges with Steve. I watched John Patrick Morgan's video "100 Hours with Steve Hardison." I started to understand him. I tried to emulate him. We can all do what he does, but we don't.

Steve loves each and every person. For some reason, when I connected with Steve, he saw ways he could help me. He has continued to do so. For some reason, out of everyone he has on his mind, I got in there too.

Steve's beautiful way of being fills me with light just writing about it. It brings tears to my eyes knowing he values who I am and what I have to say. There is no concrete reason for him to do so. Steve doesn't live with concrete. He lives with the infinite love of the Universe, a love that connects all of us and runs through our veins. Steve helps me to connect to that simply through his way of being. It's a gift that I am forever grateful for.

Vignette

Minda Pacheco

A couple of years ago, I was looking for a coach for a friend. I had a coach, but I recognized that my coach was not a good fit for him. My friend was very successful, and he needed a coach who was well suited for him and one he could really respect.

I had heard Steve's name tossed around a few times by friends and I had been to a few events by Steve Chandler where Steve Hardison's name came up. This stood out to me because Steve Hardison and my dad worked together years ago. Steve brought us these enormous stuffed animals. Even though I was only four or five, I remember Steve's personality was larger than life. But I hadn't seen or heard from him in years.

I did some homework on the internet and got on Steve's website. The tributes were phenomenal. I was especially touched by his son Blake's tribute. The more I studied his website, the more fascinated I became. Who is this person? How does he charge this amount?

I couldn't get Steve off my mind. I called my dad and said, "Hey, dad. I just spent a lot of money to go to a school for life coaches. I don't have the funds right now to hire Steve, but I feel compelled to understand who he is and how he does what he does."

My dad said, "Let me give him a call. Maybe he will meet with you."

"Great!" I was nervous about it, but I also felt very compelled.

My dad jumped on the phone with Steve, and Steve said, "Have her call me."

I dialed his number and introduced myself. He said, "What can I do for you?"

"I want to know more about who you are. Is meeting or talking on the phone a possibility?"

He gave me a whole bunch of homework. It took me six weeks to do it all. When I finished, I called him. He invited me to come to his home the next Friday.

As I drove to his house, I was drinking a cherry smoothie and I spilled it on my white shirt! I thought, "This is my life. I have this fantastic opportunity, and I spill cherry smoothie all over me." I got there fifteen minutes early. I noticed the front and back of my shirt were the same, so I ripped the tag out of my shirt and turned the shirt around. I thought, "I am not going to go in there and be uncomfortable. I am not going to be distracted thinking about my shirt. I want to get everything I can from this opportunity."

Steve answered the door wearing a red leather jacket. I love how bold he is in everything he does. He greeted me warmly and invited me in. He asked what I had learned while I was doing the things he had assigned. After I shared for a while, he invited me to go to his office.

I spent the next three hours and seventeen minutes in his office. I don't remember a lot about what I said, but I absolutely remember how I felt. I can only describe it as unconditional love. The experience is so rare and so special that it's hard to put into words. It felt like God's love. It allowed me to let my guard down, be exactly who I am, and listen to what he had to say. He didn't go easy on me. He was brutally honest. I could receive it because it was wrapped in unconditional love.

Steve allowed me to see the possibility of who I can become. I made a promise to myself and to God that I will become that. I have a son with reactive attachment disorder. We adopted him when he was six. He doesn't know how to love or to connect. My life's mission is to love him unconditionally with zero expectations of him returning that love. To do this, I have had to learn how to love myself unconditionally. I am still on that journey. The progress I have made is a direct result of me feeling unconditional love from Steve. I want to help my family experience that and then eventually teach other women how to love themselves unconditionally.

At the end of my three hours and seventeen minutes with Steve, I went to the restroom. When I came back, Steve had an apple for me and one for him. He ate the whole apple, including the seeds.

I laughed and said, "You just ate the whole apple!"

He said, "I don't waste anything."

The moment he said that, I knew. I said, "My time with you will not be wasted."

It was a sacred time for me. I am so grateful for it, and will be for the rest of my life.

Vignette

Will Moreland

About nine years ago, I was at a conference. I met a woman named Nadine Larder. We were talking about the conference and how it was going when she stopped and said, "Do you know what the most amazing thing is that has happened to me at this conference?"

I said, "No. What is it?"

She said, "I met this man. I don't know how to describe him, but it was magical."

I said, "I met a man yesterday at the conference and I had that same type of feeling. I don't know who this gentleman is. I don't know where he came from, but it just felt magical." As we were talking, Steve Hardison happened to walk up.

At the same time, we both said, "That's the guy!" Steve came over and gave Nadine a book he had promised to give her.

When he walked away, we both said, "Whoever this guy is, we need him in our lives."

Immediately after that, I went home. I found Steve on Facebook and reached out to him. I told him I would love to take him out to lunch. I just wanted to talk with him. Steve said, "I know there is this book out there that says never eat alone. But to be honest with you, I don't do lunches." I was so bummed out. How was I going to get to know this guy? At this time, I didn't know Steve was a coach. I just knew that I needed this guy in my life.

[Steve doesn't do lunches, but he did offer to spend a couple of hours with Will. Those two hours were momentous. Will reflects:]

I'm an African American man. I come from the inner city. Steve is the reason why I can't hate white people. He is the absolute reason why I can't. Because if I did, I would miss out on the most magical person I've ever met in my life, and investing time with Steve has transformed my life.

A lot of times we say someone changed our life or an experience changed our life. People say, "I went over to India or Africa and that trip changed my life." That's what I feel about every text, every email, every encounter I have with Steve. No matter how crazy the world gets or how much hate I see in the world, it just takes one conversation with Steve to remind me of the abundance of love that's in the world. It supersedes any negative thoughts I could have. That day, nine years ago, my life was forever transformed because of this gentleman.

Steve always reminds me that we are humans. And that supersedes our political being. That supersedes our religious being. That supersedes our ethnicity. Steve always grounds me back into the fact that we're just humans having this experience and trying to figure it out. He's the reason why I go back to my community and say there is hope.

Chapter 36

Amy on Love, Marriage, and Life with Steve

If Steve is an enigma, so is Amy. But not in the same way or for the same reasons. Amy does not polish her toenails with attention-getting exclamation marks. She does not act in ways that leave people shaking their heads and saying, "Who does that?" She definitely doesn't dance in the aisles of Home Depot, something Steve does with regularity.

The enigma of Amy is generated from the general quandary of "What kind of person is the chosen sweetheart of someone who flies so high?" It is also generated by the fact that Steve unabashedly adores her. He sings her praises to his clients and on Facebook. Yet, she is largely off stage. Many clients meet her, but five or ten minutes affords only a cursory glance of Amy. Some clients get more time with her. Those who do sense she has a power equal to Steve's. But it is a quiet power. It is the power of kindness, steadiness, and intelligence. It is a power of spiritual depth and emotional graciousness.

Amy is comfortable in her own skin and is content that her power whispers instead of shouts. Still, her voice needs to be heard, since Steve insists there is no Steve without Amy. The following email exchange between Amy and Lorraine Warren allows us to hear her voice.

Nov 13, 2018

Hello Mrs. Hardison,

My name is Rain Warren. I have had about two or three conversations with Steve and we are Facebook friends. Every encounter I have with your husband becomes a growth opportunity for me. Being around him compels me to be a better person, or the best that I can be. I hold him in the highest regard.

On my visit with him, my spirit told me to connect with you. I have always wanted to meet the woman who has Steve Hardison show up the way he does. His enthusiasm and generosity of spirit is wonderful to be around. I was just a little disappointed that you were not home.

I love the way Steve is so devoted to you and cherishes you. He speaks about you with so much regard and love. I know that you two have been together for a long time. I just wonder what you would say about what it takes for women to create such a sacred marriage and partnership? Who would a woman have to be?

I ask because I feel that God is directing me towards a sacred partnership and I have no idea how it will manifest.

It feels awkward to approach you in this way. I respect whatever your response may be. I am just following guidance here and taking a chance in reaching out.

Many blessings to you and all those you love.

Rain

November 19, 2018

Hi Rain,

I love your questions, "What would you say that it takes for a woman to create a sacred marriage and partnership? Who would a woman have to be?" Obviously, my answers are from my perspective, based on my (our) experience. I don't assume that what works for me would work for everyone. My answers are from my heart. I am not going to try to make my answers politically correct. For instance, I have chosen to be a stay-at-home mom for my career. Not every woman can or wants to do that. I totally honor that. My answers will reflect my choice, without intending to make it superior or inferior to other options.

Amy, 1997

First of all, as anyone who knows or knows of Steve is well aware, Steve is a powerful, dynamic, amazing, unique man. Part of what gives him his power is he doesn't see the world in the same way as other people. He can see into people's souls. This requires at least two things from his partner. First, I am totally fine with him taking center stage. That is not because I am overly meek and timid. Rather it is because I am confident in my role and my contribution as a human being. Also, there are areas where I am in the spotlight and Steve is the support person. He is awesome at that. But more often, Steve is in the spotlight. I am totally content with that. It does not threaten me because I see the limelight person and the support person as having equally important, just different, roles. As a stay-at-home mother and wife, I find being the person who helps others thrive a sweet role.

Second, as I said, Steve is amazing and unique. He definitely marches to the beat of his own drummer. On the other hand, I am quite conventional. Bringing those two disparate ways of being together requires patience, love, and generosity. It took us a while to get proficient at that. Being able to grant each other the space to be uniquely him- or herself is an essential part of creating a sacred marriage and partnership. It is not easy to do. It takes years of practice, with a lot of failed attempts along the way. So along with granting space comes the need to forgive, forgive often, and forgive well. We will do "do-overs" if we get off on the wrong path. Occasionally, we even have a "delete day."

Another thing that is essential is absolute trust and fidelity. You can imagine that being as powerful, handsome, and charming as Steve is, many women would like to edge me out. Steve honors our love and our exclusivity perfectly. He speaks his love for me to others and declares his fidelity publicly so women know he is off-limits. I trust him explicitly. And he trusts me absolutely.

In addition, we honor the path we have walked together. In a few short weeks, we will have been married 41 years. We met when I was 17 years old and Steve was 21. We have seen a lot of life together. We have experienced a lot of heartaches, joy, growth, and healing. We have had children together and raised them to become amazing, talented, loving, capable human beings, with our unique Steve-and-Amy imprint. We cherish this path as uniquely ours. That enables us to embrace aging as a witness to our ever-deepening love. Steve frequently tells me I am the most beautiful woman in the world to him. He truly believes that, regardless of wrinkles. I can live with great peace and confidence knowing that the most important person in my world loves me for who I am. I am not worried that Steve will toss me aside "for a younger model." We know that our love will become even richer and sweeter as the years go on.

Finally, we support each other in what is important to us. I have LOVED being a stay-at-home mother. I believe with all my heart that there is nothing more important than family. Often people ask what I do for work and I say I am a stay-at-home mom. When they ask how old my children are, I say "39-37-34-31." They are usually quite puzzled. I love having been able to spend both quality and quantity time with my kids. It is obvious that young children need a lot of time and attention. But so do teenagers. And so do adult kids. And so do grandkids. Consequently, I still claim being a stay-at-home mom, even though we are empty nesters. Steve both supported me in doing this and also honored it. This is important because being a stay-at-home mother isn't always regarded as highly as being a career woman. When our kids were little, Steve would always say to me, "You have the harder job. It is so much easier to go out to work." He also speaks powerfully of me and my talents to others.

In addition to this, Steve has supported me in the other things I have loved. For twenty-four years, I was a volunteer religion instructor, teaching a couple of classes each week. Next to my family, this was my passion. I loved the preparation. I loved teaching. And I loved the class members. Steve generously supported both my prep time and my time away because he could see that it was something that gave me so much joy. In return, the thing that is important to Steve is to have a partner to talk with, to connect with on and off throughout the day, and to have pillow talk with. That connection keeps him grounded, joyful, and fueled to go out and help others change their lives. In other words, we have given each other the thing that was important to the other.

I hope this gives you a sense of me, of us, and of how we work. It has been a wonderful adventure and an incredible privilege to love and be loved by Steve.

Best to you. Have a wonderful Thanksgiving.

Amy

Chapter 37

We'll Have Fun, Fun, Fun

Jeff Dinsdale is a close friend with Steve's son, Blake. He also hired Steve as a coach when he was twenty-three years old. In 2010, Jeff went with Steve, Blake, and Blake's wife Maryn to an auto show in Los Angeles. He relates:

> We were spending the night at Steve's buddy's house in Redlands, California. Blake and Maryn were sharing a room and Steve and I were sharing a room. Early the next morning, I woke up and looked over at Steve. He was getting dressed in this kaftan thing. By the time he was finished, he looked like a Middle Eastern prince. He had even painted his face a little bit. This was out of nowhere. There had been no discussion about this. I started laughing and said, "Where are you going, man?" He just said he was going out. When he finally came back, we went to McDonald's for breakfast. He was still totally in costume. I asked him where he had gone. He said he had gone to LA Fitness. He had been walking

around meeting people.

That stands out to me because I think a lot of people think of Steve only as this powerful, transformational guy. They don't see how fun Steve is. It's the fun that makes the magic. What is life if you're powerful and you have all this money and you can do all this stuff, but you don't enjoy life? Steve enjoys life at a level that I have never seen with anyone else.

Steve definitely enjoys life. He enjoys chortling with comedians, Dry Bar Comedy being his special favorite. He has a penchant for practical jokes. Amy, his kids, and even his grandkids know that if they leave the dining table for a minute, they are going to have to look for their food when they return. They know who is responsible. Steve delights in being playful. He always has.

Steve, Burford, England, 2019

Steve and Amy became close friends with Rick and Nan Glauser when both couples were newlyweds. They shared a lot of life's milestones together, especially having babies. They stayed close even when Steve and Amy moved to Arizona and Rick and Nan moved to St. George, Utah. Rick and Steve had an ongoing joke of "tag, you're it." The designated item was a stinky baby diaper. Since Steve and Amy had four kids and Rick and Nan had eight, there were years of fun. Nan relates:

Rick and Steve had this joke where they would hide the current baby's poopy diaper in an odd place, under their pillow or something of the other person's. Stinky! In 1985, Rick was visiting Arizona, selling water softeners, and he stayed with Steve and Amy. When Clint had a poopy diaper, Steve hid it under the driver's seat of Rick's rental car. Rick kept complaining about his car, saying it smelled like Limburger cheese. It was summer and we all know Arizona is hot. Rick drove around with the windows down. The heat was more bearable than the smell. After a few days of this, Steve suggested to Rick that he check under his seat. When he did, he found the diaper. Several weeks later, Steve went golfing. When he unzipped his bag to get the golf balls out, his bag reeked! Rick had found the perfect place to put the next poopy diaper.

Steve's siblings have plenty of stories to share. Steve's sister, Jayme, recalls:

We were all together in Utah when my mother passed away in 1993. A couple of days after the funeral, we all went to a mall in Salt Lake. There were benches in the middle of the walkways that were set up back to back. We were on one side and some strangers were on the other side. There wasn't enough seating for all of us, so Steve got up and walked away and took Kresta, our niece with him. In a few minutes, they came back and he said to the people on the other side of the bench, "We are with mall maintenance. We need to move this bench. Could we ask you to get up?" So, of course, the people got up and walked off. Then he and Kresta moved the bench two inches and then we all sat down.

Amy was embarrassed. You would think she would have been used to his shenanigans by then. So, she got up and walked down the walkway, looking at store windows. Steve is calling after her, "Amy Hardison, you can't get away that easily." He kept on calling after her and she was like, "Who is this person?"

We always have a lot of fun when we are together.

The "mall security" gag is one Steve recycles. He loves to see what people will do when someone speaks with authority when asking them to do preposterous things. One hot summer day, Steve and his family were floating down the Salt River. There are several starting points for tubing this river. All that is needed is a parking area and a bank with a gentle slope into the river. There are no park rangers around for miles. At the location Steve and Amy had chosen, a crowd of sixty or so people were wading into the water. Steve raised his voice and spoke in his most official tone, "Excuse me. We need to inspect your ice chests. Please line up over here." Almost everyone did. Some even got out of the river, went back on shore, and got in line to comply.

On another occasion, Steve and his family and some friends were attending an Easter pageant. Several temporary restrooms were set up. When Steve walked into the men's restroom, he decided to have some fun. He announced that they needed to move the restrooms over a few feet. Would everyone please hold on. The men complied, with sidelong glances of "What the heck?"

Steve's fun is spontaneous. When a joke or a way to heckle reality pops into his mind, he goes with it. When Steve, Jeff, Blake, and Maryn were pulling up to Paul and Melanie Waite's house on their way to Los Angeles, Steve said, "Jeff, I am going to tell Melanie that you are deaf and mute. Just go with it."

"Done deal," said Jeff.

The friends greeted each other and started catching up on the latest. Jeff says, "Everyone is talking, except for me. Steve explains I'm a client, a friend of Blake's—and deaf and mute. Melanie is as sweet as it gets. She is a sweet, wonderful lady. She was so sympathetic." After a while, they started to make dinner plans. "They wanted to go somewhere nice for dinner. Steve asked me through pantomime where I wanted to go. I pulled out this coupon I had from McDonald's for free fries and I started pointing to the word 'McDonalds.' You could tell Melanie didn't want to go to McDonalds, but she didn't want to go against me, this poor guy that couldn't hear and speak."

Steve's fun often has an impish quality. Shanti Zimmerman currently lives in Switzerland, but she is originally from Arizona. When she returned to Arizona for a visit, she posted that she was in Phoenix. Steve responded and invited her to work out with him at CrossFit. She accepted. She was doing handstands—not an easy feat. She says, "You have to fight for a handstand. Every time I was doing one, Steve would come over and kick it out from underneath me. He was being really, really, really cheeky. There is definitely a part of him that is mischievous and playful."

Every few years, Amy and her sisters take a sisters' trip. Steve takes the opportunity to do his favorite kind of vacation: no hard and fast plans, no museums, no touristy destinations—just free flow, spontaneous adventure, just friends to visit and people to meet. When Amy and her sisters prepared to go to Boston to visit their brother, Steve posted that he was driving to Salt Lake. If anyone wanted to meet up en route, let him know.

Lisa Berkovitz was in Los Angeles at the time. She had been traveling nomadically for about three months. She says, "I had been speaking in L.A. I was staying for a couple weeks, just hanging out and not knowing where I was going next. I literally had no plan. I kind of make things up as I go." Sounds like Steve's kindred spirit. She was the first to respond to his posting. She wrote, "I have a mind to get myself somewhere on your route."

Steve replied in capital letters, "DO IT!!" So, she did.

When Lisa met Steve in Salt Lake City, he told her he had some other people he had to meet that day. He invited her to join him for the day if she didn't have any other plans. She was available and delighted. "And so off we went on this absolutely magical adventure," says Lisa. "It was total superflow, just meandering in and out of the day." Lisa calls it her "ten-and-a-half-hour lunch." They flowed from one thing to the next.

"We talked about why he was so in love with Amy and all the things that he loves about her. When I said, 'Oh, tell me more,' he said, 'I could talk about that for six hours.' He also shared stories of his life." What did Lisa learn about Steve after spending all day with him? "He's got a trickster quality to him. He's got a rock-and-roll quality to him. He's got a sass, a charm, and a wild streak. He's such a paradox. He has a wild, unbridled force through which life flows."

Steve regenerates by being spontaneous. He gets power from connecting with people. His week-long wanderings are pure bliss.

But he takes bliss in smaller amounts too. One day, Amy and Steve were out running some errands. She had a book on hold at the library. Steve parked while Amy ran in. She was only gone a few minutes. When she came out, she could see two African American women talking to someone, but a van was blocking her view so she couldn't see to whom they were talking. The women were smiling and laughing. Amy knew they were talking to Steve. The van pulled away. Amy was right.

Fun on the Internet

"Social media is so often an outlet for self-indulgence and glorification," observes Adam Amin Mahboubi. "Everyone I know, including myself, plays into that. I think it's interesting that Steve

Steve, 1994

posts things you would never expect to be posted, super random, super joyful things." John Vehr says more candidly, "You've seen Facebook posts from him, right? They are crazy. He posts shit that the rest of us would say, 'I need to edit that.'" Steve doesn't care. He is having fun.

One of the things that Steve loves to do is to create contests and post them on his Facebook page. He has sponsored a "Guess what is the last thing I do before I go to sleep" contest and a "Fill in the blank: Amy says I should have been a _____" contest. The first person to respond with the correct answer wins a prize. Sometimes it is a $500 gift card. Sometimes it is simply going to lunch with him. However, since Steve rarely does business lunches, that is a treat.

Steve's favorite contests have been for concert tickets. Amy is not a hard rock fan, so when a group comes to town that Steve wants to see, he creates a contest. He asks people to tell him why he or she should be the one to go with him to the concert. He has done it twice. Once for Jethro Tull and once for the Rolling Stones. The answers are fascinating. Sometimes the answers are so good Steve buys additional tickets. With the Rolling Stones concert, Steve upped the ante. Steve embedded in his contest rules the requirement of mentioning the name of his turtle. If you were a regular follower of his Facebook posts, the answer was easy.

The winners of the Rolling Stones contest were Gary Mahler, Bryan Samuels, and Curtis Marsh. Gary is a client of Steve's. He flew in from Canada to attend the concert. Curtis and Bryan flew in from out of state. Curtis says of the evening, "We danced, sang, and laughed like it was the last concert we would ever be attending. Four guys, three of whom had never met until that night, and we created a memory that is forever tattooed on my heart. Sometimes one gets to catch lightning in a bottle."

Bryan Samuels shares his experience:

I put on some pure 70s rocker wear, platform heels and leather pants. In Phoenix. During August. Never said I was the sharpest knife in the drawer. Curtis Marsh, Gary Mahler and I met up at the Hyatt Regency hotel. Curtis' excitement was infectious. Gary is quietly confident, and the gentlest of souls. Shortly after we got there and introduced ourselves, Steve pulled up and we piled in.

Suddenly it became obvious that meeting Steve Hardison is a somewhat ineffable experience. The first light we stopped at has Steve throwing the gear lever into park as he drops the windows, exits the car and dances around it to "Start Me Up." As a stalwart Mormon, I know he has not had a drop of liquor. This isn't a typical sixty-something-year-old.

We had a fabulous evening. Our dinner discussion was as tasty as the steaks. Steve continued his generosity as he bought each of us a concert shirt. The show was magnificent, far exceeding my expectations. And where was Steve? Dancing in the aisle. Making friends with a dozen strangers. Having the time of his life.

After the concert, we chatted as Steve drove. At times the topics were serious, at times light. When we said our goodbyes, we hugged like brothers.

These are the contests to date, but you can be sure there will be more in the future.

And in case you are wondering, the last thing Steve does each night is squirt on some cologne. And Amy thinks this master delegator missed his calling. He should have been a king.

Dancing like a Star

"While Steve is a human dynamo wherever he is," says Curtis Marsh, "that's most true where the music's loud, live, and rocking"—especially if the music just happens to be "Walk This Way" or "Play That Funky Music White Boy" or "All Right Now." When Steve hears those songs, it is a dance party, wherever he is. Jackie Skinner connected with Steve during his driving adventure to Salt Lake City. She relates:

> I met Steve in downtown Salt Lake. We only had ten minutes because he was meeting with someone right after me. He accidentally left a gift he had been given at our table. I didn't notice this until about fifteen minutes after he left. I texted him about the forgotten gift, and in about ten minutes, Steve showed up in his awesome white car (I don't know cars well, but it's a nice one!) with the music full blast. He pulled up to grab the gift, and ended up getting out of the car, music still fully blasted, and the two of us danced on the busy sidewalk. A window washer was right next to us and just laughed. It was a solid minute-long dance party, and then he zoomed off.

On that same day, Steve met up with Curtis Marsh and Bryan Samuels. Lisa Berkovitz says, "All of a sudden, Curtis has The Rolling Stones' "Start Me Up" blasting at full volume from his Range Rover. The three of them begin dancing right there in the parking lot. They are dancing like no one is watching—strutting around like Mick Jagger and playing air guitar!"

Steve dances with abandon. He doesn't care if he is at a concert or on a busy city street or in a store or a mall—or anywhere else. When he feels the music, his energy surges and he starts to move.

Steve in his Halloween costume, 2019

He merges with the music. Steve is in a zone of absolute self-expression and pure bliss.

Melanie Waite recalls when she and her husband Paul went on a cruise with Steve and Amy:

> We were in one of the larger venues that had a bar area, a stage, a dance floor, and general seating. It was really full. The MC announced they were having a Tina Turner impersonation competition. He asked for volunteers. Five people volunteered—four women and Steve. They went backstage.

When they came out, they were all in Tina Turner outfits and wearing Tina Turner wigs. Steve had this sparkly silver, sequined mini dress on. One by one, each participant danced to one of Tina Turner's songs. When it was Steve's turn, he let loose. He had absolutely no inhibitions. He danced like he was a rock star performing on stage. His energy was astounding. Amy and I never laughed as much as we did that night. It was so, so funny. Of course, he won the competition.

Emma Holmes says, "Steve is pure light, love, kindness and generosity. He is also playful, fun and energized." Indeed, he is enlightened and outrageous. He is intensely focused with his work and gleefully cheeky in his life. He is not either/or. He is both/and. As Carla Rotering says, "His playfulness is intertwined with the rest of who he is, which is really delightful."

Chapter 38

Making Sense of Steve

The nuns in the abbey break out in a song that is so snappy it is hard not to sing along. It is the second scene in the classic movie, *The Sound of Music*, just after Maria twirls in an alpine meadow in her beloved Austrian Alps. The nuns in the abbey are trying to make sense of Maria, their atypical novitiate. They differ in their opinions about Maria but agree that the task of understanding her is as challenging as catching a cloud, pinning a wave upon the sand, and holding a moonbeam in your hand.

The same could be said for Steve. He defies easy explanation. He does not fit in classic categories. He simply isn't standard. Jason Jaggard reflects:

> Steve goes to a pedicure place and has exclamation marks painted on his toenails. Who does that? That is not normal. He does these weird things. That's probably the headline for Steve Hardison: "Who does that?" And that's what makes him so wonderful. His way of being is a threat to normality.

He radically accepts normality and radically disrupts it at the same time. And that is a really fascinating experience.

Steve warps normality the way gravity warps time and space. He produces perplexity. The consensus is that there is no one quite like Steve. Here is a sampling from a friend, family member, and client. John Goodie says, "I've never met a person like him in my life. And I've met a lot of people." Steve's sister, Teresa, says, "Steve is not like a lot of people. There's not another Steve, not that I know of." Clate Mask says, "Steve is so different than anybody I've ever met. Everybody you meet is different, but he's more different than anybody."

Indeed, most people don't turn their son's wisdom teeth into pendants for a necklace, which they wear. Most people don't keep their kidney stones and use them for the center stone of a ring. Most people don't frame an MRI of their brain and hang it in their house. Most people don't frame a close up of an ant so they can tell people, "This is my favorite ant (aunt)." Most men don't wear patent leather, fuchsia Oxfords. But Steve is unique, pathologically unique. Is it any surprise he pronounces "unique" as "**you**-ni-Q"? He thrives on zigging when others zag. He delights in leaving people slightly befuddled.

Scott Law says, "People who observe Steve from afar don't really know how to take him. He's very, very interesting, even quirky. People don't get it. They think there has to be some sort of a motive behind it. He is so unusual, so peculiar that you just don't know."

Patrick Provost says:

He can be different than what people are used to. It can be polarizing. People either love him or fatally they don't. He can be very intense, especially when he has an intention or a commitment to do something. Actually, he can be intense even when there isn't an obvious intention. Maybe it's just a function of who he is. I'd say that most of the time people really like him. And when they don't, they really don't. It's pretty rare that I find somebody who doesn't like Steve, but it has happened.

John Vehr says it this way:

If you look at a bell curve, something like 80 percent of people are in the middle. And then 10 percent are on each side, the outliers. Steve doesn't fit on the bell curve. He doesn't even fit with the outliers. He is kind of broken. He doesn't have the thing inside of him that judges others. I don't think he has a thing that judges himself. He does what he does because he's broken, and I mean that in the most loving, kind, and honoring way I can say it. Because he is broken, he doesn't see the world the way the rest of us do.

No doubt, Steve is difficult to decipher, but that doesn't mean we aren't going to try.

How to Make Sense of Steve

In interviewing people for this book, Alan asked nearly every interviewee what they thought makes Steve Steve. Some proverbially threw their hands up in the air and surrendered to the mystery, but most people weighed in, offering a variety of possibilities. Steve's daughter, Lil, summed it up well when she said, "I think he was born naturally more sensitive, more in tune with people and the world around him. His early life experiences created more of that. He has worked to develop his strengths. And then there is his energy. He was given a gift. It's a gift that I don't think you can completely create, and yet it is a gift that can be cultivated."

We will touch on these things and then plunge into speculation, but not wild speculation. We will consider theories that offer solid possibilities. They will provide some aha moments. They may even dispel some of the mystery. Will they completely explicate Steve? Not even close. But until we can take a MRI of Steve's personality or do an autopsy on his state of being, this may be the closest anyone will come to figuring out the enigma that is Steve.

Nature

Without a doubt, Steve entered this world with genes from two powerhouses. "My mom," says Steve's sister, Teresa, "was intuitive and perceptive. She could figure out people really fast. She was very intelligent. Our father was intelligent and very creative. That is in Steve's DNA. Steve has always thought at a higher, more creative plane."

Steve's sister, Jayme, adds this insight:

Steve would have known our dad less than anybody, and Steve is the most like him as far as charm, personality, and making friends. My dad was tall and very good-looking. There are a lot of similarities. Steve is not like him in the bad aspects. In my dad's later years, he did a lot of things that nobody would be proud of. But Steve was never like that. Where my dad chose some self-destructive paths, Steve chose to make something of his life.

Particularly interesting is Jayme's remark that of all the family members, Steve knew their father the least. Steve only has a few memories of him. His opportunities for direct modeling were limited. This suggests that when Steve exhibits his father's traits and behaviors, genetics is in play.

In 1995, Steve and Amy made a trip to Adairville, Kentucky, where Roy Hardison grew up over sixty years before. It was like stepping into Mayberry. It had an old-fashioned town center built around a square park with mature, shady trees. There was a colonial-style town hall in the town center, complete with a clock tower. There was a barbershop with a red, white, and blue pole and a wooden bench that invited folks to sit a spell and gab. Three elderly men sat on the bench. As Steve approached them to ask directions, one man raised his voice and said, "You must be Roy Hardison's son." It stopped Steve in his tracks.

"How did you know?"

"You walk just like him."

The power of genetics is amazing, and slightly creepy. In Steve's case, it accounts for his charm, his fastidiousness, his propensity for practical jokes, his ability to talk the birds out of the trees, and probably several other unrecognized connections to a father who was absent yet present, if only at a molecular level.

Nurture

Maurine Hardison had a bit of the rebel in her. She abandoned her Mormon upbringing for a more unbridled lifestyle, which she kept even after returning to conservative Clearfield after her divorce. For Pioneer Day, the holiday celebrating the pioneers' arrival in Utah, she shaved Steve's and Phil's hair into mohawks. It got them kicked out of grade school. It was just too edgy for 1962. Decades later, Amy remembers Maurine dropping one-liners here and there,

Steve (left), Phil (right), with mohawks,
Matt Mason (center) 1963

encouraging her to question authority. It was a lost cause. Amy colors inside the lines. Maurine was more successful with Steve. He questions authority, organizations, rules, paradigms, and all status quo thinking. Maurine would be proud.

This was not the only attitude Maurine bequeathed to Steve. Maurine had moxie. She was a natural-born CEO. She radiated: "Don't mess with me—or even think about it." No doubt there is a genetic component to the transmission of these assertive traits, but there was also plenty of modeling. In addition, Maurine gave her children a lot of leeway to experience life, to fail, and to learn through natural consequences. Maybe this was by choice, maybe by necessity. In a pre-cell phone era, Maurine simply couldn't be too hands-on as a mom when she was rarely at home.

Maurine Hardison Echols, about 1985

In the 1960s, single-parent homes were not as common as they are today. At times, curious friends asked Steve, "What's it like growing up without a dad?" Steve's answer was always, "It's great! I have so much freedom." It was a hybrid answer, part bravado and part truth. Steve would have loved a *Leave it to Beaver*-style home, but it's doubtful he would have become who he is today without the untethered freedom he experienced.

Teresa notes, "In the early years, Steven wasn't constrained. My mother wasn't teaching him a lot of things. My dad wasn't there. As siblings, we were all doing our own thing. No one was putting restraints on Steve's creativity." No one was reining in his ideas. No one was demanding he adhere to social conventions. He was a free spirit with plenty of space.

Steve's son, Clint, observes:

I have a unique dad. He's unique in a lot of ways. I have spent a lot of my life pondering, "Who is this guy? Why is he like this?" I think he came that way. I think that he is wired differently. I think the nature of his childhood added to it. He had to learn to survive and he had to be creative in ways other kids didn't have to. That cultivated skills in him that other people don't have to cultivate.

Amy certainly never had to get creative to make sure she ate. Neither did Steve's kids. When Steve was young, he bounded down the stairs in the morning hoping there would be $.35 on the table for lunch money. It was hit and miss. But hunger is a great motivator. It kicked Steve's creativity into high gear. He came up with a lot of ways to get food, some of which were even legal.

So many of the exceptional talents and abilities that Steve has today can be traced back to his childhood experiences. But there was also a dark side. There was trauma. There was a sense of abandonment. There was literally living on the wrong side of the tracks and being the kid that parents didn't want their children hanging out with. There was not fitting into the establishment, be it church, school, or community. There was having too much energy, too many words, and too much unbounded zest—aka a penchant for trouble. Steve internalized all these things and adapted accordingly. Some of his adaptations were empowering. Some haunted him for years.

Louise Phipps Senft observes, "I think Steve was deeply wounded as a child and has probably spent his whole life trying to overcome his woundedness. It is a lifetime journey. He will possibly never be fully healed until he moves over the veil into pure spirit. But he's wired as a fighter. His big fight kept him alive."

Teresa's thoughts align with Louise's. She says, "Steven is extraordinary. What makes him extraordinary? I do not know. I think that some things he came to earth with. Some things he developed as he worked to make the best out of what was given to him. But I think at his core there is that little boy that felt a sense of trauma."

Ten Thousand Hours

In his book, *Outliers,* Malcolm Gladwell popularized his 10,000-hour rule, the amount of time it takes to achieve mastery. Ten thousand hours roughly equates to ten years of focused work. Gladwell points to Mozart, the Beatles, and Bill Gates as examples. He applies the 10,000-hour rule to things as varied as computer programming, hockey, and chess. What does it have to do with Steve?

Steve was given the raw materials—the genes, the modeling, the freedom, and the environment—to become who he is today. But those things were the possibility of Steve. Between possibility and fruition, Steve buffed and polished, developed and refined his gifts and talents for years. From the time he was eight, and maybe younger, he was having conversations with strangers. He was engaging them, delighting them, and enrolling them to help him. As a missionary and when he traveled in his Rodel days, Steve was always talking to people, asking pointed questions and pushing the limits of conversational propriety to learn about human nature.

Steve has spent 10,000 hours healing his life. In his almost thirty-year career as a coach, he has spent well over 10,000 hours coaching. Clearly, Steve's coaching ability didn't just happen. "Steve is rare and unique," says Shanti Zimmerman. "His capacity is so broad that sometimes people forget that there's a human being behind that. They don't see the sheer magnitude of work that he has done within himself to be that person."

Personality

"Steve, you have to see this movie. The main guy reminds me so much of you." Steve hears this a lot. The star is always bold, brash, and visionary. He goes against the grain. He makes a difference. Steve always sees the movies. Usually he sees himself. Always he sees how others see him.

Steve doppelgangers also show up in books. When Amy was reading Walter Isaacson's *Steve Jobs*, she kept saying to Steve, "You are so much like Steve Jobs." She highlighted passage after passage of similarities. Midway in the book, their personalities diverged and Amy adjusted her assessment. Saloni Singh saw similarities between Steve and the protagonist in Ayn Rand's *Fountainhead*, Howard Rorak, specifically their "sheer amount of self-confidence, trust in oneself, and closeness to divinity." Hana Callaghan was reminded of Steve as she read Czech fairy tales to her daughter Hani: "A hero is born from nothing, accomplishes the unimaginable—while never for a moment thinking it was impossible—and then just goes about his life."

When reading, *War at the End of the World: Douglas MacArthur and the Forgotten Fight for New Guinea, 1942-1945*, by James P. Duffy, Amy found another match. Douglas MacArthur was the Supreme Commander of the Southwest Pacific Area. Admiral Ernest King was the Commander in Chief of the U.S. Fleet and the Chief of Naval Operations, the only officer to hold this combined command. More than anyone else, these two powerful men shaped the Allied strategy in the Pacific Theater—and they were at cross purposes on almost every important issue. According to Kyle Beckman, General MacArthur and Admiral King both had dominant personalities. "Each was confident to the point of arrogance, tenacious to the point of obstinacy, and possessed practical intelligence bordering on genius." Sounds familiar.

The movie heroes, Steve Jobs, the Admiral, the General all point to the fact that there are certain personality types that movers and shakers share. It is something that has been studied extensively under different names, such as "dominant personality." Katrina Faust writes, "People who are high in 'D' [dominant personality] are extroverted and outgoing and task-oriented. They tend to be direct, decisive, driven and demanding. They typically have high confidence, are self-motivated, and are comfortable taking risks. They like to focus on the big picture, not details." It sounds like a description of Steve. Faust reveals the shadow side of High Ds. "When the Dominant trait is overdeveloped, or when people high in D become stressed, they can become impatient, blunt to the point of being insensitive." That shoe fits too.

Another study is Gallup's research on the qualities of highly successful entrepreneurs. They studied more than a thousand entrepreneurs and came up with a short list of ten common qualities. These are:

1. Business Focus
2. Confidence
3. Creative Thinker
4. Delegator
5. Determination
6. Independent
7. Knowledge-Seeker
8. Promoter
9. Relationship-Builder
10. Risk-Taker

Steve is strong in all these areas.

Particularly interesting, Gallup cited research showing that these entrepreneurial characteristics are between 37 percent and 48 percent genetic. Once again, the Steve Hardison we know goes back to Maurine and Roy. Steve inherited the mix of characteristics that generated a dynamic, confident, creative leader with pit bull tenacity.

The Dichotomy

Steve is crazy about black and white. Just look at his toenails. He frequently sports black polish with white exclamation marks, a replica of his business card. Or if the fancy strikes him, he goes with black and white checks. Sixty percent of his clothing is black or white or both. His cars are black or white. Birthday and Christmas gifts are often black and white: black-and-white-striped shirts, black-and-white Oxfords and customized Vans—black with white

Steve, 2017

exclamation marks. Just as form follows function, Steve's partialities reflect his personality. He is awash in dichotomy. It is part of the enigma.

Deanna Chesley says, "Steve is one of the most reverent and irreverent people I know." Scott Law notes that Steve is both humble and confident at the same time. Many clients consider Steve eminently enlightened, making "the Porsches and the California teeth and the chiseled body so unexpected. It is a paradox in so many ways, and I love it" (Mandy Lehto).

Amy says, "If you walk into a furniture store, a jewelry store, or onto a car lot and ask Steve to identify his favorite, he immediately points to the most expensive item. He has an eye for quality. And then he does things like enlarge his senior picture from high school and use a toilet seat for its frame. He thinks it is hilarious. That went in the garage!"

Steve, 66 years old, 2021

The dichotomies are ubiquitous. Steve loves hard rock and pan flute music. He is an extreme extrovert and basks in his alone time. He is both edgy and conservative. He is extremely picky when it comes to the taste of meat and he delights in odd culinary combinations, like a sandwich of peanut butter, jelly, cheese, pickles, and ham. He is a veritable noise machine, loud, talkative, and boisterous—and he is disrupted by loud noises. He is absolutely enlightened and transformed—and he has meltdowns that are anything but enlightened.

His dichotomy is evident in his coaching. He kisses the feet of his clients and then gets in their face with sound and fury. Theresa Campbell relates:

> At one point I was sitting on the couch and he was on his knees in front of me. I remember feeling almost cared for, like I was a baby again. And then there was this crescendo until he was screaming at me, "Are you going to get this message, lady?!" I'll never forget it. He was yelling, "You are as talented as anyone who has ever sat in this office. You could be running the Ford Motor Company, if you wanted to." It was intense, but it was really nice. I felt like he gave me a million-dollar coaching session.

Ollie Trew says:

> The guy is a complete enigma. One minute I feel like I'm being massively challenged, as though he is poking a hot dagger into my heart and twisting it around. The next minute, I feel like I'm being hugged by a Care Bear and receiving all of his love. That's the best I can describe it: a hot poker in the heart; compassionate Care Bear. I love that those two things go hand in hand.

It is perplexing. He is perplexing. As Carla Rotering notes, "He's a rascal. He's a motorcycle guy. He's a Mormon. He's all of those incredible, conflicting polarities." And then some.

A Highly Sensitive Person

Perhaps you have noticed. When asked what makes Steve Steve, the people who know him best—his siblings, Amy, his children—all mention, "He came like that." But what is the "that"? Could that "that" hold the secret of Steve?

Fifteen to twenty percent of people are born with a neurological system that is prewired to be highly sensitive. They are considered "highly sensitive persons" (HSP), a term coined by Elaine Aron, a clinical research psychologist and pioneer in the field of high sensitivity. High sensitivity exists on a continuum. Some HSPs consider themselves extremely sensitive, others quite a bit sensitive, and still others just moderately so. Steve never does things part way. He definitely falls into the extremely sensitive category. Many, but not all, HSPs are quiet and reserved. Thirty percent are extroverts. An extremely sensitive, extroverted HSP, like Steve, would fall into a narrow category of people who might be born "like that."

There are four main traits of HSPs, arranged in an order to make the acronym D.O.E.S.

1. **D**epth of Processing

The fundamental characteristic of HSPs is their depth of processing sensory information. HSPs "notice levels of stimulation that go unobserved by others. This is true whether we are talking about subtle sounds, sights, or physical sensations like pain . . . We [HSPs] sort things into finer distinctions. Like those machines that grade fruit by size—we sort into ten sizes while others sort into two or three."

2. **O**verstimulation

People perform best when their nervous systems are moderately alert and aroused. Too little arousal and life is bland and boring. Too much arousal and life is like Times Square Everlasting. The optimal level of arousal is somewhere in the middle. This is true for everyone, both HSPs and non-HSPs. The difference is the tipping point. Aron notes, "What is moderately arousing for most people is highly arousing for HSPs. What is highly arousing for most people causes an HSP to become very frazzled indeed."

HSPs are constantly processing every detail, all the time, whether they are aware of it or not. Thus, HSPs' nervous systems are frequently overstimulated, overtaxed, and overwhelmed. Consequently, HSPs needs plenty of down time. They may marvel and even envy those who can keep going and going and going, like the energizer bunny.

3. **E**motional Reactivity / **E**mpathy

The "E" in D.O.E.S. does double duty. It stands for emotional reactivity, which means HSPs have stronger reactions to both positive and negative experiences and to external and internal stimuli. External stimuli include pain, light, and noise. While most people tune out sirens, glaring lights, strange odors, clutter and chaos, HSPs are disturbed by them. They may even find them physically painful. Internal stimuli include thoughts, emotions, and realizations.

The "E" also stands for empathy. HSPs are more aware of others' emotions and are intensely affected by them. This can be traced to a phenomenon discovered by scientists in the early 1990s called mirror neurons. When humans watch someone do something, a clump of neurons fires in the same way as the neurons fire in the person who is actually doing that thing. For example, whether you are kicking a soccer ball or watching someone kick a soccer ball, the same neurons fire. These mirror neurons help us perceive others' feelings and intentions and are partly responsible for the universal human capacity for empathy. They are especially active in HSPs, who excel at knowing how someone else feels.

4. Sensitive to Subtleties

HSPs will notice small sounds, tiny distractions, smells, or tastes that others aren't even aware of. This awareness is both physical and emotional. Aron explains, "Most people walk into a room and perhaps notice the furniture, the people—and that's about it. HSPs are instantly aware, whether they wish to be or not, of the mood, the friendships, the amenities, the freshness or staleness of the air, [and] the personality of the one who arranged the flowers."

Humans are not the only ones who are highly sensitive. Mice, cats, dogs, horses, and monkeys—all higher animals—exhibit these traits. There may be an evolutionary reason for high sensitivity. Highly sensitive animals may serve as an early warning system, alerting the less sensitive animals of imminent danger, whether that danger be a predator or a natural disaster. Duly warned, the less sensitive animals can escape to safety. Such watchmen on the savannah and in the forest are assets in their animal communities. But you can't have a whole gaggle of watchmen. Some animals need to charge into the unknown, blissfully unaware of every threat. Thus, according to Aron, "those with the sensitive survival strategy will always be in a minority."

Highly sensitive people have strengths beyond boosting the odds of survival. They are often very intelligent, creative, exceptionally intuitive, compassionate, and spiritual. Their oversensitivities enrich and amplify their talents, so much so that they veer into the domain of giftedness. On the flip side, because they take in so much sensory information, they are more easily overwhelmed and stressed out than non-HSPs. When the onslaught of sights, sounds, and emotions becomes too much, they may get upset, frazzled, and angry.

This is only a brief overview of sensory-processing sensitivity (the trait's scientific term). For those interested, Elaine Aron's *The Highly Sensitive Person* is the bible in the field. For us, this survey is enough. We can move on to looking at the nature of highly sensitive persons in terms of Steve's life and personality.

Inheritance

Having a highly sensitive nervous system is an inherited trait, but not entirely. Some people become highly sensitive because of abuse, trauma, or extreme stress in their childhood. Steve, it appears, has a double source for high sensitivity.

No doubt, Maurine was an HSP. When describing their mother, each of her children remark on Maurine's extraordinary ability to read people. And there was the spraying of the fields, the purses from China, the smell of new carpet, paint, and perfume that made Maurine's life nearly unbearable at times. Of course, most people notice and may even dislike the smell of a newly painted room or a newly carpeted house. But for Maurine, it was painful. When Steve and Amy remodeled, it was well over a year before Maurine could step inside their house. In her last decade, Maurine couldn't stay in hotels because of the fumes emitted by the carpet. It didn't even have to be new carpet. She bought a small travel trailer so she could take a clean room on the road. Elaine Aron notes that HSPs are more sensitive to all things airborne. They suffer more hay fever and skin rashes. That explains the spraying of the fields.

Not Your Average Joe

Many HSPs feel like they don't fit in. They fear they are broken, out of step with the rest of humanity. For instance, Mel Collins writes, "For the first three decades of my life, I was convinced that there was something wrong with me. I seemed to feel things more deeply than those around me and processed my emotions for longer . . . As a child, I heard consistent messages of 'stop being so sensitive,' but I didn't know how to stop something that was naturally a part of me."

Steve has never seen his unique abilities as a liability. He loves who he is. His gifts are an invaluable asset. His clients would agree. Still, that doesn't negate the fact that Steve, a super-HSP, is truly different, as in "from a different planet." Dustin Venekamp says, "Steve is just someone like no one has ever seen on the planet." Steve is definitely different. It's not our imagination.

For years, Amy has said that Steve's senses are acute and supersensitive. Steve can smell something in the kitchen that is off three days before Amy. Steve sees details from a hundred feet that Amy is oblivious to at three feet. Steve rarely goes outside without sunglasses, even for a few minutes. The sun is brutal on his eyes. Even at night, Steve likes minimal indoor lighting. Normal lighting is too glaring. But in actuality, it is probably not Steve's senses at all.

Elaine Aron explains that HSPs' hearing, vision or other senses are not superior. Rather, the difference is in the brain. An HSP's brain processes information differently, more carefully. This difference is observable. Jadzia Jagiellowicz and her colleagues studied the brain activation of HSPs and non-HSPs and found HSPs use more of the part of the brain that is associated with the deeper processing of information. HSPs also have more activity in the right side of their brain. They have more norepinephrine, which is the brain's version of adrenaline, and more cortisol, which is the hormone present in higher concentrations when a person is in a constant state of arousal or wariness. The Russian physiologist Ivan Pavlov believed that the most basic inherited difference among people is how soon they reach the point where their system is overwhelmed by stimuli. He concludes that those who are quick to shut down (i.e., HSPs) have a fundamentally different type of nervous system.

The essential point from the studies of Pavlov, Jagiellowicz, and others is that HSPs don't just behave differently; their brains actually *work* differently than the brains of non-HSPs. Jerome Kagan of Harvard concludes that HSPs "are a special breed. They are genetically quite different, although still utterly human, just as bloodhounds and border collies are quite different, although both are still definitely dogs." Little wonder HSPs feel out of step with their world and that non-HSPs are left scratching their heads when they are with an HSP. No surprise that most of us don't know quite how to explain Steve. John Patrick Morgan says:

> There are very few people I meet that I can't understand where they're coming from or what their reality is, especially after spending some time with them. Usually I can anticipate what they will say. But Steve's responses continuously come

out of left field. I definitely can't anticipate them. It's like he blindsides me every time, in a good way. My interest in working with Steve is to be able to see the world that he sees.

Awareness and Intuition

One of the central traits of HSPs is that they pick up on the subtleties around them. Be it sights, sounds, or emotions, they are aware of things that a non-HSP would never see. When Steve and Amy pick up a rental car or accept delivery on a piece of furniture or do a walk through with a contractor, it is Steve's job to inspect. He sees everything, from the smallest scratch to the tiniest variance in alignment. It is a remarkable ability—and it can be frustrating. It sets a high bar for contractors. Steve can be seen as picky. When younger, the relentless awareness of a flawed world was a constant, low-grade irritation, but Steve learned to let go of that.

To non-HSPs, particularly the forty-two percent of people who consider themselves "not at all" sensitive, an HSP's ability to see, hear, and feel things that are below their radar is mind-boggling. It is, as Aron notes, like talking to Laplanders about coconuts. Aron gives an example of the different ways an HSP and non-HSP experience life. "Imagine Rob and Rebecca coming to school one morning. Rebecca sees the same classroom, teacher, and children as were there yesterday. She runs off to play. Rob notices that the teacher is in a bad mood, one of the children is looking angry, and some bags are in the corner that were not there before." Steve wouldn't miss the emotional temperature or the bags in the corner. Such things are like the E on the eye chart for him. For non-HSPs, they are the smallest line of letters.

Steve clearly responds to subtle visual and audio cues from his clients and derives remarkably accurate conclusions about them. But that isn't the whole story. "HSPs' systems are very porous," says Hary McBride. "That is, external stimuli seem to be more directly absorbed into their bodies. It has been said that HSPs hardly have skin at all to protect them from the outside stimuli." A less porous system, such as the skin of non-HSPs, diffuses outside stimuli and thereby keeps the nervous system from taking in too much and overloading. It is interesting that John Goodie says of Steve, "He thinks beyond the body. He thinks beyond the real." Steve, himself, when asked how he is able to see into a person's soul, says, "It is seeing, feeling, hearing. It is also something else I can't put into words. I am a huge receptor." That is unintelligible to those of us whose skin does its job.

This hyperawareness is why HSPs are highly intuitive. An HSP processes sensory information both consciously and subconsciously, whether they want to or not. It is the subconscious processing that leads HSPs to say they "just know things" without knowing how they know them. In fact, Aron defines intuition as "picking up and working through information in a semiconscious or unconscious way." Aron elaborates, "You 'just know' how things got to be the way they are or how they are going to turn out. This is that 'sixth sense' people talk about. It can be wrong, of course, just as your eyes and ears can be wrong, but your intuition is right often enough that HSPs tend to be visionaries."

Holly Profitt-Venekamp relates her experience of Steve's awareness and intuition:

> We were filming a podcast at our home and Steve came over. I introduced him to the three other people that were at our house, Christie, Lauren and Paul. Paul was in my kitchen, about twenty feet away. Lauren was on the other side of the family room. She was not facing Paul. They were not even

in the same room. Steve said, "Oh, are you guys married?" These are just random people he has never met before. They say no, but apparently, they had just kissed the night before. How does Steve know stuff like that? I don't know. He's magical. He had them pegged right away. They are married now.

Creativity

Pearl S. Buck once said:

The truly creative mind in any field is no more than this: A human creature born abnormally, inhumanly sensitive. To him . . . a touch is a blow, a sound is a noise, a misfortune is a tragedy, a joy is an ecstasy, a friend is a lover, a lover is a god, and failure is death. Add to this cruelly delicate organism the overpowering necessity to create, create, create—so that without the creating of music or poetry or books or buildings or something of meaning, his very breath is cut off from him. He must create, must pour out creation. By some strange, unknown, inward urgency he is not really alive unless he is creating.

It sounds like Buck is speaking from experience. It also sounds like she is speaking of Steve. Indeed, for Steve, a "touch is a blow"—and a cold is a dire illness, but more on that later. Studies have shown that HSPs are very creative. Perhaps it is because they are often more right-brained and less linear in their thinking. Perhaps it is because many HSPs tend to link and combine different ideas in new and creative ways.

Creativity is Steve's lifeblood. It is the heart of his coaching and the essence of every conversation. "With every question, with every answer, with every conversation, I am creating," says Steve. "It's all I do all day long. It gives me energy. I could talk about creation for forty days."

Love and Tenderness

HSPs, says Aron, "fall in love harder than others." Bryan Samuels notes, "Steve honors his wife to a degree that approaches worship." Enough said. HSPs also cry more easily. They are moved to tears by movies, music, and art. Steve can be seen wiping away a tear or two while experiencing musical performances, from Freddie Mercury to *The Lamb of God*. He is also profoundly moved by underdogs, the courage of everyday heroes—especially his clients— the miracle of a strawberry growing out of dirt, and grocery store grand openings. Steve is sensitive, tender, and susceptible to awe.

Many HSP traits are traditionally associated with females. That is why Amy calls Steve, "my metrosexual." In fact, Amy and Steve experience several role reversals. Steve talks more, talks more about feelings, loves to shop more, is more disturbed by violence in a movie, loves clothes more, and loves shoes a whole lot more. Amy is happy with two pairs of flip flops.

Think About Thinking

Steve's son Clint recalls many summer evenings, lying on the grass with Steve, looking up at the stars. Sometimes they talked about eternity. Sometimes it got even deeper. Clint says, "I remember him explaining to me how the self doesn't exist. I thought, 'What are you talking about? Dude, I'm nine.'"

HSPs love to think about life and death and how complicated everything is, and they spend more time doing it than non-HSPs.

They love to think about thinking. Steve loves to ponder the mysteries of life, space, and existence. And "thinking about thinking" is an apt description of the Forum, Byron Katie, the Enneagram, and USM. It also sounds a lot like the twelve-year old Steve in the shed behind his grandpa's house, the forty-something Steve gazing at the stars with his son, and the current Steve as he meditates in his Zen garden.

Zen gardens are made-to-order for HSPs. Meditation is how they thrive. Aron says:

> HSPs need plenty of downtime just for unwinding and thinking over the day . . . Yet another form of rest, perhaps the most essential, is transcendence—rising above it all, usually in the form of mediation, contemplation, or prayer. At least some of your transcendent time should be aimed at taking you out of all ordinary thinking into pure consciousness, pure being, pure unity, or oneness with God. Even if your transcendence falls short of this when you return, you will have a bigger, fresher perspective on your life.

Keeping it Simple

"Keep my toys simple and my life uncomplicated." Aron gives this advice to parents of highly sensitive children, speaking from the child's perspective. It's not something an HSP outgrows. Steve's toys are more expensive and go a whole lot faster than a child's toys, but they are still simple. A nice—*really* nice—car is the only toy Steve really wants. And he definitely wants his life uncomplicated.

Jenara Nerenberg, an HSP and the author of *Divergent Mind: Thriving in a World that Wasn't Designed for You,* says, "I find it unpleasant to have a lot going on at once." Steve has a busy mind. If his outside world moves at the same velocity, it is too much. Steve gets frazzled. At such moments, Amy consciously slows her speaking. In general, she works to keeps the chaos at bay. Steve practices and advocates slowing down and just being present.

Hary McBride, an HSP, says, "It doesn't take much to make me happy . . . I am capable of being happy all day long just because I saw a parakeet flying in the wind. It's not a 'Hallelujah! My life is complete' kind of happiness, but more of a childish excitement. And who wouldn't want to feel that awe so easily?"

Jason Jaggard experienced Steve's parakeet happiness. During one session, Steve spent a significant amount of time walking Jason through his Zen garden, pointing out all the flowers, plants, and trees. Jason says, "He was like, 'Look at that! Look at this! Look! Look!' It was almost like a five-year old showing a parent. He was modeling wonder and awe and how beautiful the world is. I'll be honest. I was having a lot of judgments come up. This sixty-five-year old man is delighting in a flower and I'm thinking, 'What the hell?'" Eventually, Jason saw the beauty and wonder of it. He reflects, "That's what Steve does. He creates a space that is so big that you judge it at first. But then when you step into it, you expand, and it makes sense."

Clint offers this insight:

One thing that strikes me about my dad is that he'll have an experience that I would have brushed off. For instance, let's say I am on my way from A to B, and this little thing happens. I wouldn't even tell anybody about it. And my dad is on his way from A to B, the same thing happens and he sees divinity in it. He picks up the phone and calls people. He says, "You are not going to believe what happened to me." No one else would have made that phone call because no one else would have viewed it that way. I've gotten that call from him so many times.

Simple, uncomplicated joy.

Extracurricular Traits

The following traits don't have a direct bearing on coaching, but they still capture Steve in ways his clients may or may not have experienced.

Low Threshold for Pain

"Amy! I've cut myself. I need help." Amy used to run to Steve. Now she walks. She knows she will probably have a hard time seeing the wound. When she gets to Steve, they both laugh.

"Looks like you need stitches," says Amy. "I'm just not sure where."

HSPs are typically very sensitive to all forms of pain. For Steve, a muscle cramp feels like a vice. A sore throat feels like knives slicing his throat. And a cold—well, get out the last will and testament.

Amy used to think Steve was kind of a baby. Now she understands they have different baselines for pain. Still, she can't help teasing Steve just a little when she brings him his meals in bed when he has a cold.

Nostalgia

Aron writes, "The deeper processing of subtle details causes you to consider the past or future more." Steve is highly nostalgic. Every visit to Utah includes driving by his childhood home, his grade school, junior high, and high school—with ample narration. He still remembers his junior high locker combination. He tears up when he hears music he loved as a teenager. Anything that happened pre-1976 has elite status in Steve's mind and memory. It is only with the greatest difficulty that Amy has kept a conversation pit out of their home. They do have shag carpeting.

Physical Sensations

Hary McBride says, "I love the feeling of a soft blanket against my skin. The touch of a loved one has a similar effect. When I walk out the door and the smell of spring hits me, I am instantly in a good mood for the rest of the day." Physical sensations are intense for an HSP.

Steve loves to be touched. It is probably the real reason he loves pedicures. He purrs like a kitten when Amy rubs his arm nightly. He wiggles his arm if she gets distracted and stops. He has toyed with hiring someone to rub his arm all night long so he can sleep deeply. Amy nixed that idea.

Steve loves Arizona in March when the outdoors smells like orange blossoms. He loves cologne and wears it lavishly. Strong odors, like cooked broccoli, assault his senses and trigger olfactory distress.

Sensitive to Criticism

HSPs tend to react—and overreact—strongly to criticism. They often feel like they are being attacked personally.

In his interview, Ward Andrews says, "Steve has very few weaknesses, but I think one is that if he is challenged or thinks someone isn't listening to him, he can take it as a personal affront. He feels like he has to justify himself, which he certainly doesn't have to do. I think there's a growth edge there for him, a little bit."

Hate to Forget

HSPs may try to avoid making mistakes or forgetting things.

It irritates Steve to no end when he has to get out of his car, go back in the house, and get his car keys, or whatever else he may have forgotten. Except in dire circumstances, once Steve drives away from the house, he does not return if he forgot something.

One-Liners

Finally, some one-liners, all of which apply to Steve:

- HSPs are often rattled by unexpected changes. It can take quite a while for them to adapt to a new situation.
- HSPs tend to not do well in multitasking and find it unpleasant to have a lot going on at once.
- Most people's feet are tired at the end of a day at the mall. HSPs' nervous systems are exhausted.
- HSPs tend to startle easily, are easily stressed by loud noises, strong odors and bright lights.
- HSPs are especially good at tasks requiring vigilance, accuracy, speed, and the detection of minor differences.
- HSPs hate to be rushed and may get rattled when they have to do a lot in a short amount of time.

The Exceptions

Most of the HSP traits fit Steve like an exquisitely tailored suit. But there are certain characteristics that don't fit Steve at all. For instance, an HSP may take more time to fully process information. They may need a few days before they can sort out how they feel or think about something. Steve processes information rapidly and decides quickly. Needlessly drawn out decision-making drives him nuts. HSPs tend to proceed much more cautiously than non-HSPs. Steve loves being spontaneous. He does not proceed with caution. HSPs may find public speaking more challenging. Their key to success is "to prepare, prepare, prepare." Not so for Steve, who won the National Extemporaneous Speaking Competition in 1980. HSPs are "more often cooperative than competitive." Laughable. Steve thrives on competition. These exceptions don't kick Steve out of the HSP club. Rather, they reveal that even within a limited category of people who are different, Steve is still different.

Energy and Intensity

Having looked at nature, nurture, intentional development, personality, and being an HSP, there is still one more component to consider in our attempt to understand Steve—his energy and intensity.

Steve Chandler, who knows Steve as well as anyone outside of his immediate family, attributes Steve's uniqueness to three things: 1) His ability to see into another person and his belief system after talking to him for a very short time. 2) His power of creation. 3) His energy. Regarding this last one, Chandler says, "His energy is simply higher than anyone's I have ever met. Sometimes it's overwhelming to people. Sometimes it's just too much, even though it's benign, even though it's loving."

To get a sense of Steve's energy, picture Niagara Falls—colossal, commanding, dynamic. Steve's sister Teresa says, "Steve is not for a faint-hearted person because his energy will burn other people out." That's not hyperbole. He burned out companions on his mission. When in the midst of a project, like sharing TBOLITNFL with the world, he can put in twenty-hour days while his family lags in exhaustion. When he sees possibility, he is like a horse with blinders, running at top speed and barely aware of the horses dropping out of the race. On the upside, his energy produces unbelievable results.

Riding shotgun to his energy is Steve's intensity. Steve is intense as a way of being, but at the same time his intensity is not always activated. Think of a sports car that goes zero to sixty in 1.9 seconds. Steve's intensity is always there in potential, ready to respond when he hits the gas. Amy explains, "He may be having a totally normal conversation on the phone and the next thing I know, he is yelling and gesticulating. When the phone call is over, he is totally calm and says, 'I just needed to wake someone up.' The passion erupts because he cares so much."

Like his extreme energy, his intensity can be difficult. Adam Amin Mahboubi says, "I would say one of my most challenging things with Steve has been his intensity. He is by far the most intense person I know. And that comes across in his emails, his phone calls, and his Facebook posts. But once you accept that this is actually who this guy is and that he's not messing around, that's really amazing."

There are some incredible benefits to Steve's intensity, if you can handle it. Jason Jaggard says, "Steve trains you how to take things seriously. He trains you how to engage in things with an intensity that most people simply don't have the courage to engage in." In an email to Steve, Bryan Samuels wrote, "There's an intensity, a pressure to your presence. You turn coal into diamonds. And that, my friend, is the rarest of all gifts. It towers above the kindness, enthusiasm and generosity you show to all."

Recently, Stephanie Hoi-Nga Wong, a journalist for nearly twenty years and now a life coach, reached out to Steve. Shortly thereafter, she engaged Steve for a Chocolate Chip Cookie agreement (the ten-hour agreement). She is invigorated by the power and verve of Steve's intensity. She wrote in an email:

Dear Steve,

I'm drawn to your humility, intense passion, authenticity and sincerity . . . Sometimes I coach people with such intensity that I'm worried I will offend them. I almost feel like yelling, yet I try to stay calm . . . I can't help but think to myself: I wish someone would do the same for me (like freaking wake me up and shake me to the core so I can FEEL big and powerful!) . . . I enjoy your intensity and admire your authenticity as well as your courage in showing your vulnerability and emotions. You are genuine and down to earth and emanate love. Big smile.

With love, joy, peace, hope,

Stephanie Hoi-Nga Wong

No doubt, when Steve coaches people who are willing to stand inside the fire of his intensity, they get lit up. They glow with possibility. They burn brightly, so brightly that others notice. But in terms of understanding Steve, that is secondary. Steve's intensity means that every characteristic he has, every trait he embodies and everything mentioned in this chapter is supercharged. He is not just emotionally sensitive. He is *extremely* emotionally sensitive. He is not just high energy. He has more energy than most people have ever seen. He is not just amazing. "He is a walking miracle" (Steven Sainato).

Conclusion

So, what makes Steve Steve? Is it nature? Nurture? Steve's life experiences, the trauma he endured, or the intentional development of his abilities? Is it his personality, his high sensitivity, or his energy and intensity?

Yes.

All of these. All of them together.

And more.

There is undoubtedly a wild card, something else we just can't put our finger on. John Goodie said of Steve, "There are a few people walking this earth who have been blessed with something that is hard to explain." That is the "that" we may never pin down, like the wave upon the sand.

Vignette

Wayne Hoffman

When I met Steve Hardison, I was performing on cruise ships as a mentalist and an illusionist. The ships held 3,000 passengers, so I met a lot of people. In my profession, it is helpful to profile people. I have come up with seven different categories of people, three main categories and four subsets. Steve did not fall into any of those categories. It was a bit off-putting. I read people for a living, yet I couldn't figure him out. Steve was one of very few people I couldn't get a take on right away.

I had two interactions with Steve on the ship that really stood out because they weren't normal. I performed several shows during each cruise, so I was pretty high-profile. As I walked around on the ship, passengers often came up and said they loved my show. Steve walked up to me and said, "I've been looking for you." That was a little out there.

"Is this good or bad?" I asked.

He handed me a book and said, "I want to give you this book. This is for you. But I want you to promise me that you'll read it."

"Well, sure. Absolutely." It was a book by Steve Chandler. No one ever gives me physical objects. They'll say a nice compliment, but not give me something. I was perplexed. "Who is this guy? Is this some kind of sales pitch?" Right away, I knew Steve was not like the average person.

My second experience with Steve was after one of my final shows. There was a little hallway next to the stage. It went back into the kitchen area for the staff. No passengers went there unless they were lost. I was finishing packing up in this hallway and Steve walked up to me and said, "All right, I have a challenge for you. If you can tell me my middle name, I will be your biggest fan and I will book you a show in Los Angeles, guaranteed."

"Oh, really?" I said. I love these moments because I have the ability to actually do things that some people—most people—would say are impossible. I said, "Well, I have something for you. I have been carrying this around all day and I didn't know why until right now." I pulled out a folded piece of paper that was in my wallet. As I handed it to Steve, I asked him what time he was born. He didn't know because he was born in Germany and it wasn't on his German birth certificate. Steve unfolded the piece of paper and saw the words "Forbes 10:10." As you can imagine, he freaked out. He fulfilled his commitment. He called Ron Hulnick at the University of Santa Monica. They have a big fundraiser each year called "The Night of Magic." They bring in a magician. Steve called him and said, "You need to hire Wayne Hoffman to do your event."

Ron said, "Steve, we already have someone booked. I can't book Wayne."

Steve said, "Listen, pay the other magician whatever he wants. Pay him his fee, but you have to get Wayne. You just have to." He was convincing enough that Ron actually told the other performer to only do half of his set. Ron paid me to perform the second half of the show. It was fantastic. I've been back several times. At that very first show, I met my best friend, Scott. We travel the world together and have a really close bond, which is the biggest gift I could ever receive. I am grateful to Steve for that.

I can tell you point blank: Steve Hardison is not your average Joe. I wouldn't even call him a human being, because he takes the physical embodiment of a human being as nothing more than a vehicle to move energy. He does it in such a way that it affects everyone. I would compare it to one of my favorite movies, *The Matrix*. Steve has the ability to not live in the matrix and to create his own reality.

It's so hard to explain Steve Hardison. If somebody has never met him, it's almost nearly impossible. I've never told Steve this, but when I tell people about Steve, I tell them I have given him a moniker: the most intense human I've ever met.

I don't know how he does it, but he creates things. He creates things for himself and for other people. He attracts people. If Steve wanted to wield his powers for evil, he most certainly could. He could start a cult tomorrow. But he uses his power for good. I think he has the ability to do in life what I do on stage. As a mentalist and illusionist, I don't come from "I'm magical. Look at me." Rather, I say to my audience, "I'm magical, and you are too."

That is how Steve lives his life, helping others find their magic.

Steve, Hunedoara Castle, Romania, 2015

A Note from Steve Hardison

To You, the reader:

Thank you for taking your time to read this book. I hope that there was something of immense value for you in these pages. Thank you for being wonderful you. Please know that you make a difference. Your life makes a difference. Your "being" impacts your entire world, beginning with yourself and then with everyone you encounter each and every day of your life. Know that I love you. Know that others love you. Know that you are love.

To Alan D. Thompson, the researcher:

As you may recall, on more than one occasion when you invited me to write a book, I declined. You asked me why and I told you that if I ever wrote a book it would be on Being. I also shared with you that if I wrote a book on Being it would not be on Being, it would simply be about Being. I was of the belief that it could not be done.

I let you know that my life was my book and the people that shared time, space, and presence were the chapters in my book. What moved me off that position was your email in April of 2020 wherein you wrote, "Steve, last night God nudged me to write a biography on your life." The rest, as they say, is history. Thank you for your persistence. Thank you for your dedication. Thank you for your efforts. Thank you for the hundreds of interviews you did. Thank you for the hundreds of hours you dedicated to this work. And especially, thank you for your brilliance and your magnificent way of being.

To Amy, the writer:

Amy, it is not very often that one's girlfriend invests over a year of her life to write about her boyfriend. I was and am totally blown away by your commitment and dedication to this and to me. I watched you each day for the duration of this project. I have never witnessed such focus, such tenacity, such creation. And you did this for over a year, six days a week, eight hours (or more) a day. The amazing thing about it is the grace with which you did it all.

As I have often said, you are more talented than any client I have ever sat with. You are more loving than anyone I have ever met. You are a miracle. No wonder when John Patrick Morgan asked his wife if she would like to do a *Be With* session with me, she responded, something like, "To be totally honest, I would rather have a *Be With* session with Amy." I totally understand that.

Thank you for the life you gave to write *The Ultimate Coach*. Thank you for the life you gave to *create* the Ultimate Coach. I have frequently said, "No Amy Blake Hardison, no Ultimate Coach." You have loved me. You have healed me. And you have created me. I truly am blessed. I love you, my dear, sweet Amy.

The End

Scan the QR code below to join

The Ultimate Coach **Facebook Group**

A community for of *The Ultimate Coach* to share their
experiences of how the book has impacted them.

www.facebook.com/groups/theultimatecoach

*Thank you for reading! If you enjoyed this book and would like to
share your thoughts, please feel free to leave a review on
Amazon or a similar site. Book reviews can spread the
word and help readers find great books.*

Acknowledgments

Amy

Thanks to **Stephanie Wong** and **Victor Boc** for your brilliance and generosity.

Thanks to **Marena Hales, Steve Chandler, Iyanla Vanzant, Cathy Thomas, Karan Rai,** and **John Patrick Morgan** for proofreading our manuscript with such precision, acumen, and expertise.

Thanks to **Lydia** for opening my eyes to something more.

Thanks to **Angela** for sharing your amazing graphic design talents so generously and for creating a cover with class and artistry.

Thanks to **Rob, Debbie, Jayme, and Teresa** for all the phone calls, emails, and conversations as I fact checked Hardison history. Thank you for loving me as one of the family from the first moment I met you.

Thanks to **Chris** for your extraordinary skill in editing and for taking this project from manuscript to book with such ease.

Thanks to **Alan** for generating this project and for giving it lift. Thank you for your hours and hours of interviews, for your meticulous organization, and especially for your graciousness.

Thanks to all those who took their time to share their stories, experiences, thoughts, and acknowledgments.

Thanks to all those who read advanced copies and shared valuable feedback. Thank you for your unstinting encouragement.

Thanks to **Steve**. It has been a sheer delight to record your magnificence, to see you as others see you, and to be your sweetheart and wife.

Alan

Much like the many painters of the Sistine Chapel, there have been many reliable supporters of this massive project, particularly in the research phase.

Steve: I am incredibly grateful to you for allowing me to be both gently assimilative and ruthlessly forensic. I have been amazed at your commitment to supporting this record of your life. Thank you for listening to your intuition (though I do wonder whether texting your current inspiration while sleepwalking to the bathroom at 1:30am really is good for you!). PPC. MIM. Peak Performance Commitment and Mastery in Motion. My appreciation to you is documented in this book, and yet can never be fully expressed. Thank you.

Linda Kwan: thank you for being available for anything and everything, your transcribing, note-taking, and all-around mastery have transposed many of the most beautiful melodies in this symphony. Your being is appreciated in every moment.

Steve's clients, friends, and strangers: your willingness to open yourself, to put yourself on record, and to reveal your heart, speaks volumes about who you are. To each of you: thank you for who you be.

Acknowledgments

The Hardison family: Amy, Steff, Lil, Clint, Blake, thank you for opening your doors to me, and revealing the real magic that is Steve.

Jody Vehr: thank you for being available as a listening ear, sounding board, and touchstone.

Steve Chandler: thank you for your gracious presence and giving to this project. Your written record of Steve across so many of your books has been a wonderful giant's shoulders on which to stand.

Immense gratitude to **Dylan Jones** for your generous legal review of our consent release forms during the research phase.

Other authors: biography is the ultimate form of literature. I probably own more biographies (including autobiographies) than anyone I know. I have been most grateful to stand on the highest scaffolding: Herbert Breslin's biography of Pavarotti (The King & I), Kristin Williamson's biography of her husband (David Williamson: Behind the Scenes), James Gleick's biography of Richard Feynman (Genius). Thank you for your contribution to the planet.

Soundtrack: for this project, my grateful thanks to Aussie singer Guy Sebastian, British-Aussie singer Passenger (Michael David Rosenberg), Canadian composer Howard Shore, Argentine countertenor Fernando Lima, English vocalist Michael Ball, French-Canadian composers Guy Dubuc and Marc Lessard (Bob & Bill), and American-Swiss rockstar Tina Turner (inspired by a story in this book).

Amy: The Ultimate Author of course, but more than that, The Ultimate Human Being. I see you.

Endnotes

The source material for Steve Hardison's words, memories, insights, and perspectives are from personal interviews with Amy Hardison and from Amy's personal experience.

Chapter 1. An Enigma

Interviews with Steve Chandler (June 17, 2020 and Nov 18, 2020).
Trent La Marsh, "Where Did We Meet?" Steve Hardison's Facebook page, *Facebook,* March 2020
https://www.facebook.com/steve.hardison.14

Chapter 2. Growing Up

Interviews with Rob Hardison (May 14, 2020); Jayme Hardison Harris (May 14, 2020); Teresa Hardison Holdaway (June 30, 2020); personal correspondence and phone conversations with Rob, Jayme, and Teresa (October 14-20, 2020).
Kate McLaughlin, "Five Things Women Couldn't do in the 1960s," *CNN,* updated August 25, 2014
https://www.cnn.com/2014/08/07/living/sixties-women-5-things/index.html
Carol McGrath Nash shared with Amy Hardison (November 2, 2020)

Chapter 3. Roots

Interviews with Rob Hardison (May 14, 2020); Jayme Hardison Harris (May 14, 2020); Teresa Hardison Holdaway (June 30, 2020); personal correspondence and conversations (October 14-20, 2020).

Chapter 4. At Risk

Interview with Larry Belnap (July 21, 2020).

Chapter 6. Gainfully Employed

Interview with Larry Belnap (July 21, 2020).

Chapter 7. A Man on a Mission

Interview with Scott W. Parker (May 5, 2020).
Linda Eyre, Richard Eyre emails to Alan D. Thompson (2020).

Chapter 9. Newlyweds

Darlene Loves, "The Most Truly Loving Relationship," Interview, transcript shared with Amy Hardison, July 10, 2021.

Chapter 10. Weber State

Jim Barlow, email to Alan D. Thompson, May 22, 2020.

Chapter 12. Family

Interviews with Lindsey Hardison Eskey (June 28, 2020); Clint Hardison (July 8, 2020), Blake Hardison (July 7, 2020).
Email from Steffany Hardison (August 1, 2020).

Chapter 13. Rodel.

Interviews with Don Budinger (July 7, 2020).
Terry Hays-Sapp, "Where Did We Meet?" Steve Hardison's Facebook page, *Facebook,* March 2020
https://www.facebook.com/steve.hardison.14

Chapter 16. Demolition

Interview with Lloyd Fickett (June 15, 2020).

Chapter 17. The Birth of Coaching

"International Coaching Federation Releases 2020 Global Coaching Study," *ICF: International Coaching Federation,* accessed May 27, 2021, https://coachingfederation.org/blog/international-coachingfederation-releases-2020-global-coaching-study.

Greg Faxon, "The 21 Most Profitable Life Coaching Niches," *Greg Faxon Blog,* updated 2021, https://www.gregfaxon.com/blog/21-coaching-niches.

Reece Bawden, email to Alan D. Thompson (2020)

Chapter 18. Steve Chandler

Interviews with Steve Chandler (June 17, 2020 and Nov 18, 2020); Patrick Provost (Aug 1, 2020).

Chandler, *Seventeen Lies That Are Holding You Back and the Truth That Will Set You Free,* manuscript emailed to Amy Hardison, (Nov 9, 2020).

Chapter 19. University of Santa Monica

Interviews with Carla Rotering (May 29, 2020), Lisa Haisha (June 29, 2020), and Clint Hardison (July 8, 2020).

Chapter 20. Iyanla

Interview with Iyanla Vanzant (June 13, 2020).

"Iyanla Vanzant," *Wikipedia*, Wikimedia Foundation, 29 April 2021, https://en.wikipedia.org/wiki/Iyanla_Vanzant.

Iyanla Vanzant, Peace from Broken Pieces, How to Get Through What You're Going Through (New York: Smiley Books, 2010), 152-156.

Iyanla Vanzant, The Art of Living Retreat Center, 2021, accessed January 2021, https://artoflivingretreatcenter.org/faculty-members/iyanla-vanzant/.

Chapter 22. The Office

Interviews with Lisa Hale (June 6, 2020); Yayati Desai (June 3, 2020); Norma Bachoura (May 20, 2020); Stephen McGhee (July 14, 2020); Lisa Berkovitz (June 7, 2020); Steve Chandler (June 17, 2020); Jason Jaggard (June 9, 2020); Iyanla Vanzant (June 13, 2020); Devon Bandison (June 3, 2020); Kai Jordan (June 21, 2020).

Gina Carlson, "Tributes," *Steve Hardison The Ultimate Coach,* accessed September 20, 2020, https://theultimatecoach.com/tributes/

Daniel Harner, "Where Did We Meet?" Steve Hardison's Facebook page, *Facebook,* March 2020
https://www.facebook.com/steve.hardison.14

"Metamorphose," *Edition Strassacker,* accessed January 2021, https://edition-strassacker.de/en/maria-luise-bodirsky/metamorphose-84207.

Chapter 23. Fasten Your Seat Belt

Interviews with Scott Parker (May 5, 2020); David Orton (May 17, 2020); Karan Rai (June 21, 2020); Lisa Haisha (June 29, 2020); James Malinousky (May 8, 2020); Mandy Lehto (June 24, 2020); Iyanla Vanzant (June 13, 2020).

Scott Parker, "Tributes," *Steve Hardison The Ultimate Coach,* accessed September 20, 2020, https://theultimatecoach.com/tributes/

Mandy Lehto, email to Amy Hardison (December 21, 2020)

Chapter 24. The Coaching Experience

Interviews with Devon Bandison (June 3, 2020); Iyanla Vanzant (June 13, 2020); Jered Schager (July 9, 2020); Norma Bachoura (May 20, 2020); Jason Jaggard (June 9, 2020); Shanti Zimmerman (May 28, 2020); Teresa Walding (May 23, 2020); Michael Serwa (May 16, 2020); Aaron Benes (May 11, 2020); Tom McGovern (July 7, 2020); Martine Cannon (May 22, 2020); Scott Parker (May 5, 2020); Carla Rotering (May 29, 2020); Lisa Berkovitz (June 7, 2020); James Malinousky (May 8, 2020); Steve Chandler (June 17, 2020); Stephen McGhee (July 14, 2020); Gary Gietz (2020); Greg Hiller (2020); Daniel Harner (August 27, 2020); Billy Woodmansee (June 5, 2020); John Vehr (August 5, 2020); Jayalalita Branscum (June 20, 2020); Gary Mahler (May 16, 2020); David Orton (May 17, 2020).

Greg Hiller, "Where Did We Meet?" Steve Hardison's Facebook page, *Facebook,* March 2020
https://www.facebook.com/steve.hardison.14

Allison Watts, email to Alan D. Thompson (2020).

Aaron Benes, email to Alan D. Thompson (2020).

Michael Schantz, "Tributes," *Steve Hardison The Ultimate Coach,*

accessed September 20, 2020
https://theultimatecoach.com/tributes/

John Patrick Morgan, "100 hours with Steve Hardison," *YouTube*, uploaded 4 April 2019
https://www.youtube.com/watch?v=z6G4Jpafbs8.

Ollie Trew, Facebook post to Steve Hardison (August 28, 2020).

Steve Chandler, *Creating Great Relationships* (Maurice Bassett, 2017), 133.

Chip and Dan Heath, *Decisive,* Kindle (New York: Crown Publishing Group, 2013), location 2492. They cite Suzy Welch, a business writer for publications such as Bloomberg Businessweek and O magazine, as the creator of the idea 10/10/10.

Van Dunham, email to Alan Thompson (May 26, 2020).

Matt Laughlin, email to Alan Thompson (2020).

Rich Litvin, "Tributes," *Steve Hardison The Ultimate Coach,* accessed September 20, 2020
https://theultimatecoach.com/tributes/

Vignette: Heidi Boyd

Email to Alan D. Thompson (2020).

Vignette: Jody Vehr

Interview (February 18, 2020).

Chapter 25. The Sky's the Limit

Interviews with Luna Viva Ananda (July 31, 2020); Melanie Waite (June 8, 2020); Carla Rotering (May 29, 2020); Billy Woodmansee (June 5, 2020); Clate Mask (July 15, 2020); Brandon Sulser (May 1, 2020).

Jenn Walter, email to Alan D. Thompson (May 1, 2020).

Lewis Carroll, *Through the Looking Glass,* (Digireads.com Publication, 2004), 38.

Nicholas Smith, "Where Did We Meet?" Steve Hardison's Facebook page, *Facebook,* March 2020
https://www.facebook.com/steve.hardison.14.

Michael Neill, *The Inside Out Revolution* (Carlsbad, California: Hay House, 2013).

Jordan Dangelo, to Amy Hardison (2020).

Sebastian Hidalgo, email to Alan D. Thompson (July 11, 2020).

John Vehr to Steve Hardison (2020).

Vignette: Lisa Haisha

Interview (June 29, 2020).

Chapter 26. Listening

Interviews with Tom McGovern (July 7, 2020); Greg Hiller (2020); Patrick Provost (Aug 1, 2020); Jeff Dinsdale (June 22, 2020); Scott Parker (May 5, 2020); Oren Harris (July 10, 2020); A.J. Richards (July 1, 2020); Devon Bandison (June 3, 2020); Steve Chandler (June 17, 2020).

Steven Pothier, email to Alan D. Thompson, June 5, 2020.

John Patrick Morgan, "100 hours with Steve Hardison," *YouTube*, uploaded 4 April 2019 https://www.youtube.com/watch?v=z6G4Jpafbs8.

Chapter 27. Creation

Interviews with Carla Rotering (May 29, 2020); Karan Rai (June 21, 2020); Mary Turner (May 24, 2020); Gina Carlson (2020.) Steve Chandler (June 17, 2020); Jeff Dinsdale (June 22, 2020); Jered Schager (July 9, 2020); Ward Andrews (May 13, 2020); Lisa Hale (June 6, 2020).

Cherryl Blake Vernon, email to Alan D. Thompson (August 2, 2020).

John Vehr, personal note to Steve Hardison (May 21, 2020).

Allison Watts, email to Alan D. Thompson (2020).

Vignette: Kai Jordan

Interview (May 6, 2020).

Chapter 28. The Document

Interviews with Daniel Harner (August 27, 2020; May 4, 2020); John Vehr (August 27, 2020); Norma Bachoura (May 20, 2020); Marina Lazarus (May 23, 2020); Dave Orton (May 17, 2020); Chris Dorris (May 26, 2020); Alisha Das (April 29, 2020); A. J. Richards (July 1, 2020); Jeff Dinsdale (June 22, 2020); Karan Rai (June 21, 2020); Abigail Olaya (August 28, 2020).

Vignette: Nadine Larder

Conquering Fears to Create Masterpieces, (Printerbees: 2017).

Chapter 29: Being Your Word, Commitment, and Integrity

Interviews with Brandon Craig (June 24, 2020); Tom McGovern (July 7, 2020); Martine Cannon (May 22, 2020); Jeff Dinsdale (June 22, 2020); Chris Dorris (May 26, 2020), Oren Harris (2020);

Byron Applegate, email to Alan D. Thompson (2020).

Matt Laughlin, personal correspondence with Amy Hardison, July 15, 2020.

Michael C. Jensen, "Integrity: Without It Nothing Works," *Negotiation, Organizations, and Markets Research Papers*, Harvard NOM Research Paper No. 10-042; Interview by Karen Christensen, from *Rotman: The Magazine of the Rotman School of Management*, (Fall 2009, pp 16-20) 18. http://vsacoaching.com/wp-content/uploads/2012/04/Integrity-Without-it-Nothing-Works-042610.pdf

Vignette: Cathy (M. Catherine) Thomas,

Document sent to Alan D. Thompson (May 1, 2020).

Chapter 31: Sacred Connections

Interviews with Melanie Waite (June 8, 2020); Michael Serwa (May 16, 2020); Norma Bachoura (May 20, 2020); Edith Croteau (September 24, 2020); Karen Davis (May 27, 2020, May 14, 2021); Martine Cannon (2020).

Gina Carlson, "Tributes," *Steve Hardison The Ultimate Coach*, accessed September 20, 2020, https://theultimatecoach.com/tributes/

Roxane Beck, email to Steve Hardison (Dec 3, 2017).

Laura Minard, email to Amy Hardison (July 30, 2021), interview (Aug 2, 2021).

Aaron Benes, personal note to Steve Hardison.

Chris Baek, email to Amy Hardison (March 15, 2020).

Electra Ariail, email to Alan D. Thompson (July 31, 2020).

Vignette: Shenal Fernando

Interview (2020).

Vignette: Byron L. Applegate

Email to Alan D. Thompson (2020).

Chapter 32. The Cost of Coaching

Interviews with Lisa Hale (June 6, 2020); Scott Parker (May 5, 2020); Lisa Haisha (June 29, 2020); Townsend Wardlaw (August 6, 2020); Gina Carlson (2020); Martine Cannon (May 22, 2020); Jeff Dinsdale (June 22, 2020); Tom McGovern (July 7, 2020); Aaron Benes (2020).

Rich Litvin. "Tributes," *Steve Hardison The Ultimate Coach,* accessed September 20, 2020, https://theultimatecoach.com/tributes/.

Jordan Dangelo, email to Amy Hardison.

Stephen McGhee, "Tributes," *Steve Hardison The Ultimate Coach,* accessed September 20, 2020, https://theultimatecoach.com/tributes/.

Ethan Okura, "Tributes," *Steve Hardison The Ultimate Coach,* accessed September 20, 2020, https://theultimatecoach.com/tributes/.

Vignette: John Patrick Morgan

"100 hours with Steve Hardison," *YouTube,* uploaded 4 April 2019, https://www.youtube.com/watch?v=z6G4Jpafbs8.

Vignette: Clate Mask

Interview with Alan D. Thompson (July 15, 2020).

Chapter 33. The Millennials

From interviews with Robert Harding (July 30, 2020); Todd Runyan (May 16, 2020); Sebastian Hidalgo (August 12, 2020); David Bennett (May 9, 2020).

Sebastian Hidalgo, email to Alan D. Thompson (11 July 2020).

Chapter 34. TBOLITNFL

Interviews with Chris Dorris (May 26, 2020); Rosie Bernardo (May 29, 2020).

Lorrain Warren, email to Alan D. Thompson (28 April 2020).

James Strock, "W H Murray, Until One is Committed," *Serve to Lead,* 1 January 2021, https://servetolead.org/w-h-murray-until-one-is-committed/

Isla Morrison, personal communication with Steve Hardison.

Fred Beljaars, personal communication with Steve Hardison.

David Gerber, "Where Did We Meet?" Steve Hardison's Facebook page, *Facebook,* March 2020, https://www.facebook.com/steve.hardison.14

Eric Lofholm, "Where Did We Meet?" Steve Hardison's Facebook page, *Facebook,* March 2020 https://www.facebook.com/steve.hardison.14

Jenn Walter, email to Alan D. Thompson (May 1, 2020).

Emma Holmes, text to Steve Hardison (March 13, 2021).

Will Keiper, *Life Expectancy* (Scottsdale, Arizona: FirstGlobal Media dba FirstGlobal Partners LLC, 2012), 142-153.

Vignette: Chris Dorris.

Interview with Alan D. Thompson (May 26, 2020).

Vignette: Luisa Molano

Facebook Post, Jan 19, 2021. https://www.facebook.com/lulu.molano/posts/10158893684764770?comment_id=10158893996224770

Vignette: Stephen Sainato

Interview with Alan D. Thompson (May 5, 2020).

Chapter 35. Love

Interview with Yayati Desai (June 3, 2020); Iyanla Vanzant (June 13, 2020); Lyn McCright (May 23, 2020); Lisa Hale (June 6, 2020); Louise Phipps Senft (July 6, 2020); Patrick Provost (August 1, 2020); Paul Waite (July 14, 2020); Michael Serwa (May 16, 2020); Lisa Berkovitz (June 7, 2020); Ward Andrews (May 13, 2020); Bill Jensen (July 6, 2020); Stephen McGhee (July 14, 2020); Karan Rai (June 21, 2020); Clint Hardison (July 8, 2020);

Gary Mahler, document to Alan D. Thompson (2020).

Lorraine Warren, email to Alan D. Thompson (28 April 2020).

Bryan Samuels, email to Alan D. Thompson (May 19, 2020).

Van Dunham, email to Alan D. Thompson (May 26, 2020).

Lisa Haisha, "Where Did We Meet?" Steve Hardison's Facebook page, *Facebook,* March 2020 https://www.facebook.com/steve.hardison.14.

Marena Hales, personal correspondence with Amy Hardison (May 4, 2020).

Stephen McGhee, "Where Did We Meet?" Steve Hardison's Facebook page, *Facebook,* March 2020 https://www.facebook.com/steve.hardison.14

John Patrick Morgan, "The Window Cleaner," originally written July 22, 2014; *JP Morgan Creating*, 2021, https://jpmorganjr.com/steve-hardison-the-window-cleaner/

Deanna Chesley, "Where Did We Meet?" Steve Hardison's Facebook page, *Facebook,* March 2020 https://www.facebook.com/steve.hardison.14

Sylvia Carter, email to Alan D. Thompson (2020).

Nanette Glauser, email to Alan D. Thompson (8 June 2020).

Tara LaRue Stradling, "Where Did We Meet?" Steve Hardison's Facebook page, *Facebook,* March 2020 https://www.facebook.com/steve.hardison.14

Michael Schantz, Tributes," *Steve Hardison The Ultimate Coach,* accessed September 20, 2020, https://theultimatecoach.com/tributes/

Allison Watts, email to Alan D. Thompson

John Patrick Morgan, "100 hours with Steve Hardison," *YouTube*, uploaded 4 April 2019, https://www.youtube.com/watch?v=z6G4Jpafbs8

LaTrina Williams, email to Alan D. Thompson (2020).

Stephen Pothier, email to Alan D. Thompson (5 June 2020).

Vignette: Gary Mahler

Email to Alan D. Thompson (2020).

Vignette: Rephoel Wolf

Email to Alan D. Thompson (April 30, 2020).

Vignette: Minda Pacheco

Interview with Amy Hardison (March 12, 2021).

Chapter 37. We'll Have Fun, Fun, Fun

Interviews with Jeff Dinsdale (June 22, 2020); Jayme Hardison Harris (May 14, 2020); Shanti Zimmerman (May 28, 2020); Lisa Berkovitz (June 7, 2020); Adam Amin Mahboubi (June 10, 2020); John Vehr (August 5, 2020); Clint Hardison (July 8, 2020); Melanie Waite (June 8, 2020); Carla Rotering (May 29, 2020).

Nanette Glauser, email to Alan D. Thompson (8 June 2020).

Curtis Marsh, text to Steve Hardison (March 14, 2021).

Bryan Samuels, email to Alan D. Thompson (May 19, 2020).

Jackie Skinner, email to Alan D. Thompson (June 8, 2020)

Emma Holmes, "Where Did We Meet?" Steve Hardison's Facebook page, *Facebook,* March 2020 https://www.facebook.com/steve.hardison.14

Chapter 38. Making Sense of Steve

Interviews with Jason Jaggard (June 9, 2020); John Goodie (August 3, 2020); Teresa Hardison Holdaway (June 30, 2020); Clate Mask (July 15, 2020); Scott Law (May 31, 2020); Patrick Provost (August 1, 2020); John Vehr (August 5, 2020); Lindsey (Lil) Hardison Eskey (June 28, 2020); Jayme Hardison Harris (May 14, 2020); Clint Hardison (July 8, 2020); Louise Phipps Senft (July 6, 2020); Shanti Zimmerman (May 28,

2020); Michael Serwa (May 16, 2020); Mandy Lehto (June 24, 2020); Teresa Campbell (June 18, 2020); Ollie Trew (July 19, 2020); Carla Rotering (May 29, 2020); Iyanla Vanzant (June 13, 2020); Dustin Venekamp (May 21, 2020); John Patrick Morgan (April 29, 2020); John Goodie (August 3, 2020); Holly Profitt-Venekamp (May 21, 2020); Ward Andrews (May 13, 2020); Steve Chandler (June 17, 2020); Lisa Hale (June 6, 2020); David Bennett (May 9, 2020); Teresa Walding (May 23, 2020); Adam Amin Mahboubi (June 10, 2020); Stephen Sainato (May 5, 2020).

Malcolm Gladwell, *Outliers, The Story of Success,* Kindle, ed. (New York: Little, Brown and Company, 2008). 34-66.

Saloni Singh, email to Amy Hardison (July 31, 2021).

Hana Callaghan, email to Amy Hardison (July 28, 2021).

Kyle B. Beckman, *Personality and Strategy,* Kindle, (Pickle Partners Publishing, 2015) 20.

Katrina Faust, "Personality Types of DISC: D Personality (Dominant)", January 10, 2019, https://leadx.org/articles/disc-personality-types-d-drive/, accessed 3-1-21.

Elaine Pofeldt, "Gallup: The 10 Qualities of Highly Successful Entrepreneurs," May 31, 2014, https://www.forbes.com/sites/elainepofeldt/2014/05/31/gallup-the-10-qualities-of-highly-successful-entrepreneurs/?sh=57e696ac21fc, accessed 4-1-21.

Deanna Chesley, Steve Hardison's Facebook page, *Facebook,* March 2020 https://www.facebook.com/steve.hardison.14.

Elaine N. Aron, *The Highly Sensitive Person,* (New York: Citadel Press Books, 2020), xxix, 4, 7, 28-30; 56, 63, 110, 140.

Hary McBride, *Highly Sensitive Person: The Highly Sensitive Person,* Audible, 2019, https://www.audible.com/pd/Highly-Sensitive-Person-The-Highly-Sensitive-Person-Is-a-Guide-on-How-to-Handle-Positive-and-Negative-Emotions-It-Teaches-How-to-Manage-Anxiety-Overcome-Fears-and-Live-Better-Audiobook/B07WW5YRST?qid=1617826403&sr=1-16&ref=a_search_c3_lProduct_1_16&pf_rd_p=83218cca-c308-412f-bfcf-90198b687a2f&pf_rd_r=PJMA1S2QFJN3QGN7ZTXN

Bianca P. Acevedo, Alaine N. Aron, Arthur Aron, Matthew-Donald Sangster, Nancy Collins, and Lucy L. Brown, "The Highly Sensitive

Brain: an FMRI Study of Sensory Processing Sensitivity and Response to Others' Emotions," *Brain and Behavior*, US National Library of Medicine, National Institute of Health, Jun 23, 2014. https://www.ncbi.nlm.nih.gov/pmc/articles/PMC4086365/

Mel Collins, "The Top 7 Challenges of Highly Sensitive People, According to a Therapist", *Highly Sensitive Refuge,* Oct 7, 2020, https://highlysensitiverefuge.com/top-7-challenges-of-highly-sensitive-people-according-to-a-therapist/

Pearl S. Buck, "Quotes," Goodreads, https://www.goodreads.com/quotes/31946-the-truly-creative-mind-in-any-field-is-no-more

Jenara Nerenberg, *Divergent Mind: Thriving in a World that Wasn't Designed for You,* Kindle ed., HarperOne, 2020.

"Eight, The Challenger," The Enneagram Institute, accessed April 1, 2020, https://www.enneagraminstitute.com/type-8.

Stephanie Hoi-Nga Wong, email to Steve Hardison (April 2, 2021).

Vignette: Wayne Hoffman

Interview with Alan D. Thompson (June 12, 2020).

Index

About the Authors

Amy Hardison

Along with *The Ultimate Coach,* Amy Blake Hardison is the author of *How to Feel Great About Being a Mother* (1987) and *Understanding the Symbols, Covenants and Ordinances of the Temple* (2016). She has also participated in five Sperry Symposiums at BYU. Her articles were published in the accompanying volumes.

Amy graduated magna cum laude from Weber State University in 1980 in English. She chose to be a stay-at-home mother, focusing her time and energy on her family. She has been married to Steve Hardison for forty-four years. It has been a wonderful adventure. They have four children and eleven grandchildren.

Throughout her life, Amy has pursued a passion for learning. She also loves to exercise, read, listen to audiobooks, travel, and spend time with her family.

Alan D. Thompson

Dr. Alan D. Thompson is a world expert in the fields of AI, intelligence, high performance, and personal development. He is a former chairman for Mensa International's gifted families committee, a co-founder of the Australia-Asia Positive Psychology Institute and author of the best-selling parenting book, *Bright,* a copy of which was sent to the moon aboard the Peregrine lunar lander.

Alan advises international media in the fields of exceptional ability and personal development. He completed his Bachelor of Science (Computer Science, AI, and Psychology) at Edith Cowan University, 2004; studied Gifted Education at Flinders University, 2017; became a Fellow of the Institute of Coaching affiliated with Harvard Medical School, 2017; and received his doctorate from Emerson, 2021. Alan's dissertation was adapted into a book featuring Dr Rupert Sheldrake, *Connected: Intuition and Resonance in Smart People.* You can connect with Alan at: www.LifeArchitect.ai

For community, extras and more:

www.theultimatecoachbook.com

To learn more about Steve Hardison:

www.theultimatecoach.com

Printed in Great Britain
by Amazon

39360090R10290